heritage in
WALES

heritage in WALES

A Guide to the Ancient and Historic Sites in the care of Cadw: Welsh Historic Monuments

David Robinson

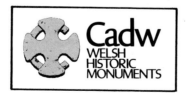

Macdonald
Queen Anne Press

A *Queen Anne Press* BOOK

First published in Great Britain in 1989 by
Queen Anne Press, a division of
Macdonald & Co (Publishers) Ltd
66–73 Shoe Lane
London EC4P 4AB

A member of Maxwell Pergamon Publishing Corporation
plc

British Library Cataloguing in Publication Data

Robinson, David M. (David Martin), *1953–*
    Heritage in Wales.
    1. Wales. Antiquities
    I. Title
    936.2'9
    ISBN 0-356-17278-3

Picture credits

Bibliothèque Municipale Dijon, 129B; Bodleian Library 84;
British Library 15, 40, 43, 127, 132, 155B, 189T; Cambridge
University Collection of Air Photography 18; Chepstow
Museum 115; Peter Humphries 22, 23B, 25, 27, 34, 36T, 40,
41B, 46B, 49T, 67, 83T, 91, 92, 97, 102T, 103, 113T, 117,
119B, 122B, 139B, 151, 159, 166, 176, 181, 191; Marquess of
Salisbury 178; Musée de Poitiers 133B; National Library of
Wales 48, 73T, 180; National Museum of Wales 37, 49B,
100T, 111B, 174, 184, 186; Public Record Office 138;
Skyscan Aerial Photography 31, 71, 85, 116, 125T, 131, 146;
Trustees of the British Museum 123; Wales Tourist Board
17T, 17B, 19, 53, 61, 75, 94, 96, 113B, 120, 137T, 141, 143,
154, 164, 177, 185; Walker Art Gallery 145; Robert
Williams 12T, 20, 36B, 41T.

All other illustrations courtesy of Cadw: Welsh Historic
Monuments.

Typeset by Tradespools Ltd, Frome, Somerset
Printed and bound in Great Britain by Butler and Tanner
Ltd, Frome, Somerset

CONTENTS

The turrets of the outer gate at Harlech castle.

PREFACE

Despite the inevitable difficulties, writing this book has proved a great luxury. It is a rare privilege to have had the opportunity to seek out and prepare the material, covering some of the most historically and archaeologically significant monuments in Wales. In turn, the importance of these monuments, and the vast quantities of literature they have inspired over many years, now stand at the centre of my frustrations. Alongside the major works of scholarship, which underpin virtually every point of substance, the entries are overshadowed and appear all too brief. I hope, of course, that the volume will contain something of interest for all those concerned with the built heritage of Wales, though the specialist is unlikely to find much that is brand new. A more accomplished scholar may well have produced a very different book – mine must snuggle modestly under the shadow of those authors with greater talent.

The text can, therefore, make no pretensions to being exhaustive. In each entry, within the compass of a few hundred words, I have tried to share my enthusiasm and interest in the history and architecture of the site with general readers both within and beyond Wales. I very much hope the book will encourage them to look still deeper and to travel yet further.

In preparing the text, I have been helped by many friends and colleagues, and it is a pleasure to record my thanks here. My first and greatest debt is to all those hard-working scholars whose published material I have, of necessity, drawn upon anonymously. I can only crave their indulgence and understanding for the wholesale plundering and consequent simplification which a book such as this often entails. At Cadw, my colleagues within the Inspectorate of Ancient Monuments have been particularly helpful. Richard Avent, Jeremy Knight and Sian Rees not only read and commented upon sections of the typescript, but were also kind enough to supply details of their own work in advance of publication. Again, I am pleased to express my gratitude and appreciation to Jack Spurgeon and to Peter Smith (Secretary) at the Royal Commission on Ancient and Historical Monuments (Wales), who were generous enough to allow me to draw on the Commission's superb forthcoming surveys of Glamorgan castles. I should further like to extend my warmest thanks to Professor Glanmor Williams who, despite one of the busiest retirements on record, has once more given so freely of his time and rich experience. Many other friends within Cadw provided additional support and assistance in various ways, especially Lizbeth Barrett, Peter Humphries, David Jones, Jean Paskell and Diane Williams. I am grateful to them all, though none of course can be associated with any factual errors or idiosyncracies in approach.

I would also like to thank Christine Davis at Queen Anne Press, who has been a model of editorial patience and efficiency. Finally, I owe a particular debt of gratitude to the Director of Cadw: Welsh Historic Monuments, Mr John Carr. Without his firm commitment and enthusiasm, the project would certainly not have moved beyond the stage of a 'good idea'. For several years now, it has been my singular good fortune to be a recipient of his constant support and cheering words of encouragement.

David M. Robinson
Cardiff, April 1989

INTRODUCTION
The work of Cadw: Welsh Historic Monuments

The choice of title for this book, *Heritage in Wales*, is no accident. As many readers will already be aware, it is the name given to the membership scheme administered by Cadw: Welsh Historic Monuments – the new body set up by the Secretary of State for Wales in 1984 to look after the rich legacy of ancient monuments and historic buildings situated throughout the principality. Yet it must be admitted that the meaning of the word 'Cadw' is generally less well known, and people unfamiliar with the Welsh language can perhaps be forgiven for taking it to be an acronym. In fact, its English translation is 'to keep' or 'to preserve', and – in so far as one word can – it sums up the many challenging and varied tasks faced by the organization.

At the centre of Cadw's work lie the statutory responsibilities for protecting, conserving and presenting the 'built heritage' of Wales on behalf of the Secretary of State. Indeed, it is interesting to note that the origins of these important duties can be traced back as far as 1882, when the nation initially acknowledged the need to preserve the best of our ancient monuments as an archaeological and historical record for the future. For it was in that year that the first Ancient Monuments Protection Act appeared on the statute book. Thereafter, under subsequent legislation, the Ministry of Public Building and Works, and later the Department of the Environment, became the relevant Government guardians, with the Inspectorate of Ancient Monuments acting as adviser on all such matters. In Wales, more recently, the work passed to the Conservation and Land Division of the Welsh Office, and has since been absorbed into the new structure of Cadw:

Welsh Historic Monuments. In much the same way, the duties in England are now carried out by the sister organization, English Heritage.

In relation to the responsibilities themselves, Cadw plays an often complex and inevitably wide-ranging role. One of the major tasks, for example, is the protection of the current statutory list of some 12,000 buildings of architectural or historic interest. Moreover, over the next decade or so it is envisaged that this list could expand to take in a total of up to 40,000 buildings and other structures. It will include an immense range, from country mansions to terraced houses, from churches to farm buildings, from bridges to cinemas, from mills to lighthouses and even early telephone boxes. Linked to this sphere of work, on the advice of the Historic Buildings Council for Wales, the Secretary of State – via Cadw – provides grant-aid to the owners of 'outstanding' properties. Such aid ensures the preservation of a highly significant selection of some of the very best buildings in Wales.

Once again, under the present legislation, some 2,700 ancient monuments of all periods are protected as sites of national importance. In the coming years Cadw plans to increase this 'schedule' considerably, extending the statutory protection to a much wider representative sample. The schedule will eventually include the best preserved, as well as the more vulnerable, examples of monuments such as Bronze Age barrows, Iron Age hillforts, Roman forts and farmsteads and deserted medieval villages, right through to industrial sites of the nineteenth century. Alas, conservation in this way is not always possible. Pressures for building development, road schemes, or modern farming and forestry, often present a real and irreversible threat to the historic environment. In these circumstances, Cadw as the sponsoring body provides funds to the four Trusts for rescue archaeology in Wales. In this way important archaeological sites are carefully recorded before they are totally destroyed and the details lost forever.

All of these tasks, of course, relate to 'Heritage in Wales' in its broadest sense. This book, however, focuses upon a particularly distinct selection of buildings and monuments: a group of more than 120 castles and monasteries, churches and palaces, prehistoric tombs and Roman remains – all regularly open to the public. Despite the range of other statutory duties, there can be little doubt that the conservation, management, presentation, promotion and educational use of these so-called 'properties in care' will continue to represent the best-known aspect of Cadw's work. Not that this is any way surprising, since they include some of the most celebrated historic sites in Wales. In the north, for example, the awe-inspiring castles raised by King Edward I at Beaumaris, Caernarfon, Conwy and Harlech are justly world famous. Similarly, in the south, few locations surpass the haunting beauty of the Cistercian abbey at Tintern in the Wye valley, or can match the vast scale of the great baronial stronghold at Caerphilly. Other sites, it is true to say, are probably less familiar, though often just as intriguing in their own way. The chambered tomb at Bryn Celli Ddu on Anglesey, for instance, is one of the most evocative prehistoric sites in Britain. Again, visitors will readily appreciate why the castles raised by the native princes of Gwynedd at Dolbadarn and Dolwyddelan frequently stir the heart of many a Welshman.

This volume is a comprehensive record of all these properties, from the least-known standing stone to the most famous castle. Every site

covered is in the direct care of the Secretary of State for Wales and administered on his behalf by Cadw: Welsh Historic Monuments. From Neolithic chambered tombs, to the Victorian Gothic fantasy at Castell Coch, they reflect up to 6,000 years of history in the principality. Each one represents an expression of personal or communal aspirations, and many can be seen as the most tangible demonstrations of power, wealth and status that have come down to us from earlier centuries. They bear testimony to aspects of daily life; to ritual and burial; to religious belief and practice; to phases of ruthless military conquest and peaceful occupation; and even to dramatically changing cultures and physical conditions – they are at the very heart of heritage in Wales.

Readers of the book, as much as visitors to the sites, are encouraged to become involved and contribute to all aspects of Cadw's work by enrolling in the membership scheme itself. The built heritage of Wales is a unique and precious national asset to be shared with everyone for the benefit of future generations.

Finally, a word or two should be said on the arrangement of the volume. The various chapters, by and large, follow the modern administrative counties of the principality. The chief exception to this is the decision to devote a separate chapter to the Isle of Anglesey. Although now part of Gwynedd, as an island it has always had a rather distinct personality of its own. In the south, however, the monuments in the three Glamorgans have been grouped together. Within these sections the entries are then arranged alphabetically. The details on each site stand alone, though of course many are contemporary and share something of a common history. The volume ends with a summary of dates, placing all of the monuments in context. The maps and concluding gazetteer should help visitors find even the smallest and most remote of locations.

ANGLESEY
Mona the Mother
of Wales

As many writers have observed, Anglesey is an island, and it is this simple fact which gives it a distinct and lasting personality all of its own. Until the local government reorganization of 1974, it was of course a shire county – an administrative, judicial and financial unit first created at the end of the thirteenth century. Anglesey's distinctiveness, however, is rooted in far more than political circumstance or territorial division. Sheltered and physically protected in the lee of Snowdonia, it is the only area of generally fertile and reasonably accessible land in a region of high and barren mountains. As such, man has always been attracted to the island, resulting in an unbroken chain of settlement from the dawn of history and beyond. By the early Middle Ages – at the latest – Anglesey had become fundamental to the agricultural economy of the native rulers of north-west Wales. It was Gerald of Wales who, at the end of the twelfth century, quoted the island's age-old name of 'Mon mam Cymru' – Mona the Mother of Wales. Exaggerated through the claim may have been, Gerald recorded that 'when crops have failed in all other regions, this island, from the richness of its soil and its abundant produce, has been able to supply all Wales'.

Anglesey certainly lay at the heart of the ancient kingdom of Gwynedd. It was there at Aberffraw, on the south-west coast, that the principal court of the kingdom's rulers and great princes lay from post-Roman times right through to the extinction of native independence. We know, for example, that from 1230 Llywelyn ab Iorwerth ('Llywelyn the Great') began to style himself prince of Aberffraw and lord of Snowdon, demonstrating to all where he

saw the roots of his power. The final eclipse of this native rule came with the conquests of King Edward I. It was under the Statute of Wales, issued at Rhuddlan in 1284, that Anglesey emerged as a separate county with its own sheriff and shire governance based on English lines. This lasted essentially until 1974 when the island once more became part of Gwynedd – a further new county with very much older origins.

Anglesey has never been particularly difficult to reach. The Roman author Tacitus tells us how auxiliary soldiers invaded it in the late 70s AD by swimming across the Menai Strait. Visitors crossing the Strait today will notice a much more recent landmark, Thomas Telford's celebrated suspension bridge built in 1818–26. The island itself has a gently undulating and attractive landscape, with much of the 125-mile coastline designated an area of outstanding natural beauty.

Cadw cares for a wide variety of ancient and historic sites on Anglesey. Many of these, it must be said, are small in comparison to some of the spectacular medieval castles for which Wales is so well known. They are sometimes rather isolated in fields away from the main roads. None the less, in return for a little effort, there is much to see. Fascinating prehistoric monuments offer insights into the ways of life, belief and customs of some of the island's earliest permanent settlers. The native hut group at Din Lligwy and small fortlet at Caer Gybi represent developments in the Roman period. Most famous of all, however, is undoubtedly Beaumaris Castle – the last and the most sophisticated of all King Edward I's strongholds in north Wales.

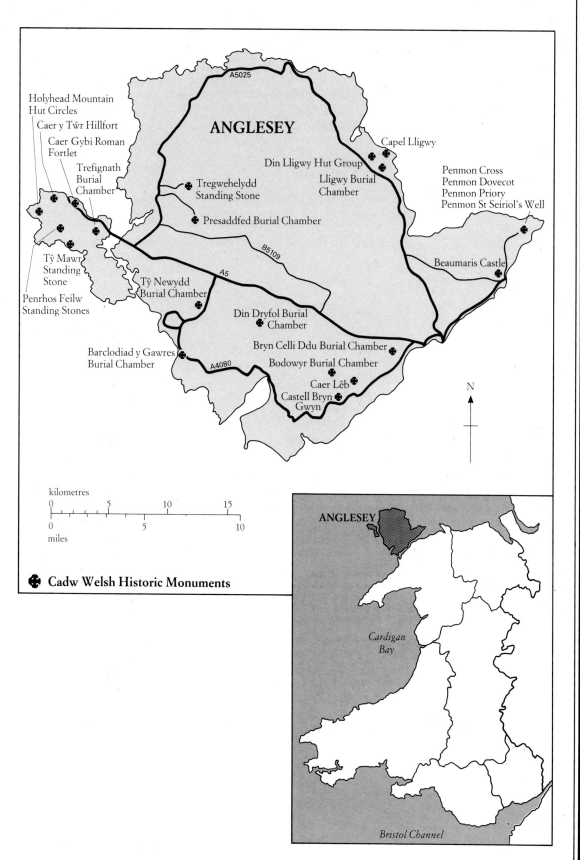

ANGLESEY

Holyhead Mountain
Hut Circles

Caer y Tŵr Hillfort

Caer Gybi Roman
Fortlet

Trefignath
Burial
Chamber

Tregwehelydd
Standing Stone

Din Lligwy Hut Group

Capel Lligwy

Lligwy Burial
Chamber

Penmon Cross
Penmon Dovecot
Penmon Priory
Penmon St Seiriol's Well

Presaddfed Burial Chamber

Tŷ Mawr
Standing
Stone

Penrhos Feilw
Standing Stones

Beaumaris Castle

Tŷ Newydd
Burial Chamber

Din Dryfol Burial
Chamber

Barclodiad y Gawres
Burial Chamber

Bryn Celli Ddu Burial Chamber

Bodowyr Burial Chamber

Caer Lêb

Castell Bryn
Gwyn

N

kilometres

0   5   10   15

0   5   10

miles

✣ Cadw Welsh Historic Monuments

ANGLESEY

Cardigan
Bay

Bristol Channel

The earthen mound of Barclodiad y Gawres stands on the headland above Porth Trecastell beach.

Barclodiad y Gawres Burial Chamber

In a spectacular cliffside position, overlooking the beach at Porth Trecastell, this is one of the most fascinating of all the Welsh Neolithic tombs. Barclodiad y Gawres – 'the Apronful of the Giantess' – had been used mercilessly as a stone 'quarry' in the eighteenth century and was thought to hold little of value. However, the results of excavations in 1952–53 were as much a rewarding surprise to the excavators – the late Professors Terence Powell and Glyn Daniel – as they are to visitors today. Five of the stones in the passage and chambers were found to be decorated with a variety of incised lozenge, chevron, spiral and zig-zag patterns. It remains one of the most striking modern finds in a chambered tomb, and is the foremost assembly of megalithic art in Wales. The present Director of the British Museum, Sir David Wilson, gained some of his archaeological experience as a young Cambridge undergraduate on this excavation.

The mound of the tomb is restored, but copies the original which was almost 90 feet in diameter and constructed partly of rubble and partly of turves. Inside, a passage some 23 feet long leads to a central chamber, from which open three smaller side ('transeptal') chambers. Each of these would have been covered with a capstone, but only that to the south survives. In the undisturbed west chamber, the cremated remains of two men were discovered. The central chamber does not appear to have been used for burial, but possibly for 'magical' practices. It contained a hearth on which a stew – a 'witches' brew' of frogs, toads, snails, snakes and fish – was poured. Indeed, both this hearth and the decorated stones were probably of powerful ritual and symbolic significance to the late Neolithic builders of the tomb.

As at Bryn Celli Ddu, the overall form of Barclodiad y Gawres, together with the curvilinear patterns on some of the slabs, seems to represent a direct copy of traditions seen elsewhere. In particular, it is very similar to the passage graves found in the Boyne valley of Ireland. On this basis, the tomb could have been constructed around 2700 BC.

The tomb passage at Barclodiad y Gawres.

Beaumaris Castle

It is difficult to find words adequate to express the genius behind the construction of Beaumaris. Quite simply, it is probably the most sophisticated example of medieval military architecture in the British Isles, the final fruit of a rich experience that had come close to bankrupting the kingdom. Raised on an entirely new and level site, without earlier structures to fetter its designer's ambitious creativity, it is without doubt the ultimate 'concentric' castle – built with an almost geometric symmetry. Conceived as a unified and integral whole, a high inner ring of defences was to be surrounded by a lower outer circuit of walls, combining an almost unprecedented level of strength and firepower. Huge sums were invested in the works, totalling more than £6,000 in the first six months of construction. Never before had so much royal treasure been applied so swiftly to one single operation. Yet for all this, Beaumaris was never completely finished. Remarkable though it may seem, the ground plan remained something of a blueprint for an awe-inspiring fortress that was never fully realized.

Today, after the dramatic skylines at Caernarfon, Conwy or Harlech, the low, squat walls and drum towers at Beaumaris may appear a little disappointing. This is largely because the great towers of the inner ward never received their top storeys, and the startling array of planned turrets was never so much as begun. It is only when the visitor walks around the moat, and begins to explore the intricacies of the defence capabilities, that the true significance and immense scale of the castle are appreciated. Not so many years ago, there were several tennis courts within the inner ward – with plenty of room to spare!

A castle was almost certainly planned when King Edward I visited Anglesey in August 1283. The following year the island was given shire status, with the Welsh town of Llanfaes as its seat of government. At this time, however, resources were already stretched with castle-building on the mainland, and any such scheme was postponed. Then, in October 1294, the Welsh rose in serious revolt under Madog ap Llywelyn, who even assumed the title 'prince of Wales'. The revolt took the king completely by surprise. The rebels were only crushed after an arduous winter campaign, during which

Beaumaris, the island castle, with the mountains of Snowdonia rising in the distance.

Edward himself was pinned down at Conwy from January to March 1295. With the advent of spring, surviving pockets of resistance soon collapsed. Even so, in their fury, the Welsh had massacred English royal officials, including the sheriff of Anglesey, Sir Roger Puleston, who was hanged. Without doubt the reoccupation of the island was foremost in the king's subsequent plans. Edward seems to have been determined upon one last show of strength, on the construction of one last magnificent castle to finally break the spirit of the Welsh. Thus it was that work began on a site at the northern edge of the Menai Strait, a site given the Norman-French name of *Beau Mareys* – the 'fair marsh'. The extent of English power is emphasized by the fact that the entire Welsh population of Llanfaes was summarily evicted 12 miles away, to the newly established settlement at Newborough.

Paralleled by huge investment, building work progressed initially at astonishing speed. In sole charge of the operations was Master James of St George, now in his late fifties, with already seven major Welsh castles to his credit. In 1296 he was at the head of a labour force of some 400 masons, 200 quarrymen, 30 smiths and carpenters, and 2,000 labourers. In addition, 30 boats, 60 waggons and 100 carts were used to bring stone to the site and to transport coal for the limekilns. In February of that year, Master James and his clerk wrote to the Exchequer officials, reporting progress and estimating further expenses. They pointed out 'the work we are doing is very costly and we need a great deal of money', and concluded with a desperate postscript: 'And, Sirs, for God's sake be quick . . . otherwise everything done up till now will have been to no avail'. In the event, work continued at a slower rate until 1298 when the money seems to have dried up altogether. King Edward's ever increasing commitments in Scotland inevitably diminished the resources for Wales. None the less, by this time Beaumaris was in a defensible condition, with the inner curtain wall standing between 20 and 28 feet high. Further works were eventually undertaken after 1306. The barbican was added to the southern gatehouse, and a gap in the still vulnerable circuit of the outer curtain was closed. The walls and towers were raised to the level much as we see today.

Even after 700 years it is not difficult to appreciate the tremendous sophistication in the overall design by Master James. The first line of

The moat and outer curtain wall at Beaumaris Castle.

A fifteenth-century manuscript illustration, showing the use of spiral scaffolding to build round towers such as those at Beaumaris.

defence was provided by a water-filled moat, some 18 feet wide. At the southern end was a tidal dock, where vessels of 40 tons laden weight could sail right up to the main gate. The dock was protected by a shooting deck, known as 'Gunners' Walk' since the nineteenth century. Across the moat is the low curtain wall of the outer ward, its circuit punctuated by 16 towers and two gates, providing some 300 firing positions for defending crossbow men. On the northern side, raised after 1306, the Llanfaes gate was probably never completed. The 'Gate next the Sea', on the other hand, preserves evidence of its stout wooden doors and 'murder holes' above. If an assailant broke through, there was then an awkward corner immediately to the right, with 11 more obstacles to negotiate before entering the heart of the castle. These included the barbican, further 'murder holes', three portcullises and several sets of doors. If the daunting prospect of the gate-passage proved too much, the would-be attacker caught hesitating between the inner and outer walls could not have survived for long. A rain of heavy crossfire would have poured down from all directions.

The striking thing about the inner ward is its great size. Covering about three-quarters of an acre, it was surrounded by a further six towers and two great gatehouses. Within, it is clear that the intention was to provide lavish suites of accommodation. Both gatehouses were planned as residential fortresses, with grand arrangements of state rooms at their rear – much as the completed gatehouse at Harlech. The north gate, however, was only raised as far as its hall level and the projected second storey was never built. Even as it stands, with its five great windows, it dominates the courtyard. Another block, of equal size, was planned for the south gate, but this was never to rise further than its footings. Around the edges of the ward further buildings were projected, and must have included a hall, kitchens, stables and perhaps a granary. There is some evidence for their existence in the face of the curtain wall, but it is not certain they were ever completed.

The curtain walls, like those at Caernarfon, are pierced throughout at main or first-floor level by long passages, linking the rooms in the flanking towers and giving access to latrines. On the east side of the inner ward is the chapel tower, where the vaulted basement now houses an exhibition on the castles of Edward I in Wales. The chapel proper, on the first floor, is a lovely room ended with a ribbed-stone vault.

The visitor may be left wondering why all this lavish accommodation was contemplated. Halls and chambers, and at least 19 good rooms in the towers of the inner ward, would perhaps appear greatly excessive. In short, Master James was intent upon a creation more splendid than his last. He was anxious to provide the most luxurious apartments for his patron the king, and – if he should marry again – his queen and her household. Moreover, Edward's son, the Prince of Wales, was fast approaching marriageable age. Considering the size of such entourages, plus the need to accommodate royal officials, the constable, and even the sheriff of Anglesey, the scale of these domestic arrangements is put into perspective.

Ironically, Beaumaris saw very little action. A survey in 1343 recorded the still incomplete nature of the works. By 1543 'there was scarcely a single chamber . . . where a man could lie dry'. The castle did play some part in the Civil War, and was held for the king until 1646 when it was surrendered to Parliament – marking the end of its active life. Nevertheless, in 1988 the quality, sophistication and genius behind this glorious masterpiece were formally recognized when it was inscribed on the 'World Heritage List' as a site of outstanding universal value.

Bodowyr
Burial Chamber

Bodowyr – a Neolithic burial chamber.

Although it has never been excavated, Bodowyr may well belong to one of the earliest groups of chambered tombs in north-west Wales. The polygonal chamber is thought to represent the remains of a simple 'passage grave', built by Neolithic farmers more than 5,000 years ago. The large mushroom-shaped capstone is now supported by three upright stones, and a fourth upright now lies fallen. Access to the tomb would have been gained by a short passage, with the low sill-stone on the east side marking the position of the entrance. Originally, the chamber was probably covered by a small cairn of stones.

Bryn Celli Ddu
Burial Chamber

Bryn Celli Ddu – 'the Mound in the Dark Grove' – is one of the most evocative prehistoric sites in Britain, and was probably one of the last megalithic tombs to be built on the Isle of Anglesey. Excavations in 1928 revealed a long and complex history, and it is now generally recognized that the tomb superseded an earlier

'henge' monument. Henges themselves were introduced from southern England about 2500 BC, and so the burial chamber must be somewhat later than this. The site has been so restored that something of both these monuments can be appreciated.

The henge, in the same tradition as the earlier phases of the much more elaborate Stonehenge, was a circular enclosure some 69 feet in diameter. This enclosure was defined by a wide ditch, and probably an outer bank which has not survived. Inside the ditch was a circular setting of stone pillars, only two of which remain unbroken and can be seen today. Henges are generally interpreted as ritual monuments, though some of the stones at Bryn Celli Ddu had cremated burials associated with them.

At a later date, the henge was deliberately wrecked and concealed by the builders of an impressive passage grave. The covering mound which can be seen today is only a partial reconstruction; the original must have been some 80 feet across. The edge of the mound was revetted by a kerb of stones bedded in the henge ditch, and at the entrance to the tomb this kerb joins up with the dry-stone walling of the outer passage to present an elaborate forecourt. The passage is 27 feet long, though only the inner 16 feet was roofed. It leads into a polygonal chamber, where a free-standing pillar, and carved spiral on one of the stones of the south wall, were probably of ritual or symbolic significance. Both burnt and unburnt bones were found in the passage and the central chamber. When the tomb was finally sealed, the outer

The entrance passage at Bryn Celli Ddu.

Bryn Celli Ddu – a late Neolithic passage grave raised within a circular henge.

passage was systematically blocked with earth and stones.

The forecourt may have served for elaborate ceremonial rites – a small ox was found buried in an enclosure framed with stone and timber. Finally, just behind the chamber, the excavations revealed a pit lying at the centre of the pre-existing stone circle. This had been the focus of a curious ceremony before the passage grave was built. It was covered with a stone, decorated with wavy and spiral lines carved on the sides and top. A cast of this now stands on the spot, and the original can be seen at the National Museum of Wales. Possibly the builders of the passage grave replaced some central feature of the henge with their own ritualistic pillar. This in turn would have then been covered by the large mound over the tomb.

The form of the passage grave, together with the curvilinear art style, is similar to Barclodiad y Gawres and can be compared cautiously to tombs elsewhere. In this instance, the best parallels are in Brittany, but of course the exact relationship is far from clear. Bryn Celli Ddu is a splendid structure, yet it must represent the last expression of a very long tradition of megalithic architecture in north-west Wales.

Caer Gybi Roman Fortlet

The parish church of St Cybi, which overlooks Holyhead harbour, is surrounded by the walls of a late Roman fortlet. Caer Gybi – 'Cybi's Fort' – was probably built towards the end of the third century as a base for a small Roman

'Cybi's Fort' at Holyhead.

naval flotilla. Recent archaeological excavations elsewhere in Wales, notably at Cardiff, Loughor and Neath, have demonstrated a definite pattern of coastal defences established at this time, and suggest that Caer Gybi was part of a consolidated network defending the Welsh coast from Irish raiders.

The walls of the sub-rectangular fortlet enclose less than an acre. Originally, there were circular towers at all four corners, but that in the south-east corner is a modern rebuild. The pattern of diagonally laid courses of 'herringbone' masonry, particularly in the west wall and north-west tower, is typical of the late Roman period. The site of the Roman quay was probably on the east side, and the fortlet may well have operated in conjunction with the signal station recently identified within the hillfort at Caer y Twr.

Caer Gybi is held to be the site of a monastic foundation, granted to St Cybi by King Maelgwn of Gwynedd in the sixth century. The saint is also associated, of course, with the holy well which bears his name on the Lleyn peninsula. By the south wall of the fortlet there is a small chapel known as Eglwys y Bedd – 'Church of the Grave' – which is traditionally believed to cover the grave of St Cybi. However, an Anglo-Saxon silver penny dug up within the churchyard suggests a later use of the deserted fort by Viking raiders.

Caer Lêb

This low-lying rectilinear enclosure is defined by double banks and ditches, though the outer bank has been totally destroyed on the north and east sides. The size of the enclosure, together with its marshy location, have sometimes led to its interpretation as a medieval moated homestead. Excavations in the last century, however, revealed a third-century brooch and a fourth-century coin, indicating that the site was in use in the late Roman period, if not earlier. Traces of stone buildings were also recovered, and the platform visible along the

Caer y Twr – the rocky hillfort on Holyhead Mountain, seen from the air.

The small twelfth-century chapel known as Capel Lligwy.

north side yielded a medieval coin. Only through further archaeological investigation might we expect a fuller history of this intriguing monument.

late Roman watchtower. It would have commanded excellent views over Holyhead harbour, and probably operated in conjunction with the fortlet at Caer Gybi.

Caer y Tŵr Hillfort

Visitors pursuing the lengthy walk to the top of Holyhead Mountain are rewarded with superb views from the rocky interior of Caer y Tŵr. Although not closely dated, there is little doubt that this was an Iron Age hillfort, similar to other examples in north-west Wales. On the north and east sides, the stone rampart wall stands to a height of ten feet in places, and encloses an area of some 17 acres. There is an inturned entrance in the north-east corner, where the walls are around 12 feet wide, thick enough to have included a rampart walk. The south-western side of the enclosure ends in a sheer precipice, with little need for artificial protection. It is now impossible to trace any signs of late prehistoric occupation in the barren and uneven interior.

At the very summit of the site, however, recent excavations have revealed the base of a

Capel Lligwy

Standing isolated in a field, within the large parish of Penrhos Lligwy, the origins of this little chapel are obscure, though its initial construction in stone probably dates to the first half of the twelfth century. By 1100 Anglesey was finally free from Viking raids, and the Normans had abandoned their effort to hold the island. It was at this time, during the settled conditions brought about under the patronage of Gruffudd ap Cynan and his son Owain Gwynedd, that many churches were built in masonry for the first time.

Capel Lligwy is a simple rectangular building, with no structural division between the nave and chancel. The south doorway has a plain round-headed arch. The upper parts of the walls, which stand almost to full height, were rebuilt in the fourteenth century, and a bellcot survives on the western gable. The small chapel was added to the south side in the sixteenth century.

19

Castell Bryn Gwyn

Today, visitors to Castell Bryn Gwyn are greeted by little more than a single bank, standing some 12 feet high and enclosing a circular area about 180 feet in diameter. However, excavations in 1959–60 revealed a long and complex history hidden beneath the turf. The earliest monument was raised in the late Neolithic or early Bronze Age period, more than 3,500 years ago. It comprised a bank with an external ditch, and has been considered by some to be a 'henge' monument. There are difficulties with this interpretation, particularly since henges generally have a ditch inside the bank (though the ditch is outside at the famous Stonehenge in Wiltshire).

The site was later remodelled on at least two different occasions, culminating in a timber-revetted rampart with a deep V-shaped ditch on the exterior. This last form of enclosure was common in the Iron Age. Moreover, a few sherds of Roman pottery were recovered from the excavation, and indicate occupation extending into the later first century.

Din Dryfol Burial Chamber

From Fferam Rhosydd, a pleasant walk across several fields takes the visitor to one of the more intriguing megalithic monuments in Wales. Din Dryfol is situated on a narrow ledge at the foot of a rocky hill, and it is clear that the shape of the monument was undoubtedly influenced by its location. A huge portal stone survives at the east end, marking the entrance to what must have been a series of up to four rectangular chambers stretching some 40 feet behind. The whole was covered by a long and narrow cairn, probably as much as 200 feet in length, and representing a huge investment in terms of manpower for construction.

Recent excavations have revealed several periods of construction, and during an early phase the entrance to one of the chambers was built of wood. The excavator has suggested that this may have been more common in Neolithic tombs than we now think. The composite nature of Din Dryfol bears some comparison to the evidence from Trefignath but it, too, shares features found at a distinct family of 'long graves' located in the Clyde area of Scotland.

The chambered tomb at Din Dryfol.

The use of large slabs is a notable feature in the construction of the huts at Din Lligwy.

Din Lligwy Hut Group

A short walk across several fields, past Hen Capel Lligwy, takes the visitor to the best-known example of a Romano-British 'farmstead' in north Wales. It is, however, just one of almost 300 such sites which dot the hillslopes between the Dyfi and the Clwyd, sometimes referred to by the traditional but misleading name of 'cytiau'r Gwyddelod' – 'Irishmen's houses'. Although very few of these stone hut groups have been excavated, there is little reason to believe that they owe their origin to Irish settlers. In fact, where excavations have taken place, most of the material recovered dates to the later Roman period, chiefly to the third and fourth centuries. Such is the density of these settlements that some scholars have suggested a deliberate plantation of farmers under Roman military influence.

Din Lligwy is one of the larger sites, but is likely to have been no more than a single profitable homestead. The enclosure wall surrounds two circular huts and a series of rectangular buildings now standing up to five feet high. The single narrow entrance passes through a 'porch' or lodge, and the circular structures almost certainly represent houses. The various other rectangular buildings were probably barns and workshops. Excavations in the early part of this century recovered third- and fourth-century Roman coins, pottery and glass, together with considerable evidence for ironworking. Indeed, agricultural production was perhaps a relatively minor element in a more profitable mixed economy. It has been argued that Din Lligwy was a local centre for smithing, with the inhabitants deriving much of their wealth from passing on the products of this work to the Roman military centres.

We still have much to learn on the history and economy of these intriguing hut groups. The recent excavations at the Holyhead settlement, for example, have emphasized the dangers of assuming too much merely on the basis of surface characteristics and the results of early archaeological investigation.

One of the hut circles at the ancient settlement on the footslopes of Holyhead Mountain.

Holyhead Mountain Hut Circles

Not far from the South Stack lighthouse, on the south facing slopes of Holyhead Mountain, the Tŷ Mawr hut circles are spread over an area of some 15 to 20 acres. Even before recent archaeological investigations, they had attracted attention for many years. About 20 buildings survive today, though originally the group was much larger with over 50 structures recorded in 1862. Such a concentration is far greater than that generally found in the enclosed hut groups of north Wales, as for example at the well-known site of Din Lligwy. Indeed, it is rare to find so many buildings of this kind outside a hillfort. About a dozen of the structures were excavated in 1862 and 1868, and the finds – pottery, coins and evidence of metalworking – were subsequently interpreted as representing a settlement dating to the late Roman period. However, radiocarbon dates derived from investigations at the eastern group of huts in 1978–82 have indicated that this part of the settlement, at least, goes back to the late Neolithic or early Bronze Age period. Moreover, there are hints of a prolonged occupation or reoccupation right through to the sixth century AD!

The huts themselves are constructed of drystone walling and of larger boulders set upright. Some have elaborate entrances, and they must have carried conical roofs of thatch or turf. Within several of the huts there are traces of 'furniture', such as basins and benches of stone.

The remains of a substantial field system, largely hidden by scrub, occupies the slope below the Tŷ Mawr structures. Thus, it has become increasingly clear that the huts are merely the more obvious traces of an ancient and extensive landscape of farms and fields extending back at least 4,000 years.

Lligwy Burial Chamber

The enormous capstone at Lligwy must weigh up to 28 tons, making it one of the largest in Britain. Eight upright blocks sit on the rock edge or upon crude dry-stone walling, and

The Lligwy chambered tomb.

support the capstone about six feet above the base of an irregular pit. The pit itself probably began as a natural fissure in the rock. The resulting tomb appears to have had very little formal plan, with an unusual squat appearance.

Excavations in 1909 revealed a burial deposit divided into two layers, separated by a kind of rough paving. The bones represented between 15 and 30 people – men, women and children. Other finds included mussel shells, pottery, flint tools and a bone pin. The Lligwy chamber could have been in use over a very long period, perhaps from the late fourth millennium BC through to around 2000 BC.

Penmon Cross

This free-standing pillar-cross originally stood in the deer park, a short distance to the west of the priory, but has since been moved to the nave of St Seiriol's church for protection. Like Carew and Maen Achwyfan it was erected around the year AD 1000, and its decoration bears distinct Irish and Scandinavian influences.

Standing some nine feet tall, the head, shaft and base are three separate stones mortised together. The decorative fret-patterns and plaits are interspersed with crudely-carved human and animal figures. Although much weathered, the principal scene is on the front of the cross and represents the temptation of St Anthony – of

Egyptian derivation, but a favourite Irish motif. A second cross of a similar date can be seen in the south transept of the church.

Penmon Dovecot

This charming little building must have been built about 1600, probably by Sir Richard Bulkeley (1533–1621), whose house Baron Hill – just west of Beaumaris – was completed in 1618. He was undisputed cock of the walk in Anglesey at this time and, like other new gentry landowners in Wales, was busy improving his demesne farms. Sir Richard's Anglesey property furnished him, for example, with 'excellent beef, mutton, lamb, butter and cheese', and here we see evidence of attention lavished upon another important item in the domestic economy. Indeed, in the days before improvements in feeding stuffs eased the problem of fattening stock over winter months, pigeons or doves provided a ready source of fresh meat.

The Penmon dovecot was built on a grand scale, with up to 1,000 nests lining the walls. The massive roof has a vaulted dome crowned with an open lantern, through which the birds could fly in and out. Inside, a stone pillar with corbelled steps would have carried a ladder for access to the nests.

Penmon Dovecot, built around 1600.

Penmon Priory

This peaceful setting on the eastern tip of Anglesey is traditionally the site of a monastery established in the sixth century by St Seiriol, a friend and contemporary of St Cybi. Like Cybi's foundation at Holyhead – Caer Gybi – Penmon undoubtedly became an important mother church, or *clas*, with ecclesiastical authority over much of the surrounding area. Following the arrival of the Normans, the native – 'Celtic' – community of secular clerks continued to serve the church throughout the twelfth century, and the patronage remained firmly with the Welsh princes. It was almost certainly the great prince Gruffudd ap Cynan (d. 1137), or his son, who provided the capital for the earliest stone church; this survives as the present nave, crossing and south transept at St Seiriol's. Then, around 1220–40, a new chancel more than twice the size of the existing nave was added to the eastern end. This building work marks a significant change in the nature of the native community. For some time the princes of Gwynedd and Powys had been supporters of the Augustinian house at Haughmond in Shropshire. By the early thirteenth century they had encouraged the transformation of some of the oldest and most distinguished *clasau* of north Wales – including Bardsey, Beddgelert and St

Tudwal's Island – into houses of Augustinian canons. Penmon was also reorganized at this time, and thrived as an Augustinian priory until its suppression in 1536.

A cloister was formed to the south of the church, but varies from standard monastic planning in that the court lay adjacent to the chancel rather than against the nave. The three-storeyed southern range was built in the thirteenth century, and is the focus of the remains. The ground level served as a cellar, with the canons' dining hall above, and probably their dormitory on the third floor. At the eastern end of this range there is a small two-storeyed block added in the sixteenth century. This may have had a 'warming house' – or perhaps a private apartment – on the ground floor, with a kitchen above. The prior's house probably occupied the west range of the cloister, but this has been much altered and is now a private dwelling.

Penmon, St Seiriol's Well

Situated close to the later Augustinian priory, the origins of St Seiriol's Well may go back to the initial sixth-century monastic foundation at

A print of Penmon Priory in 1742, by Samuel and Nathaniel Buck.

The well chamber associated with St Seiriol at Penmon.

Penmon. It is, like St Cybi's Well on the neighbouring Lleyn peninsula, one of the many examples of 'holy wells' in Wales associated with a local apostle. The small rectangular chamber covers a pool surrounded by a slab floor, and there are stone benches and niches at the sides. The healing powers of the well continued to attract the sick and infirm through to the eighteenth century, and the upper part of the chamber was rebuilt in brick at this time. The lower stone courses could be very much older. Just outside, there are the slight remains of a circular hut, or 'cell', reputedly associated with St Seiriol himself.

Penrhos Feilw Standing Stones

Standing stones seem to have gradually appeared throughout Britain in the earlier Bronze Age, between 2500 and 1500 BC, and are generally accepted by archaeologists as ritual monuments. In Wales, as elsewhere, their function was perhaps linked to more elaborate stone circles, and as such they provide insights into groups of people concerned with the forces of life and nature. In part, at least, both circles and individual stones were probably related to major seasonal events, or to the movements of heavenly bodies.

There is a strong tradition that the Penrhos Feilw stones originally stood near the centre of a small stone circle, and that a cist containing bones, arrowheads and spearheads was found in digging between them. The two impressive stones are almost identical in shape and stand about ten feet high.

Bronze Age standing stones at Penrhos Feilw.

Presaddfed has never been excavated, but seems to consist of two distinct burial chambers, a pattern now recognized in a number of Neolithic tombs in Wales, including Trefignath (right).

Presaddfed Burial Chamber

Although well preserved, this tomb has never been excavated and cannot be easily related to other such monuments. It lies on the floor of a marshy valley, and consists of two groups of stones about seven feet apart. This arrangement bears some resemblance to the recently excavated tomb at Trefignath, in which case the stones could represent two distinct chambers in a composite 'long grave'. Presaddfed may, therefore, have developed over a long period, with its origins extending back before 3500 BC. The southern chamber remains largely intact, its capstone supported on four uprights. It is recorded that in the eighteenth century the tomb provided shelter for a family of squatters.

Trefignath Burial Chamber

Trefignath is one of the most fully excavated chambered tombs on Anglesey, and the monument has now been laid out in such a way that visitors can appreciate the main outlines of its long and complex history. Before the work, it was thought to have been constructed as a single 'gallery' grave, divided into segments. The most important discovery of the excavation, however, was that the tomb comprised three very distinct chambers, each built as a separate phase of activity.

The earliest chamber is that at the western end. It was raised about 3750–3500 BC and its box-like structure, once surrounded by a cairn of boulders, has been interpreted as a simple passage grave. After an unknown interval, the tomb was enlarged by the construction of the central chamber. The cairn was also extended into a long wedge shape, with a deeply recessed forecourt. The resulting design was very similar to megalithic tombs in the Severn-Cotswold region, and may betray the spread of architectural ideas from the south. After a further interval, these two chambers passed out of use and were superseded by a third chamber to the east. The cairn was again extended to incorporate this final addition, and its 'horn' shaped forecourt is still clearly defined. It is yet more fascinating to note that the design of the eastern chamber seems to have been influenced by developments in tomb architecture in southwest Scotland.

Trefignath thus served as a collective burial vault over a very long period, with the final closure of the chambers perhaps dating to after 2250 BC. The continued use and elaboration of a single monument, rather than the development of a cemetery, emphasizes the ritual and ceremonial significance of such sites in the Neolithic landscape.

Trefignath – a Neolithic chambered tomb in use for up to 1,500 years.

Tregwehelydd Standing Stone

Standing isolated in a field, this stone is none the less located in a prominent location on the crest of a ridge. It is almost nine feet high, but alas is now in a fragmentary state. The three pieces are held together of necessity by bolts and bands.

Tŷ Mawr Standing Stone

Tŷ Mawr is a particularly imposing standing stone, and once again is representative of early Bronze Age ritual monuments. Some nine feet tall, it tapers slightly towards the top, and occupies an isolated position on a slight rise.

Tŷ Newydd Burial Chamber

This tomb now looks in a somewhat sorry state, with a narrow capstone needing additional support from two built-up pillars. Nevertheless, it is of much interest and may belong to the earliest tradition of megalithic building on Anglesey. Excavations in 1936 revealed that the capstone had slipped to the north and no longer covered the whole chamber, whose area was marked by a spread of charcoal. In fact, the stone may well be a fractured remnant of a wider original. There is a reliable tradition that the entire tomb had once been covered with a circular cairn, which, together with its position on top of a low hill, suggests links with simple 'passage grave' practice. As such, it was perhaps built by early Neolithic farmers before 3500 BC, and is similar to the tomb at Bodowyr and to the earliest phase of the recently excavated Trefignath.

27

CLWYD
The North-Eastern Borderlands

The new administrative unit of Clwyd was formed under the local government reorganization of 1974, and includes the historic counties of Flintshire and most of Denbighshire. Much of the landscape is greatly attractive, especially the rolling Berwyn and Clwydian mountains and the lush valley of the Dee. The heart of the region, however, is the lovely Vale of Clwyd, bounded on the east by the Clwydian range, and separated from the Conwy valley to the west by the bleak Denbigh moors. The most renowned of antiquaries, William Camden (1551–1623), thought that the 'Vale itself with its green meadows, yellow cornfields and fair houses, standing thick, and many beautiful churches, giveth wonderful great contentment to such as behold it from above'. More recently, in a classic study on *The Welsh House* (1940), Iorwerth Peate likened the scenery here to a piece of the Cheshire plain let down in Wales.

Indeed, rather like Gwent in the south, the orientation of this border area has always lain firmly, though not exclusively, eastwards. The Dee estuary might be regarded as the natural boundary with England; though borders are of course not fixed in heaven, they are shaped by men. From the eighth century, Offa's Dyke and the near contemporary Wat's Dyke began to form a comparatively clear demarcation between the two nations. Even so, this did not prevent Edward the Elder founding a Saxon *burh*, or fortified town, at Rhuddlan – *Cledemutha* – near the mouth of the Clwyd in AD 921. By the mid eleventh century English political control had once more been pushed back to the east of the Dyke by the brilliant successes of Gruffudd ap Llywelyn, prince of Gwynedd.

Gruffudd was killed at the hands of his own men in 1063, and within a decade the Welsh were facing a new threat in this border area, a threat more powerful than anything they had ever faced before – the Normans. By 1073, the ruthless enterprise of Hugh of Avranches, earl of Chester (d. 1101) and his cousin, Robert of Rhuddlan (d. 1088–93), had extended Norman control along the north Wales coast as far as the Clwyd. The site of the Saxon *burh* at Rhuddlan was now chosen for a new earthwork motte and bailey castle, which served as a base for further advance into north-west Wales.

Over the next two centuries, the tide of border warfare meant the Clwyd region was to change hands many times. Anglo-Norman domination was repeatedly challenged, and at times – notably under Owain Gwynedd (d. 1170) and Llywelyn the Great (d. 1240) – Welsh rule extended once more to the banks of the Dee, with Ewloe Castle serving as a frontier post for the princes. Not until 1277, when King Edward I launched his initial offensive against Llywelyn the Last (d. 1282), was the area finally brought into permanent English control. This campaign saw the building of the king's first two north Wales castles at Flint and Rhuddlan.

Besides the strongholds which reflect these centuries of bitter dispute, Clwyd has many more sites of historic interest, including the Cistercian abbeys at Basingwerk and Valle Crucis, and the celebrated pilgrimage centre of St Winifred at Holywell. Cadw also maintains two other important ecclesiastical sites at Llangar and Rûg. The English character of parts of the county is unmistakable, with a pastoral landscape and half-timbered buildings like those of neighbouring Cheshire and Shropshire.

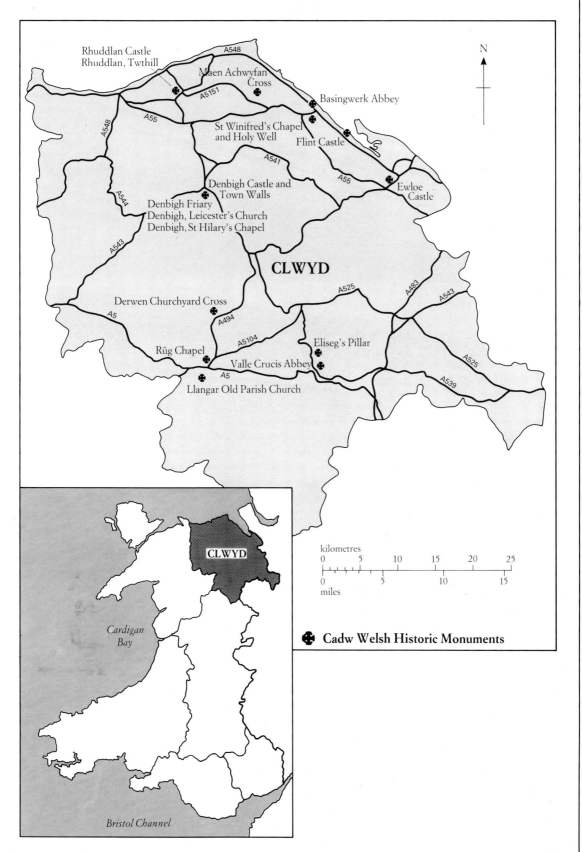

N

Rhuddlan Castle
Rhuddlan, Twthill

A548

Maen Achwyfan
Cross

A5151

Basingwerk Abbey

St Winifred's Chapel
and Holy Well

A55

Flint Castle

A541

Denbigh Castle and
Town Walls

A55

Ewloe
Castle

Denbigh Friary
Denbigh, Leicester's Church
Denbigh, St Hilary's Chapel

A548

A544

A543

CLWYD

A525

A483

A543

Derwen Churchyard Cross

A5

A494

A525

Rûg Chapel

A5104

Eliseg's Pillar

Valle Crucis Abbey

A539

A5

Llangar Old Parish Church

CLWYD

Cardigan
Bay

kilometres
0   5   10   15   20   25
0   5   10   15
miles

Bristol Channel

✠ **Cadw Welsh Historic Monuments**

The Cistercian abbey of Basingwerk, founded circa 1131.

Basingwerk Abbey

In the late fifteenth century, the bard Tudor Aled – with pardonable poetic exaggeration no doubt – praised the great beauty and setting of Basingwerk. New houses had been built for guests who flocked to the abbey in large numbers. These visitors apparently had to be accommodated for meals at two sittings, where their palates were quenched with a choice of French and Spanish wines. All this, however, was a far cry from the early ideals of the monastic community here.

The chapter house at Basingwerk.

Basingwerk was founded about 1131 by Ranulf 'de Gernon', earl of Chester, for an abbot and 12 monks of the French order of Savigny. In 1147 the houses and property of this order were absorbed by the Cistercians, and ten years later Basingwerk was placed under the oversight of Buildwas Abbey in Shropshire. The monks eventually built up substantial estates in what is now Clwyd, with further arable lands in the Wirral and an important manor at Glossop, Derbyshire. At the end of the thirteenth century there were 2,000 sheep grazing on their pastures in the Penllyn district alone. Indeed, in 1347, the Black Prince ordered his clerk to bargain for the 'excellent wools' of the abbey. As with other houses of the Cistercian order, however, the strict *Rule* and harsh conventual life at Basingwerk were severely compromised in the later Middle Ages.

The earliest buildings may have been of wood, and the first stone church seems to date from the beginning of the thirteenth century. Little of this now survives, though the plan of its aisled nave, north and south transepts, and presbytery to the east are easily traced. Parts of the chapter house and novices' lodging, on the east side of the cloister, belong to the twelfth century. In the early thirteenth century the chapter house was extended, and was divided into two by a lovely pair of arches springing from a central column. This was an important room where the monks met each day to hear a chapter of their *Rule*. Traces of the bench on which they sat can still be seen around the walls. Further south in this eastern range was the warming house, the only place in the abbey where a fire was allowed. The monks' dining hall was rebuilt at right-angles to the southern range of the cloister in the later thirteenth century. Today, it is much the most impressive surviving room, with traces of the reader's pulpit, and the hatch through which food was passed from the kitchen. In the south-east corner of the cloister, the base of the day stairs by which the monks approached their dormitory can be seen.

It was in the time of Thomas Pennant, abbot from 1488 to about 1522, that Basingwerk was praised for its hospitality. Pennant himself was described as a man 'with a fine taste for minstrelsy and a generous patron of bards'. He was succeeded by his son Nicolas! – the last abbot, who surrendered the house to the Crown in 1536.

Denbigh Castle and Town Walls

Denbigh Castle crowns the summit of what is a particularly steep outcrop dominating the Vale of Clwyd. The town walls were conceived with the castle as a complete defensive circuit. They run down the slope north and eastwards, thereby extending the fortification to the entire hilltop. Without doubt, the principal feature at the site is the great gatehouse – the link between defended town and castle ward. When John Leland – Henry VIII's self-styled king's antiquary – visited Denbigh in the 1530s, he commented that if the gatehouse had remained complete it 'might have counted among the most memorable peaces of workys yn England'. The striking originality of this triple-towered construction reflects a military architect of considerable genius.

An aerial view of Henry de Lacy's Denbigh Castle from the south.

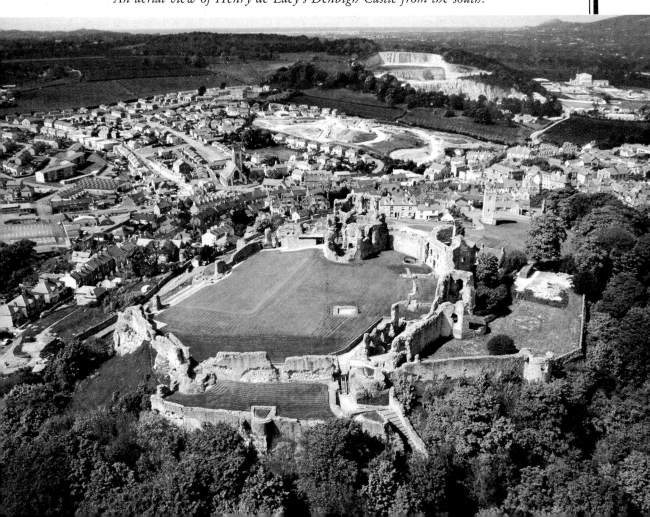

The Green Chambers and great hall along the eastern side of the castle represent the second phase of building at Denbigh, in the later 1290s.

The site was almost certainly occupied long before the construction of the present castle. In the later thirteenth century, Dafydd ap Gruffudd, Llywelyn the Last's brother, had a princely stronghold at Denbigh and it is known to have included a hall, private room, chapel, bakehouse and buttery. From this power base, it was Dafydd who swooped down on Hawarden Castle in March 1282 and threw the Welsh into open rebellion. This spark led to Edward I's second campaign in Wales, and to the final systematic annihilation of resistance in the north. The defences at Denbigh, whatever their nature, kept the English at bay for nearly a month. Immediately after the fall of Dafydd's capital, however, on 16 October 1282 the king granted the lordship of Denbigh to his close associate Henry de Lacy, earl of Lincoln. Edward was here with de Lacy until the end of the month, and work on construction began almost at once. Royal resources were made available, and both men were no doubt overseeing the planning of the new fortifications. The presence of the king's master mason, James of St George, at this stage may well explain the sophistication of the overall plan, particularly

the conception behind the great gatehouse. With the work well in hand, de Lacy was left to complete the scheme with his own resources.

The defences of castle and town were clearly built in two stages. In common with other sites, the initial effort went into securing a strong safe base for garrison and builders. The southern and western walls of the castle formed part of this earliest work, and the circuit was completed by the town defences. This period is marked by relatively thin walls and plain half-round towers, not unlike those in the town walls at Conwy. By 1284, de Lacy was feeling sufficiently secure to start stocking his deer park, and by 1290 he had granted the first borough charter to the English burgesses living in the town. Moreover, in the surrounding countryside Earl Hugh had made a concerted effort to create a rural enclave of English peasant settlers.

Small wonder that Denbigh was a significant target during the rising under Madog ap Llywelyn in 1294. The half-completed castle was taken by the Welsh, who then defied de Lacy's attempts to recapture the site. Only when the rebellion was finally crushed in the following year was it restored to English hands. We cannot be sure how far the defences of the castle had progressed by this time, but it seems likely that the eastern towers and curtain, together with the great gatehouse, had all begun to rise. The construction certainly continued after the revolt. These later stages are easily recognized by a different coloured stone. The curtain walls are thicker, and the angular towers and banded masonry facing the town resemble the achievements of Master James at Caernarfon.

As stated, most impressive of all is the superb gatehouse, a highly advanced building in which three octagonal towers enclosed a similarly multangular gatehouse hall. It is this central hall which is of great originality and was vaulted over with another vast chamber of identical plan above. The professional touch abounds in the contrivance of arrowloops, wall-passages, and notably in the careful planning of the latrine chutes in the north-west tower, five of which are brought together at a common cesspit into which rainwater from the roof also flowed. Beyond its powerful defensive capabilities, the gatehouse was embellished with chequered stonework and probably a carved figure of Edward I in the niche above the entrance arch.

Inside the castle, domestic buildings were ranged around the walls, including the great hall and various chambers. Their construction and modification probably extended into the fourteenth century, although they do not survive to any great height. There is some notable carving surviving in the Green Chambers. Following Madog's rebellion, the level of the walls on the west side of the castle were raised and an outer wall, or mantlet, was added as further defence.

The town walls were also strengthened in the 1290s, where the principal addition was the heavily defended section on the north-east which may still be walked by visitors. Here the wall plunges down the cliff edge from the Countess Tower to encompass the deep Goblin Tower, which protects a never-failing well. Beyond this, the wall links up with an earlier section of the defences higher up the slope. Elsewhere, at the foot of Tower Hill, the Burgess Gate is also well preserved.

On the death of Henry de Lacy in 1311, Denbigh was still unfinished. There is a strong tradition, recorded by John Leland in 1535, that the earl's eldest son, Edmund, fell to his death in the castle well and as a result Henry never

The remarkable great gatehouse at Denbigh Castle.

finished the building work. Indeed, it seems a planned second floor in the great gatehouse never progressed beyond the drawing board. None the less, both castle and town saw considerable action in the later Middle Ages. In the early fifteenth century Denbigh was held by Henry Percy – 'Hotspur' – in support of Owain Glyndŵr. Later, during the Wars of the Roses, it was again the scene of warfare when in the 1460s Jasper Tudor launched two attacks against Yorkist defenders. Castle and town were granted by Elizabeth I to her favourite Robert Dudley, earl of Leicester, but although he began work on a grand new church, he did little to the castle. Denbigh saw final action in the Civil War when it was garrisoned for the king by Colonel William Salesbury of Rûg. The colonel spent liberally in the royalist cause and entertained King Charles I here for three days in 1645. Following a six-month siege from April to October, 1646, Denbigh Castle was finally given up to the Parliamentary forces and eventual redundancy.

Denbigh Friary

This was a small house of Carmelite or 'White' friars, and may have been established in 1289 by John de Sunimore. The Carmelites were introduced to England in the mid thirteenth century, and there were eventually some 40 foundations, but Denbigh remained the only house of the order in Wales. In the fifteenth and early sixteenth centuries it enjoyed the patronage of the Salusbury family. It also had the support of the bishops of St Asaph.

Much of the late thirteenth-century church survives, with the friars' choir to the east standing to roof level. In the nineteenth century it remained largely intact and was in use as a malt house, but was destroyed by fire in 1898. The great east window is now bricked up, though it was clearly enlarged in the early fifteenth century. A further large window is set high in the north wall to avoid the brothers' choir stalls. The western part of the church was used as a preaching nave for the lay congregation. Between these two areas, a doorway to the south marks the position of the 'walking place', a lobby area divided from the choir and the nave by wooden screens. Above this was a wooden belfry, described at the Dissolution as 'a steple of tymbre like a lovere of a hall borded, the toppe therof leaded'. The doorway itself led out to the cloister, and to the living quarters of the friars.

Denbigh, Leicester's Church

Robert Dudley, earl of Leicester, a favourite of Queen Elizabeth I, was granted the lordship of Denbigh in 1563. It was here, in 1578, that he began to build a new town church more fitting to his dignity as virtual governor of north Wales. The ruins which can now be seen below the castle are quite remarkable, representing as they do the only large new church in Britain of the Elizabethan period. Dudley was the leading

Denbigh Friary, founded for Carmelite friars around 1289.

Lord Leicester's church at Denbigh, begun in 1578.

supporter of the Puritans at court, and the simple plan and plain character of the building reflect his ideals. Up to 170 feet long, the church had a broad central aisle, with narrower side aisles, but there are no surviving details of the internal ritual arrangements. It may well be, as is reputed, that Leicester intended his church to replace St Asaph as the cathedral of the diocese. The first vicar here was William Morgan, later bishop of St Asaph itself, and famed for his translation of the Bible into Welsh. Building work at Denbigh, however, proceeded slowly and appears to have been abandoned in 1584. The church remained unfinished when Leicester died in 1588.

Denbigh, St Hilary's Chapel

The tower and west wall are all that survive of this chapel, which was built about 1300 to serve the new town established below the castle. It was referred to in 1334 as 'the chapel within the walls', laying at a central point between the castle's great gatehouse and the Burgess Gate. The nave and chancel lay on the flat ground to the east of the tower, and both were modified over the centuries. An aisle on the north side of the nave was completely rebuilt in 1707–11. St

35

Hilary's was demolished in 1923, having fallen into disuse at the end of the nineteenth century. The tower has a western doorway, and the battlemented top probably dates from the fifteenth century.

Derwen Churchyard Cross

This once very fine pillar cross dates from the mid to late fifteenth century, and stands in the circular churchyard on the south side of St Mary's. Under little cusped canopies, there are four niches around the head, and each still retains traces of the original sculptured scene. Although much weathered, the carvings include the coronation of the virgin, the crucifixion, the virgin and child, and an angel – possibly St Michael, with scales. The chamfered corners of the cross shaft also bear worn traces of sculpture.

The churchyard cross at Derwen.

The ninth-century Pillar of Eliseg.

Eliseg's Pillar

The cross from which Valle Crucis took its name is known as the Pillar of Eliseg, and sits on a more ancient burial mound, isolated in a field just to the north of the abbey. The pillar was thrown down during the Civil War, and lay broken in two pieces when the antiquary Edward Llwyd recorded its Latin inscription in 1696. This inscription is now badly weathered and no longer intelligible, but from Llwyd's transcription we know there were once at least 31 lines celebrating the glories of the royal house of Powys. It is particularly notable as the most elaborate record of its kind surviving from early Christian Britain. The cross was erected by Cyngen – the last of the kings of Powys – who died in 854, in honour of his great-grandfather Eliseg. The text further records that it was 'Eliseg who united the inheritance of Powys ... out of the hand of the English with fire and sword'.

Eliseg's Pillar now stands about eight feet tall, though its original height was probably close to 20 feet. Raised in the ninth century, such round-shafted crosses are a type well known in parts of the English west midlands, or the old kingdom of Mercia. The cross was restored in 1779 when the barrow on which it stands was excavated. It appears this contained a 'long cist' burial of sixth or seventh century date, though the mound itself could be prehistoric.

Ewloe Castle

The attractive pink sandstone remains of this little-known stronghold of the Welsh princes lie hidden in a wooded hollow – a location which must retain much of its medieval character. Indeed, we know the castle lay in a corner of the great forest of Ewloe, estimated in Domesday as measuring ten leagues by three leagues! Throughout the early Middle Ages this was disputed border country, and to English expeditionary forces setting out from Chester for the north Wales coast the forest must have appeared a daunting prospect. During a period of Welsh recovery and expansion Owain Gwynedd may have established a motte and bailey here in the 1140s.

The earliest surviving masonry, however, is the apsidal or D-shaped tower standing at the centre of the upper ward. It is difficult to trace a precise origin for such towers, but they are characteristically Welsh. Others may be seen, for example, at Castell y Bere, or at Criccieth where two are placed side by side to form a simple gatehouse. At Ewloe the tower is known as the Welsh Tower, and was probably raised by Llywelyn the Great around 1215. Llywelyn had just recovered the district from King John and was no doubt anxious to exert his authority, and to protect this new eastern flank of his principality. The tower must have performed the function of a keep, and was perhaps surrounded by various timber buildings. It provided a suite of limited apartments set over a basement, and was entered at first-floor level by an external flight of steps. Grooves survive around the top of the parapet wall, providing a clue to the presence of a timber fighting platform. Later in the century, around 1257, Llywelyn the Last added the circular tower to the west and surrounded the upper and lower wards with a curtain wall.

With the final English conquest of this area of Tegeingl under King Edward I, a new fortress was built at Flint. Ewloe ceased to have any military significance and gradually fell into a state of decay.

A late eighteenth-century sketch of Ewloe Castle by Moses Griffith (1747–1819).

Flint Castle

Flint was among the first of the magnificent group of castles built by King Edward I in Wales, and in many ways its design is the most intriguing and the most puzzling. In mid July 1277, the king advanced from Chester at the head of his army and established field headquarters on the Dee estuary. The site was to become known as Flint and served as the primary base from which Edward launched his offensive against Llywelyn ap Gruffudd, prince of Wales. Together with Rhuddlan, the castle was intended to bring a military permanence to the English control of this disputed area in the north-east of the country.

Even as the army pushed its way along the coast, measures were already well in hand to assemble the vast labour force required to build the castle, and by late August there were nearly 2,300 diggers alone working at the site. Some 300 of these had marched from Lincolnshire, with three mounted sergeants to prevent them from deserting on the way. Such numbers not only reflect the sense of urgency in the work, but also the fact that the king was establishing a complete new town as well as the castle – both of which required major ditching operations in the early stages of fortification. King Edward had met with striking success in the foundation of fortified towns, or *bastides*, in his French lands of Gascony. In Wales, the introduction of such boroughs provided administrative centres, underlining the royal plan for total control and lasting English settlement. At Flint, the granting of burgage plots at fixed rents began in 1278, and something of the rigid grid layout of streets established at this time can still be seen in the town today.

Progress with the stonework of the castle was less rapid, particularly after the emphasis switched to the forward post at Rhuddlan. By November 1280, however, the king's master mason, James of St George, was at Flint and there can be no doubt that 1281 saw a big push to complete the works in hand. Fascinating details come down to us from the detailed accounts which survive. Thus we know that masons and their assistants were busy cutting and dressing stone, and payments were often made for taskwork. One group, for example, was paid for dressing 2,545 stones for the sides of the moat at 1½d. each, and for making and

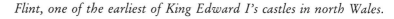

Flint, one of the earliest of King Edward I's castles in north Wales.

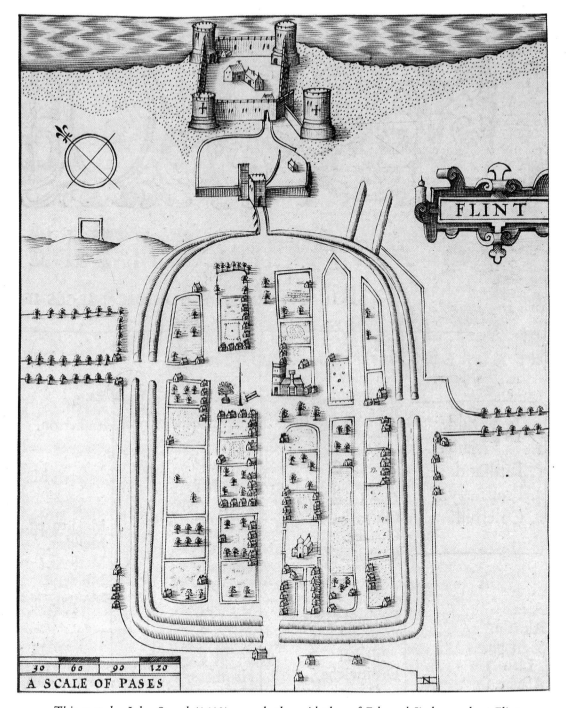

This map by John Speed (1610) reveals the grid plan of Edward I's borough at Flint.

dressing 67 steps in various towers at 1s. 8d. each. All in all, both castle and town stood substantially complete by 1284, at a total cost of around £7,000.

As stated, Flint is frequently cited as the most unusual of Edward's fortresses in Wales. The inner ward is a strongly-built square with a round tower at each angle. That in the south-east corner, however, is very much larger than the others and is detached from the main enclosure. This exceptionally well-protected Great Tower, or *donjon*, was surrounded with

39

The meeting between Richard II and Henry of Bolingbroke at Flint.

was added to the top of the tower – apparently involving a complete reroofing.

The castle played little part in the later Middle Ages, but is perhaps best known for its role in the events at the end of Richard II's reign. It was here in 1399 that the king finally awaited the arrival of Henry of Bolingbroke, hearing mass in the chapel on the upper floor of the Great Tower. The scene is immortalized in Shakespeare's *Richard II*, where the inner ward is described as 'the base court, where kings grow base'. From Flint, King Richard was taken to London where the deed of abdication was signed. Bolingbroke succeeded to the throne as Henry IV.

its own moat and was connected to the remainder of the castle by a drawbridge. In turn, the castle was encircled by a moat which was flushed out by the tidal waters of the Dee. To the south, a large outer ward stood between the core of the castle and the town.

The king's own travels may have provided some of the inspiration for the design. The Mediterranean Crusader port of Aigues Mortes may well have been in his mind when such stress was laid on the ease of access from the sea, and the great circular tower there – the Tour de Constance – has been suggested as one of the influences behind the Flint *donjon*. There is also a particularly close parallel for the overall design at the castle of Yverdon in Savoy, where James of St George had been employed in the 1260s.

In fact, the Great Tower at Flint may never have been completed as originally conceived. The basement, surrounded by a circular passage, was perhaps used for the storage of forward military supplies such as arms, armour, ammunition and clothing. The upper floor – or floors – would have provided accommodation for the constable, or possibly for the justiciar of Chester when holding court here. Further building accounts tell us that, more than 20 years after the castle was begun, a circular timber gallery

Llangar Old Parish Church

By the middle of the nineteenth century, the location of the existing parish churches in this area of the old county of Merionethshire bore little resemblance to the centres of population. In 1856, following certain changes in the parish boundaries, All Saints Llangar was replaced by a new church at nearby Cynwyd. Gradually the older edifice fell into a state of neglect and decay, although its fascinating eighteenth-century fittings survived largely intact. The deterioration continued until the north wall was in danger of collapse. Mercifully, the church was taken into State care, and since 1974 has seen a major programme of repairs and conservation. This work is now very near to completion. Soon visitors will be able to appreciate the charming details of a perfect pre-Victorian church interior.

Llangar is a small building terraced into the steep slope of the hillside on which it stands. There is a comparatively spacious and handsome porch on the south side. Despite a limited archaeological excavation of the interior, together with a close survey of the upstanding walls, the church has proved extremely difficult to date. Documentary reference to the site goes back to 1291, but none of the surviving architectural details are this early. Indeed, were it not for certain discoveries made during the conser-

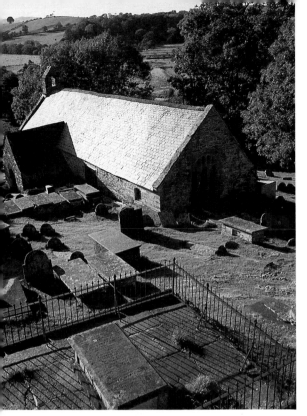

The old parish church at Llangar.

progress on the conservation of the impressive wall paintings, including the late medieval sequence which seems to have been quite elaborate.

Maen Achwyfan Cross

Situated in the corner of a field near Whitford, the so-called Maen Achwyfan cross stands almost 11 feet high. It is a free-standing cross, carved from a single slab of stone, the head of which takes the form of a disc, or wheel. Raised between the late tenth and early eleventh century, it is likely to commemorate a particular person or perhaps marks the site of some event.

The head bears a ring-cross with a prominent central boss on both the back and front. The shaft is decorated on all sides, and includes plait, knot and fret patterns, together with fairly crude human and animal figures. This decoration reflects a distinct Scandinavian element, and can be seen on several other great crosses in Wales and Northumbria. Indeed, such monuments represent some of the most notable evidence for the presence of the Vikings in these areas during this period.

Maen Achwyfan cross, raised around AD 1000.

vation works, the fabric of the building might all be attributed to two phases of rebuilding in the seventeenth and early eighteenth centuries. However, the survival of medieval wall paintings – covered by those of post-Reformation date – clearly demonstrates a somewhat earlier origin.

The churchwardens' account books survive from 1703 and record details of parish expenses. Everyday concerns are reflected, for example, in the expenditure of 2s. in 1724 for the addition of '2 railes and 12 nailes fasten'd to ye ch[urch] wall to hold hatts'. The first full description of Llangar dates from a survey of 1730 when the outside was said to be newly plastered, but inside the plaster was 'miserably decay'd dirty and foul'. Two years later a further survey recorded a much improved state of affairs: 'The windows are whole and lightsome and ye walls within new wash'd and painted, and ye floor flagg'd'.

The restored interior includes a fine timber roof, and a pulpit with a typical eighteenth-century arrangement of upper pulpit, reading pew and clerk's seat. Particular houses in the parish had their own seats in box pews along the north side of the church, whereas the poor, servants, strangers and children occupied small open benches on the other side. Work is in

Rhuddlan Castle

When, in August 1277, King Edward I led his army on from Flint to a new headquarters at Rhuddlan, the site was chosen as a second base from which to curb the ambitions of Llywelyn ap Gruffudd, the last native prince of Wales. Rhuddlan, however, had long been a place of settlement, and the tide of border warfare had already seen it change hands many times. In 921 King Alfred's son, Edward the Elder, established a fortified Anglo-Saxon *burh* here, named *Cledemutha*. By 1063 Rhuddlan had become the Welsh princely seat of Gruffudd ap Llywelyn, and 10 years later the Normans – under Robert 'of Rhuddlan' – chose the site for an earth and timber motte and bailey. Following almost two more turbulent centuries, in 1241 Henry III began building a new castle at Dyserth, just a few miles to the east.

Situated in an upland area, Dyserth was in turn cut off by the Welsh in 1263. So it was that King Edward ignored his father's hill castle, and was quick to appreciate the strategic advantages of the older Norman centre with its vital access to tidal waters. Work began in the late summer of 1277 and by the autumn of 1280 Rhuddlan Castle was substantially a finished structure, though much had still to be done in the way of fitting out. First and foremost, the initial task was to provide adequate access from the sea, some two to three miles away. This was a major feat of civil engineering, requiring enormous digging operations to create a new channel for the River Clwyd! The ditchers (*fossatores*) – the navvies of their day – came from many parts of England, some with dyking experience of the Lincolnshire fenland around Boston. By November 1280, almost £800 had been spent on the wages of these ditchers alone.

The earliest stages of the work appear to have

Rhuddlan Castle, begun in the late summer of 1277 and largely completed by 1280.

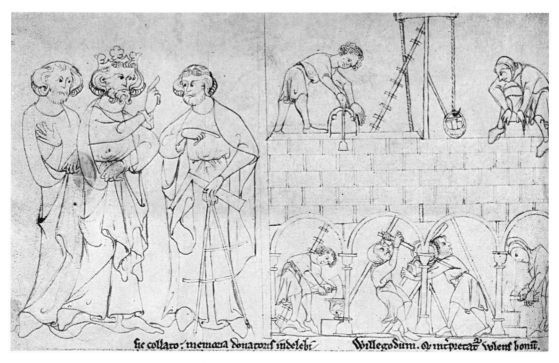

hic collato memoria donatouf indelebi.   Willegodum. q̃ inⁱpretaⁱ volenf boniⁱ.

A manuscript illustration of about 1250, showing masons at work under royal direction.

been directed by Master Bertram, but in the spring of 1278 he was superseded by the young Master James, better known to us as James of St George – the future 'master of the king's works in Wales'. Significantly, this is the first of the English royal castles where Master James can be regarded as the architect in something like the modern sense of the word. Rhuddlan was designed on what is generally known as a 'concentric' plan, with two parallel lines of defence. The outer ward was surrounded on three sides by a large flat-bottomed dry moat. On the fourth side it slopes down to the river, where there was a dock protected by Gillot's Tower – perhaps named after a mason later found at Conwy. The walls of the outer ward were of no great height, allowing archers on the inner wall-tops to fire arrows over the heads of defenders stationed there.

The diamond-shaped inner ward is perfectly symmetrical, having two massive twin-towered gatehouses, with single towers in the other two corners. Today, the empty interior belies its original appearance. At the end of the thirteenth century the walls were lined by timber-framed buildings including the King's Hall and its painted chamber, the Queen's Hall, the kitchens and the chapel. Traces of these can be seen in the beamholes and roof creasings cut in the curtain wall. The outer ward, too, was once filled with ancillary buildings such as granaries and stables, a forge and various other workshops. All was not, however, cold and stark in this essentially military establishment. Queen Eleanor was evidently anxious to add her own feminine touch, just as she was later to do with gardens at Caernarfon and Conwy. Expenditure accounts tell us that near the castle well the queen located a little fishpond, lined with four cartloads of clay brought from the marsh, and set around with seats. She also saw to it that the remainder of the courtyard was laid with 6,000 turves, and the lawn fenced with the staves of discarded casks.

Following the war between the king and Prince Llywelyn in 1282–83, Rhuddlan's pre-eminent position subsided as new and even greater fortifications began to rise beyond the Conwy river – at Caernarfon, Harlech and Conwy itself. Nevertheless, Rhuddlan was to be assured a major place in history when, in 1284, the Great Statute of Wales – the Statute of Rhuddlan as it is often known – was issued from the castle. It survived as a settlement for the country until the Act of Union in 1536 when Wales was merged with England.

The earthen motte at Rhuddlan stands above the River Clwyd.

Rhuddlan, Twthill

Near the south tower of King Edward's castle, a modern bridge crosses the dry moat and a path leads to the great Norman motte known as Twthill, situated just 300 yards upstream. Built at the command of William the Conqueror, it was established about 1073 by Robert of Rhuddlan and his cousin Hugh 'the Fat', earl of Chester. Robert has been called the exemplar of the swashbuckling Norman warrior: endless in his greed, insatiable in his lust for adventure and battle. Together, the cousins swept ruthlessly along the north Wales coast, and this motte and bailey on the River Clwyd was to provide the base from which to exploit further advances into Gwynedd. A small Norman borough was established under the protection of the castle.

Over the next two centuries Rhuddlan, along with this area of north Wales, changed hands many times. In 1157 Twthill was fortified by Henry II, only to be captured by the Welsh prince Owain Gwynedd in 1167. It was again refortified by King John in 1211, only to be taken from him by Llywelyn ab Iorwerth in 1213. The motte was recovered once more by Henry III in 1241, but fell for the last time to Llywelyn ap Gruffudd in 1263! The conclusion of this age-old border struggle came in the following decade, with the arrival of Edward I.

Robert of Rhuddlan's motte still rises some 60 feet above the banks of the Clwyd, though much of the surrounding ditch has silted up and it is difficult for us to appreciate the full defensive value of the site. When first raised, there would have been a wooden tower on the summit of the mound, and there are hints that this was later replaced in stone. The outline of the bailey can just about be traced in the fields to the north.

Rûg Chapel

Surprisingly, neither this chapel nor the attractive grounds which surround it have ever been consecrated. It is in fact a small private chapel built in 1637 by Colonel William Salesbury of Rûg (1580–1660), a rich and colourful character known as 'Old Blue Stockings'. The colonel was a staunch royalist, best known for his gallant defence of Denbigh Castle in the cause of Charles I, between 1643 and 1646. His chapel at Rûg – including its superb decoration and fittings – shows characteristic independence, as much a feature of his religious life as it was in his political career. The deed of endowment for the chapel, dated 3 January 1641, laid down that services should be taken by 'one discreet and competently learned scholar of good carriage and behaviour, being a distinct and sensible reader, and being a minister and within Holy Orders'. The curate was also required to speak Welsh, 'to read and celebrate Divine Service and other Holy exercises therin in the native and vulgarly known tongue there, both morning and evening'.

The austere external appearance, largely the

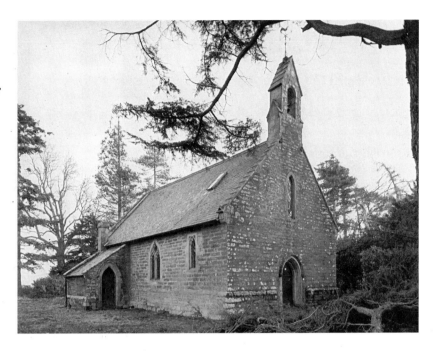

Rûg Chapel, built in 1637 for Colonel William Salesbury. The interior fittings provide a rare glimpse of seventeenth-century liturgical developments.

result of a major reconstruction in 1854–55, gives no clue to the delights of the interior. Here, it is the magnificent carved and coloured roof which is the dominant feature and the glory of Rûg. The eastern truss is carved with the date 1637, and there is no reason to suppose that the roof is essentially any earlier. The ends of the trusses, however, are carried on short brackets with cut-out wooden angels – very similar to those at Gwydir Uchaf, near Llanrwst – and these have a distinct Gothic flavour. Overall, the design at Rûg is best seen as a logical continuation of the elaborately carved and painted roofs of the later Middle Ages, so much a notable feature in this area. The sides of all the trusses are decorated with flowing floral designs, painted in reds, golds, greens, greys and blues. A remarkable wooden candelabrum, carrying painted cherubs, hangs from the central truss.

In the chancel there are handsome canopied pews on each side of the altar, and the nave is furnished with open benches of an extremely unusual design. These are joined together at the base, where the carvings include dragons, serpents, a donkey, a cow's face and even a pelican with chicks! At the west end of the nave, above the doorway, there is a wooden gallery very similar to that at Gwydir Uchaf. One further intriguing feature is the wall painting on the north wall of the nave. A quaint skeleton reclines on a pillow of coiled rope, with the prophetic inscription 'As the flame gradually consumes the tallow of the lighted candle so life under the firmament perishes daily'.

A long programme of conservation works at Rûg is currently nearing completion. Very soon visitors will be able to fully appreciate the quality of this delightful little building – a rare example surviving from the 'high church' liturgical developments of Charles I's reign.

Some of the unusual bench carvings at Rûg.

St Winifred's Chapel and Holy Well

The tradition of this holy well tells of Winifred, a virgin martyr who was beheaded in the seventh century by a ruthless local chieftain who had failed in his attempts at seduction. Winifred was miraculously restored to life by St Beuno, but where her head had fallen a spring of holy and curing water appeared. The earliest reference to the shrine as a place of pilgrimage dates from 1115 when it was held by the Benedictines at Chester Abbey. Such was the growing fame of the saint that a few years later the monks of Shrewsbury removed her remains to their own monastery. In 1240, however, the shrine was granted to the Cistercians at Basingwerk, and they continued to hold the patronage of the well until the abbey was dissolved in 1536. The importance of the site grew throughout the Middle Ages, and in 1415 it was given a

The roof of the well chamber at St Winifred's, built soon after 1500.

tremendous boost when King Henry V found time to make a pilgrimage to the site during his busy preparations before Agincourt.

The culmination of this growing fame found

St Winifred's chapel is a fine example of the Perpendicular style.

expression in the construction of the present well-building and chapel, probably in the first decade of the sixteenth century. The work was almost certainly completed largely through the munificence of Lady Margaret Beaufort, the mother of King Henry VII. It is one of the most notable examples of the Perpendicular style in Wales, with much of interest in the stone and wood carving. The handsome chapel is entered from the south, but only the chancel stands on solid ground – the nave and north aisle are built above the well. The vaulted well chamber itself is approached at a lower level and has a bath at the front. Inside, the flow of water to the well basin was once greater. It has something of a stellar pattern, and the carvings on the central pendant above the well depict scenes from the life of St Winifred.

In 1723 the chapel was converted to a school-room, at which time it was drastically altered. Happily, it is now restored to its original proportions. St Winifred's well remains one of Britain's principal Roman Catholic shrines.

Valle Crucis Abbey

Just two miles outside the Eisteddfod town of Llangollen, at the foot of the steep climb to the aptly named Horseshoe Pass, are the remains of the Cistercian abbey of Valle Crucis. Its name means 'the valley of the cross', and is taken from the ninth-century Pillar of Eliseg which stands a quarter of a mile to the north. Valle Crucis was founded in 1201 by Madog ap Gruffudd Maelor, ruler of northern Powys, and was colonized by monks from the abbey of Strata Marcella near Welshpool. The site chosen was typically Cistercian, set in a tranquil valley beside a plentiful supply of water, it remains serene and particularly attractive today. The 'white monks', as they were known from their habits of undyed wool, chose to live an austere and exacting style of life, and generally insisted upon such remote locations for their abbeys.

The east end of the Cistercian abbey church at Valle Crucis, founded in 1201.

Here, they even expelled the inhabitants of an existing settlement.

Madog granted the abbey the bulk of its early estates, and the monks soon built up considerable lands and other property in the surrounding district. Their upland farms, or granges, supplied meat, dairy products, leather and wool, whilst the lowland granges provided wheat and other crops. By the mid thirteenth century wool production had become a significant economic activity. In the early history of the house, the estates were worked by lay brothers, or *conversi*, who lived at the abbey itself. But these ideals were severely compromised in the later Middle Ages, with the bulk of the lands and other property eventually leased to tenants. In addition, despite an initial resistance on the part of the Cistercians, Valle Crucis also drew a major income from grants of tithes in seven neighbouring parishes.

Like most other Welsh abbeys, Valle Crucis suffered badly during the wars of Edward I. Indeed, the abbot had been pro-Welsh, and his community's estates became a natural target. Following the wars in 1284 the house received £160 by way of compensation. Even so, the monks' spirit was by no means dampened and they were thoroughly involved with Welsh literary activity. In particular, it seems that the continuation of *Brut y Tywysogyon* – Chronicle of the Princes – for the years 1282–1332 was compiled in the scriptorium at Valle Crucis.

Work on the construction of the abbey church began soon after the foundation, but substantial rebuilding and heightening took place after an apparently disastrous fire in the mid thirteenth century. The visitor now arrives at the west front, a glorious composition, with an elaborately-carved doorway added after the fire. The gable, with its delicately-carved rose window, was rebuilt in the fourteenth century and in good light an inscription in Latin can be seen: 'Abbot Adam carried out this work; may he rest in peace. Amen'. Within the church, the nave was used for the lay brothers' services, with their stalls situated between the pillars of the aisle arcades. Moving eastwards, beyond a stone screen wall – the *pulpitum* – the choir and presbytery were reserved for the monks themselves. Their choir stalls stood in the central crossing, between the four great piers which supported a low tower overhead. The high altar

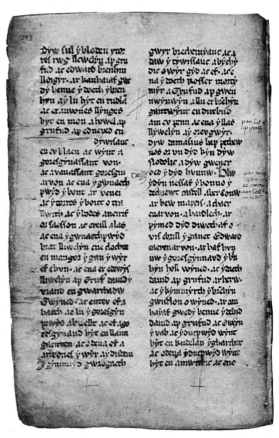

A page from the Welsh Chronicle of the Princes, compiled at Valle Crucis from 1282–1322.

stood on a raised plinth below the tall lancet windows at the east end. The south transept is very well preserved, and its two chapels retain their altar bases. From a doorway high up in the south wall the monks left their dormitory to descend a staircase into the church for services at night. The magnificent east end of the abbey church is best observed from the outside; its graceful lines and striking originality emphasized by a series of flat pilaster buttresses. Here, too, visitors will notice a surviving monastic fishpond.

The cloister and the monks' domestic buildings lay to the south, where the late fourteenth-century east range stands in particularly fine condition. It is just possible that the construction of this range was completed in the early 1400s after further destruction by fire, possibly in the Owain Glyndŵr uprising. The chapter house, with its superb rib vault, was an important room where the monks met each day to conduct business and to listen to a chapter of

The lovely stone-vaulted chapter house at Valle Crucis, where the monks met each day to hear a chapter of their Rule. It is one of the best surviving features at the abbey and dates from the late fourteenth or early fifteenth century.

their *Rule*. The floor above was originally designed as the monks' dormitory, with a latrine at the southern end. In the late fifteenth century, however, the northern half was converted to a fine new hall for the abbot. A chamber, with a fireplace, was added to the east and served as his private apartment. At the time, Valle Crucis was enjoying a modest revival in its fortunes, gaining praise for the quality of its buildings and the hospitality of its abbots. Guto'r Glyn, for example, wrote 'Of Valle Crucis Abbot good, Whose full-stocked tables ever groan'. Despite such praise, the conversions in the east range reflect a remarkable relaxation in the Cistercian way of life. Today, the dormitory houses a very fine collection of medieval memorial sculpture from graves within and near the abbey church. There is also a small exhibition on Valle Crucis and the Cistercians.

On the south side of the cloister are the excavated remains of the monks' dining hall and the kitchen. In the dining hall there is the base of the staircase which led up to a reading pulpit. The west range was initially occupied by the lay brothers, but was later given over to other uses.

In 1535, when visited by King Henry VIII's Commissioners, the abbey was said to be in 'great decay'. The house was dissolved in 1537, and with the lead stripped from the roofs the buildings soon began to fall into ruin. Not many years after the Dissolution of the Monasteries, however, the east range was converted to a private dwelling. Then, in the eighteenth century, much of the site was converted to a farm. It remained in this condition until restoration began in the 1870s.

A thirteenth-century sculptured head, inscribed +MORVS, found in the abbey dining hall.

DYFED
The Rural South-West

Since 1974 south-west Wales has been administered as one large new county known as Dyfed. It is essentially a rural area, a pastoral landscape of rich green fields and hedgerows. Many places still serve that same central market function which they have performed for centuries. Carmarthen and Cardigan, Haverfordwest and Pembroke – each with its urban origins in the Middle Ages, and each with its castle – are undoubtedly some of the most delightful towns in the principality. In the far west lies the 'city' of St Davids, with its cathedral dedicated to the national saint, and its magnificent medieval palace which speaks volumes for the power and influence of the medieval bishops. Dyfed, too, has some of the finest coastal scenery in Wales, stretching from the Dyfi estuary on Cardigan Bay, round to the mouth of the Loughor near the Gower peninsula.

Dyfed includes the historic counties of Cardiganshire, Camarthenshire and Pembrokeshire, themselves carved from earlier medieval Marcher lordships and native princedoms. Dyfed as an entity, however, can be traced back even earlier, to the dark centuries of sub-Roman Britain. It was one of the kingdoms which had emerged by the sixth century from the ruins of the earlier imperial administration. The name Dyfed is in fact derived from the Roman *Demetia*. In turn, the *Demetae* were the native people of late Iron Age south-west Wales, and during the Roman period their tribal capital was based at Carmarthen (*Moridunum*).

In the years before the Norman Conquest, the pattern of political control in Dyfed is difficult to fathom. In the tenth and eleventh centuries, internal disputes were compounded by savage Viking raids on the coastal areas. None the less, in the reign of William the Conqueror, Dyfed remained comparatively strong under the native ruler, Rhys ap Tewdwr. Following Rhys's death in 1093, the Normans seemingly crashed into the south-west from all sides, establishing their lordships along the fertile coastal areas and pushing the native dynasty into the higher and poorer forested lands to the north of Dinefwr. For a time, it seemed the entire area would be utterly smothered by the new rulers.

The tide was reversed for a time in the twelfth century, and this was in no small part due to the remarkable stamina and tenacity of Rhys ap Gruffudd (d. 1197) – the Lord Rhys as he was called by Henry II. Rhys and his sons consolidated their power in Deheubarth – as the independent areas of Dyfed were now known – and conducted spectacular raids and campaigns against their Anglo-Norman foes in the Marcher lordships, including Pembroke, Kidwelly, Llansteffan and Gower. Indeed, Rhys features in the history of many of the monuments described here; not just of the castles, but also as the founder of Talley Abbey, and as a great benefactor of Strata Florida.

As with Gwynedd in the north, the native dynasty was finally eclipsed in the late thirteenth century with King Edward I's conquests. The important Welsh castles at Carreg Cennen, Dinefwr and Dryslwyn then fell to the English.

Besides its castles, Dyfed is a county rich in ancient and historic sites, and Cadw maintains some of the finer examples from the Neolithic tomb at Pentre Ifan to the glorious Bishop's Palace at St Davids.

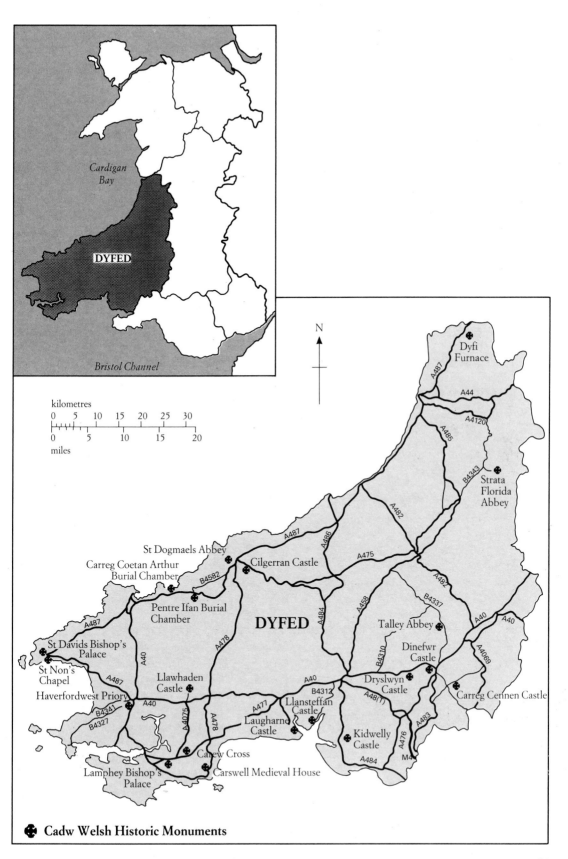

Cardigan
Bay

DYFED

Bristol Channel

kilometres

0   5   10   15   20   25   30

0   5   10   15   20

miles

N

Dyfi
Furnace

A487

A44

A4120

A485

B4343

Strata
Florida
Abbey

A482

A487

A486

A475

A482

B4337

St Dogmaels Abbey

Cilgerran Castle

Carreg Coetan Arthur
Burial Chamber

B4582

Pentre Ifan Burial
Chamber

A484

A458

DYFED

Talley Abbey

A40   A40

A487

A478

Dinefwr
Castle

A4069

St Davids Bishop's
Palace

B4310

St Non's
Chapel

A487

Llawhaden
Castle

A40

Dryslwyn
Castle

Carreg Cennen Castle

Haverfordwest Priory

B4341

A40

B4312

Llansteffan
Castle

A48(1)

B4327

A4075

A477

A483

A478

Laugharne
Castle

Kidwelly
Castle

A476

Carew Cross

A484

M4

Lamphey Bishop's
Palace

Carswell Medieval House

🟣 **Cadw Welsh Historic Monuments**

Carew Cross

Today, the distinctive head of this magnificent cross provides the inspiration for the symbol of Cadw. Indeed, it is scarcely surprising that a body charged with the guardianship of monuments in State care should choose such a milestone of Welsh art – one of the finest and best preserved eleventh-century crosses in Britain.

Situated near the entrance to Carew Castle, the cross stands nearly 14 feet high, with a free wheel-head fitted into position by a tenon. The swastika and plaitwork patterns on the shaft reveal a characteristic Viking influence, similar to that at Maen Achwyfan, and demonstrates a sculptor of considerable technical achievement. On the back face, the inscription reads: [The Cross of] Margiteut [Maredudd] son of Etguin [Edwin]. This is thought to be Maredudd ap Edwin who ruled Deheubarth (south-west Wales) with his brother from 1033 until his death in battle in 1035. As such, the Carew cross represents a royal memorial and must have been erected about this time.

The eleventh-century Carew Cross.

Carreg Cennen Castle

The powerful stone mass which is Carreg Cennen stands on a great limestone crag almost 300 feet above the River Cennen. The castle occupies a site of truly spectacular defensive qualities and demonstrates the high professionalism of late thirteenth-century military architects; making the best use of whatever natural advantages might assist in their ever more complex planning. Such is the strength of the location, archaeologists have mused over the possibility of a prehistoric stronghold here. Certainly coins of the first and fourth centuries have been found on the hill, and suggest occupation in the Roman period. The earliest mention of a castle at Carreg Cennen dates from 1248 when it was regained by Rhys Fychan, one of the Deheubarth dynasty of princes. Little can be said concerning the appearance of this Welsh castle, but in 1277 it fell to the English as a royal force moved northwards from Carmarthen during Edward I's initial campaign against Llywelyn ap Gruffudd of Gwynedd. Following the king's eventual conquest of north Wales, Carreg Cennen was granted to his loyal supporter John Giffard (d. 1299), Baron Giffard of Brimpsfield in Gloucestershire.

Virtually all of the surviving buildings were first raised in the late thirteenth to early fourteenth centuries, and belong to Giffard's time or that of his son, John the younger. However, following the local revolt of Rhys ap Maredudd in 1287, the king took control of the district and placed the castle in the hands of the earl of Hereford for two years. The details of the inner ward bear certain distinct hallmarks of this period. Indeed, overall, the site illustrates many of the principles of fortification refined in King Edward's new constructions in the north of the country. In particular, the plan is based on the use of one set of defences inside another. But there is nothing doctrinaire about the overall layout of Carreg Cennen, with no one tower the same as another. As stated, its evolution demonstrates the way in which a sophisticated castle could emerge through seizing the opportunities offered by an altogether irregular and precipitous location.

Carreg Cennen Castle on its steep limestone crag.

The inner ward is earliest, hugging the sheer limestone cliff on its southern side, and possibly incorporating sections of the Welsh castle in the west and south curtain walls. The ward is dominated by the once mighty three-storey gatehouse, with its numerous arrowslits at all levels. The entrance was defended by a draw-bridge, and there was a portcullis and door at each end of the gate-passage. Wall-galleries led from the first-floor level of the gatehouse to the two northern corner towers. Open wall-walks led off from the second floor, and these prob-ably linked the whole of the defensive circuit. Two large cisterns can be seen at the back of the gatehouse, and these held the castle's water supply. The north-west tower is round in plan, whereas that to the north-east is essentially square, though it has chamfered corners and there are large 'spur' buttresses at the base. The east side of the inner ward was occupied by the main domestic quarters. The principal rooms – kitchen, hall and private chambers – were on the first floor, with store rooms underneath. A small chapel lay on the upper floor of the square tower projecting out from the east curtain wall.

The gatehouse was subsequently streng-thened by the addition of a long stepped-ramp barbican. It would have broken the rush of any attacker with right-angle corners and two gates, each with a deep pit below a moveable bridge. Beyond this, all that was required to complete the defence of the hilltop was to add the outer ward on the most exposed eastern flank. This area was enclosed by a curtain wall with solid drum towers at the angles. One further intrigu-ing and fascinating feature of Carreg Cennen is the narrow vaulted passage which runs for some 30 yards along the cliff face from the south-east corner of the inner ward. It leads to a natural cave, which extends back from the cliff for a further 50 yards. The mouth of the cave was partly walled up and provided with pigeon holes, thus serving as a dovecot. There has been much speculation about the use of the passage, though its construction was probably contemporary with that of the outer ward. Had the cave been left exposed, there would always have been a danger of attackers establishing a foothold there.

Carreg Cennen eventually passed to the dukes of Lancaster, and on the accession of the heir, Henry of Bolingbroke, as King Henry IV it became Crown property. The castle was held by the constable John Skydmore against the forces of Owain Glyndŵr for over a year, but eventually he surrendered it and some of the walls were subsequently damaged. Finally, during the Wars of the Roses, Carreg Cennen was prised from Lancastrian hands in 1462 by the Yorkist supporters, Sir Richard Herbert of Raglan and Sir Roger Vaughan of Tretower. Although garrisoned briefly, it was soon decided to demolish the castle, probably to prevent any further occupation as a Lancastrian power base. Some 500 men 'with bars, picks and crow-bars of iron and other instruments necessary for the same purpose' set about the destruction.

Carreg Coetan Arthur Burial Chamber

Carreg Coetan is one of a little group of early Neolithic chambered tombs situated around the delightful valley of the River Nyfer, near Newport. Its form probably owes something to the tradition of tombs archaeologists call 'portal dolmen', and therefore bears some structural resemblance to nearby Pentre Ifan, or perhaps to the first phase at Dyffryn Ardudwy, Gwynedd. The hefty wedge-shaped capstone is supported by just two of the four uprights, and slopes back from the presumed entrance to the chamber. Excavations in 1979–80 revealed evidence of a circular cairn which surrounded the central chamber. It may have risen to cover the uprights, but the capstone was probably left exposed. The remains of several Neolithic pots were found to contain cremated human bone. Flint knives and a piece of a polished stone axe were also recovered during the excavation. A series of radiocarbon dates indicate that the tomb could have been in use as early as 3500 BC.

Carswell Medieval House

Somewhat off the beaten track, and situated amidst a working farmyard, this enigmatic little building cannot be closely dated and has no documented early history. It belongs, none the less, to a distinct tradition of later medieval houses in south-west Wales where the main room was sited over a vaulted basement. At its grandest, the design is seen in the first-floor halls of the upper classes, notably the palaces of the bishops of St Davids at Lamphey and St Davids itself. Substantial first-floor halls are also well represented in the predominantly early stone buildings of Glamorgan. Carswell is, of course, very much a diminutive example of this tradition, though the essential elements are present.

Perhaps of late fourteenth or fifteenth century date, the house is almost square in plan, with steep gables, a massive projecting end-chimney, and a separate entry to each floor. The ground floor with its large fireplace and barrel vault probably served as the service room. The upper floor must have been approached by an external stair, and would have provided private accommodation. In any such building, however, it is difficult to be certain if it stood alone, or if other detached or attached structures have long since disappeared.

Less than a mile away, there is a very similar house at West Tarr, though there both the upper and lower chambers are vaulted. This is another precious little medieval dwelling which may well be taken into the care of the State in the near future.

Cilgerran Castle, begun in 1223 by William Marshall the younger.

Cilgerran Castle

Cilgerran is probably to be associated with the castle of Cenarth Bychan, raised by the Norman freebooter Gerald of Windsor, and according to the *Brut y Tywysogyon* – the Chronicle of the Princes – was 'fortified with ditches and walls'. If this is so, it was from here that in 1109 the lovestruck Owain, son of the prince of Powys, risked all to abduct Gerald's wife Nest. Owain's forces attacked and burnt the castle, with Gerald himself having to make an undignified escape via a privy. The episode was to set all Wales aflame, especially as the seductive Nest – the 'Helen of Wales' – was more than suspected of arranging her own abduction. None of the present remains date to this early period, nor do we know anything of the castle buildings captured from the Normans by Rhys ap Gruffudd, prince of Deheubarth, in 1165. None the less, the Lord Rhys, as Henry II called him, held this area until his death in 1197. Seven years later Cilgerran was again recovered from the Welsh by the enterprising William Marshall, earl of Pembroke, who ap-

parently spared the lives of the garrison. His success was short lived, and this was one of the many castles in the southern March which fell to the sweeping advances of Prince Llywelyn ab Iorwerth.

In 1223 William Marshall the younger returned from Ireland with a considerable army and recaptured the castles of Carmarthen and Cardigan from Llywelyn's hands. He also finally wrested Cilgerran from Welsh control, and began the construction of the powerful stone castle we see today. Perched on a rocky crag, overlooking a steep gorge of the River Teifi, it is among the most spectacularly sited fortresses in all Wales. Indeed, the romantic ruins were much favoured by artists of the eighteenth and nineteenth centuries, with tourists of this period journeying to the site on boat trips up the river from Cardigan.

The outstanding characteristics of Earl William's castle are the two great drum towers on the most exposed face of the inner curtain wall. They stand behind a rock-cut ditch, and with a strongly constructed two-storey gatehouse they cut off and secured the promontory on which the castle stands. The towers are very much a

55

distinct mark of the period, with the walls facing the attacking side built some four feet thicker than the remainder. Each tower was of four storeys, with fireplaces in several of the upper rooms. A doorway on the second floor of both towers led on to the battlemented wall-walk. Between the towers, a small doorway through the curtain wall was protected by a portcullis operated from the battlements. The main gatehouse lay on the edge of the western scarp. It had a portcullis at either end of the passage, and there may have been a chapel above.

Later in the thirteenth century, a square tower was built next to the gatehouse and curtain walls were added to the north and east sides of the inner ward. Failure of the Marshall male line meant the castle passed to various lords, but by 1275 it was already somewhat derelict. A century later, in 1377 Cilgerran was refortified on the orders of King Edward III, who feared a threatened French invasion in this area. The buildings in the north-west corner, including a rectangular tower, could date to this time. The castle remained in use and was besieged in the Glyndŵr uprising in the early fifteenth century. Following the Wars of the Roses, it was granted to William Vaughan by Henry VII. The Vaughans continued to live at Cilgerran, perhaps until the end of the sixteenth century.

Dinefwr Castle

Even in the Middle Ages, as the seat of the ancient rulers of south Wales, Dinefwr was a fortress of immense symbolic and ancestral significance. It occupies a dramatic location, hovering precipitously on a steep cliff high above the River Tywi. In the later twelfth century it was the principal stronghold of the powerful Rhys ap Gruffudd – the Lord Rhys. From here he ruled the kingdom of De-heubarth. Indeed, it was Rhys himself who, between about 1146 and his death in 1197, so brilliantly reconstituted the strength and in-fluence of this ancient kingdom. In the early years of the thirteenth century, however, family feuding among the heirs of the Deheubarth

Dinefwr, one-time seat of the Lord Rhys.

dynasty became rampant. Brother fought brother, and castles were captured and recap-tured. Dinefwr was more or less held by Rhys's son, Rhys Gryg, who in 1220 'dismantled' the castle to prevent it falling into the hands of Llywelyn ab Iorwerth of Gwynedd. In turn, possession of the castle continued to be hotly contested by the sons of Rhys Gryg. Then in 1277 King Edward I seized Dinefwr as part of his first overwhelming campaign against the Welsh. The lord at the time, Rhys Wyndod, was evicted and a royal garrison installed. From chancery and exchequer records, we know that in 1282–83 the tower, bridge, hall, and 'little tower' were repaired, and that five buildings were erected in the outer bailey.

Following the English conquest, Rhys ap Maredudd who held nearby Dryslwyn felt he had just claim to Dinefwr. He attacked and captured the castle during his revolt of 1287, though it was quickly retaken by the king's forces. For the remainder of the Middle Ages it was essentially retained as a royal stronghold. In 1343 it passed to Edward, the Black Prince, and was found to be in need of major repairs.

Nevertheless, the castle was apparently strong enough to resist a siege by the forces of Owain Glyndŵr in 1403. In 1489 King Henry VII granted Dinefwr to his major Welsh supporter, Sir Rhys ap Thomas. The ancient pedigree of the site was certainly of huge importance to the great Sir Rhys, and he encouraged the poets to forge a link between his family and the former princes of Deheubarth.

Dinefwr is one of the most recent sites to have been taken into State care in Wales. Only in the past few years has the long process of consolidation begun on the ivy-covered walls, and it will be some years before the ruins can be made safe and fully open to visitors. The castle basically consists of two wards side by side along the edge of the river cliff. The large outer ward was surrounded by a stone wall, the remains of which can still be traced. A bridge must have crossed the rock-cut ditch leading to the curtain wall and towers of the inner ward. Here a 'bottleneck' barbican leads to the simple gate into the ward itself. Within, there is a large round tower similar to those built by southern Marcher lords in the first half of the thirteenth century, such as Skenfrith in Gwent. The Dinefwr tower now has a very curious appearance, with the present top storey added as a gazebo in the seventeenth century. The hall and private accommodation along the side away from the cliff probably date from the fifteenth century.

Whatever is said of this fascinating site at this stage, opinions will doubtless require modification as the buildings and their history are studied in greater detail over the coming years.

Dryslwyn Castle

The ruins of Dryslwyn stand on a rocky and isolated hill overlooking the flood plain of the Tywi river. It is a lush pastoral scene today, and from the hilltop there are clear views up the valley to the neighbouring castle of Dinefwr. Initially built by Welsh princes of Deheubarth,

Originally a castle of the Welsh princes, Dryslwyn stands above the lush valley of the Tywi.

much of the site has long been buried beneath centuries of debris. Dryslwyn was taken into State care in 1980 and, each summer since then, excavations have begun to recover the plan and details of a fairly extensive stronghold.

In the middle of the thirteenth century Dryslwyn was held by Maredudd ap Rhys Gryg, a member of the Deheubarth dynasty of princes. He died at the castle in 1271 and was succeeded as lord of Dryslwyn by his son Rhys ap Maredudd. Both father and son did their best to resist the expansionist policies of Prince Llywelyn ap Gruffudd of Gwynedd. Rhys in particular was fiercely loyal to Edward I during the king's wars against Llywelyn in 1277 and 1282–83. Following the English conquest, however, Rhys found himself increasingly alienated and publicly humiliated by the Crown; a situation compounded by his grievances with the new justiciar of west Wales, Robert Tibetot. The subsequent revolt of 1287 was inevitable.

In turn, the royal response was swift and crushing. A vast army of more than 11,000 men under the earl of Cornwall was mustered to besiege Dryslwyn. The army included 'sappers' whose role was to undermine the defences by digging tunnels beneath. In one such operation success came rather too quickly. A large number of men, including several knights, met a gruesome end as a collapsing wall fell upon them. None the less, the castle was apparently taken soon afterwards when the walls of the chapel were breached. Rhys himself remained at large until 1292 when he was finally taken and executed.

Following the siege Alan de Plucknet was made constable of the castle, and a small township – possibly already in existence – was given borough status. Some £300 was spent on immediate repairs and on building a new mill. Dryslwyn essentially remained in royal control throughout the fourteenth century and various documents record expenditure on the castle buildings. A bakehouse and granary were under construction in 1306, and in 1338 the 'King's Hall' was being reroofed.

In 1403 the constable betrayed Dryslwyn to Owain Glyndŵr, and some destruction may have taken place at the time. One further constable was appointed in 1439, though before the end of the century the castle had probably been abandoned and destroyed by fire.

A clear understanding of the buildings must await the results of further excavation, but the sequence of development is beginning to unfold. Greatest progress has so far been made on the inner ward, where a round 'keep' and the initial curtain wall were almost certainly the work of Maredudd ap Rhys Gryg, or his son Rhys. The hall complex could also date to before the 1287 siege, though it seems likely that this was the 'King's Hall' undergoing modification in 1338. The remainder of the castle still largely appears as grass-covered foundations stretching along the ridge to the northwest. Beyond this, further low mounds mark the position of the small borough, where there were some 34 burgages in the 1350s, with another 14 outside on 'Budge [bridge] Street'.

Dyfi Furnace

The eighteenth-century charcoal-burning blast furnace known as Dyfi is probably the best preserved example in Britain. It was the arrival of ironmaking at this north Dyfed site which appears to have given rise to the name of the village – Furnace. Visitors passing Dyfi on the modern road between Aberystwyth and Machynlleth might be deceived by its barnlike external appearance, until that is they glimpse the large waterwheel at one side. Typically, too, such furnaces had a square stack emerging from the roof, and this has now been restored at Dyfi. In fact, a comprehensive programme of conservation at the site began in 1977, and in 1985 the scheme received a 'Rural Wales Award' from the Council for the Protection of Rural Wales. Dyfi Furnace was opened to visitors in the summer of 1987, and now offers a fascinating insight into the early processes of industrialization.

The furnace was built about 1755 by Vernon, Kendall and Company, and by 1774 the Kendalls were in sole ownership. They were a family of ironmasters from the 'Black Country', with extensive interests in the Lake District and Scotland, as well as furnaces and forges in Cheshire and Staffordshire. They built Dyfi Furnace to take advantage of the local charcoal supplies, whilst iron ore was probably shipped

The recently restored early blast furnace at Dyfi.

up the Dovey river from Cumbria. The charcoal itself was produced from the surrounding woodland, but the furnace was greedy: to produce just one ton of iron, an early blast furnace like this would consume timber from up to an acre of woodland. The pig iron produced at Dyfi presumably went to the Kendalls' forges in the midlands, though a small amount was certainly purchased locally.

The working of furnaces on two levels was normal in sites such as Dyfi, and at the time they were generally built into sloping ground. This meant the charging platform and furnace charge hole were approached at a higher ground level, making it easier to cart in the bulky raw materials. Here at Dyfi, the iron ore and charcoal were probably stored in the large building overlooking the furnace. When required, they were no doubt barrowed through the opposite doorway, along the charging platform on its upper level, and tipped through the

'Gothic' shaped arch into the blast furnace itself. The draught to create a high enough temperature to smelt the iron was produced by great bellows, housed on the ground floor, and powered by an external waterwheel. The flow of water to this wheel was via a leat, and this in turn was controlled by a sluice gate near the dam above the waterfall. Eventually the molten pig iron would have been tapped off through the furnace bottom into the casthouse. It was cast into bar moulds, or 'pigs', in sand beds on the casthouse floor. Only the footings of this casthouse survive, and can be seen on the opposite side to the waterwheel.

Dyfi seems only to have been in use as a blast furnace for about 50 years and by 1810 it was abandoned. Later on, the buildings were converted for use as a sawmill, and it is to this period that the present large waterwheel belongs. Following conservation, this wheel once again functions perfectly.

Haverfordwest Priory

Until 1982, the ivy-clad ruins of the priory of St Mary and St Thomas the martyr lay neglected and much overlooked, sitting on the western bank of the River Cleddau a short way to the south of the main town. In that year the site was taken into the care of the State, and the following summer a programme of archaeological excavations commenced. The work has progressed season by season, and has gone hand in hand with essential consolidation. Eventually, the site and its extensive array of buildings will be fully conserved, and displayed in a way that visitors can appreciate the layout of one of the more important religious houses of medieval Wales.

The priory was founded for Augustinian canons, probably towards the end of the twelfth century, by Robert fitz Richard, lord of Haverford (d. 1213). Its extra-mural position, outside the medieval town, in the settlement of 'Parva Haverford', can be compared to the priory of canons at Carmarthen, and to any number of similar Augustinian houses on the fringes of the county towns of England. Unfortunately, little is known of the internal history of Haverfordwest Priory, though the canons appear to have drawn much of their wealth from tithes in a number of surrounding parishes. They also expended much energy and not a little money in building up their property holdings in the borough itself. Unlike the Cistercians of the countryside, the canons of Haverfordwest were dependent upon the bustle of urban commerce. At the suppression of the house in 1536 the priory was assessed to have a net income of just over £133.

Parts of the church still stand to a considerable height. The excavations have recovered details of the presbytery, the crossing – the canons' choir – the transepts, the chapter house and parts of the cloister. It appears that the cruciform church was built in the early to mid thirteenth century, though the internal ritual arrangements were altered as the Middle Ages progressed. In the final phase, three steps led up to the high altar at the east end of the presbytery. The floor of the church was tiled, as

The carved stone head from an effigy of a knight found at Haverfordwest Priory.

was that of the chapter house, where the pavement remained intact. This room was of some distinction, and numerous fragments of an elaborate fourteenth-century vault were discovered. One of the most notable finds was a remarkable corbel, intended to support the vault. It consists of seven conjointed and crowned heads, sharing between them six eyes. The chapter house also contained a mid thirteenth-century effigy of a knight – doubtless an important benefactor. The excavations have also uncovered information on the destruction of the buildings at the Dissolution, including evidence for melting down lead from the roofs. Further details must await several more seasons of hard work, as well as a detailed analysis of the many finds at the site.

Kidwelly Castle

During the reign of King Henry I (1100–35), the hitherto tenuous control and authority

This aerial view of Kidwelly reveals the sweeping curve of the earliest Norman stronghold.

exercised by the Normans in south Wales was significantly advanced in leaps and bounds. With a firm royal base established at Carmarthen, the south-west in particular was to witness the brutal hand of the invader. Castles were built and rebuilt in a strong chain of defence, extending right along the coastal plain and its tidal estuaries. The king exercised his overall authority above all in his choice of men behind this advance, and it was the mighty Bishop Roger of Salisbury – justiciar of England – who was given the task of establishing Norman domination in Kidwelly. The initial stronghold was raised soon after 1106 on a prominent ridge overlooking the River Gwendraeth, at the upper limit of the tidal water. Subsequently, the castle was to be extensively rebuilt, modified, and brought up to date by successive owners throughout the Middle Ages. Today it stands as a remarkably complete and well preserved ruin, one of the finest to be seen anywhere in the principality.

Bishop Roger's plans for the new stronghold were doubtless influenced by the impressive earthworks of the castle at his own episcopal seat of Old Sarum. Here at Kidwelly, the bishop's builders made use of the steep river scarp for the eastern defences, whilst they threw up a huge crescent-shaped bank with an external ditch on the exposed western flank. The bank itself was probably crowned by a timber palisade, which no doubt extended along the river front, and there must have been a substantial wooden gatehouse. So prominent were these defences, that they influenced the entire layout and development of the stone castle in later centuries.

By 1139, the castle and lordship of Kidwelly had passed to Maurice de Londres, whose family's castle-building was apparently concentrated at Ogmore in Glamorgan. A stone hall and other masonry structures may have been raised during the de Londres tenure, if not under Bishop Roger, but all traces of these have

61

The fourteenth-century great gatehouse at Kidwelly Castle.

long since disappeared. Over the next century the castle was to experience something of a chequered history. It was burnt by Prince Rhys ap Gruffudd in 1159, and rebuilt by him around 1190. Back in Norman hands by 1201, it was again attacked and partially destroyed by the Welsh on two more occasions in the first half of the thirteenth century. Then in 1244 the de Londres heiress married Patrick de Chaworth, who recovered Kidwelly from the Welsh and must have devoted considerable energy and resources to improving the defences. During the war of 1257–58, although the town was damaged by fire, the castle held out against another Welsh attack.

It was Patrick's sons, Payn and Patrick, who in the later 1270s began a major reconstruction of Kidwelly in stone. They had recently returned from King Edward I's crusade in the Holy Land, and were perhaps inspired by the fine castles they had seen there. The almost symmetrical inner ward, with its great round towers at each corner, was squeezed into Bishop Roger's existing earthwork enclosure. Its planning was very much in keeping with contemporary castle architecture, including the

king's own new castles at Flint and Rhuddlan. The ward was entered by fairly simple gates in the northern and southern curtain walls, each protected by a door and a portcullis operated from the battlements above. The towers vary in their details, though all were fitted with batteries of arrowslits. That in the south-west corner has stone vaults and floors. Fireplaces on most floors reveal that the towers would also have provided domestic accommodation.

The de Chaworth brothers were dead by 1283, and soon afterwards the infant heiress was granted in marriage by Edward I to Henry, second son of the earl of Lancaster. The actual ceremony did not take place until 1298, and it was after this date that the next phase of building was initiated. Henry of Lancaster clearly regarded Kidwelly as a great prize, and he was soon busy updating the castle as a 'concentric' construction, with a 'walls within walls' arrangement. To begin with, however, as a centre of one of the richest baronial families in the country, it was necessary to upgrade the accommodation of the inner ward. A new first-floor hall and private chamber were raised, overlooking the river, between the north-east and south-east towers. At the lower end of the hall, a chapel tower was built out on the edge of the river scarp, its angles canted off into large spur buttresses. The dressed stone of the chapel windows stands out clearly from the remaining masonry, and there is a small sacristy with a bedchamber for the priest on the southern side.

Henry of Lancaster's greatest contribution to the overall plan was the replacement of the outer timber defences by a stone curtain wall, flanked by mural towers projecting into the ditch. Much of the bank was swept away to provide firm foundations for the wall, and on the northern side two of the towers were set close together to form a gatehouse. The four towers of the inner ward were now raised in height so that archers could fire over the top of the new wall beyond. Evidence for this can be seen in the 'fossilized' battlements – walled up below the later tops of the towers. But of particular interest in the Lancastrian modernization is the emphasis placed, in the absence of an earlier keep, on a large residential gatehouse located on the south side of the outer ward. It is something of an odd construction, lacking the symmetry of the more refined earlier examples at Caerphilly or Harlech. Although work on the gatehouse began in the early fourteenth century, progress was slow. It may still have been incomplete when, in 1403, forces from France and Brittany helped Henry Don besiege Kidwelly during the Owain Glyndŵr uprising. The town fell at this time, though the castle held out for three weeks until it was relieved by an English army.

The gatehouse suffered extensive damage during the siege, and over £500 was spent on reconstruction by the Lancastrian kings, Henry IV and Henry V. It remains the most imposing feature of the castle. Three arches above the entrance allowed soldiers to drop missiles on an enemy trying to break into the gate-passage. In turn, the passage was protected by a draw-bridge, a portcullis and doorway at either end, and 'murder holes' above. Inside there were guardrooms, a dungeon, a private hall and other comfortable accommodation for the constable. Such was the design, that it could be held independently of the remainder of the castle.

In the later fifteenth century, Kidwelly passed to Sir Rhys ap Thomas who made a number of further additions. A large kitchen was built in the inner ward, and a spacious new hall and other lodgings were also raised within the outer defences. Even so, the castle was gradually abandoned in the sixteenth century, and in 1609 it was described as 'utterly ruyned and decayed'. Visitors may also be interested in the remains of an early fourteenth-century town gate which can be seen to the south-west of the castle.

Lamphey Bishop's Palace

Even before the arrival of the Normans, the Welsh bishops of St Davids may have had an episcopal residence at Lamphey. We, however, can say nothing of its character, nor for that matter can we envisage the buildings erected under the early Norman bishops. None the less, the manor of Lamphey was certainly among the more important possessions of these wealthy prelates, and by 1326 the palace had become a

Lamphey Palace, a comfortable rural retreat of the medieval bishops of St Davids.

63

favourite dwelling. In that year a great survey of the entire diocesan estates was made for Bishop David Martin (1293–1328). Known as the *Black Book of St Davids*, it not only provides insights into Lamphey's role as the centre of a manorial economy, it also reveals a lush rural retreat. The comfortable palace buildings lay amid well-stocked fishponds, orchards plump with fruit, and a no doubt extensive vegetable garden. There were also two watermills, a windmill and a dovecot, together with a park of some 144 acres which sheltered a herd of 60 deer. Here at Lamphey, far from the cares and pressures of the cathedral city, the bishop could combine the life of a powerful churchman with that of a secular 'country gentleman'.

The surviving structures represent the nucleus of a once quite considerable complex. Indeed, extensive traces of outbuildings can still be seen around the site. As at St Davids itself, all of the principal rooms lay on the first floor, and essentially comprise two halls, a large private chamber and a chapel. The smaller hall block is now much ruined, but it is probably the earliest surviving building, and was raised in the early thirteenth century. Not many years later, possibly under Bishop Richard Carew (1256–80), a large and well-appointed *camera* – a private apartment – was added to the west end of the hall. The main chamber, originally lit by tall lancet windows, was entered via an external stair up from the courtyard. On the southern side, a small projecting turret housed the bishop's bedchamber, equipped with a latrine. The ground floor may have served as quarters for his attendants.

The palace reached its greatest extent under Bishop Henry de Gower (1328–47), and the ruins still bear his unmistakable imprint. It was de Gower who raised the new great hall, a resplendent first-floor chamber over 70 feet long, set above a vaulted basement. Again, the main door of this dignified and well built structure was approached by an external stair, and a passage in the north-west corner led through the old hall to the bishop's private apartment. But it is the distinct arcaded parapet which represents the hallmark of de Gower's work. It served the same purpose as that at St Davids – allowing rainwater from the roof to be thrown clear of the wall face – though the Lamphey workmanship is simpler, and possibly

Bishop Henry de Gower's distinctive arcaded parapet at Lamphey Palace.

reflects the use of less skilled masons. Bishop Henry also remodelled the inner courtyard, enclosing it with a battlemented wall, and building a gatehouse again crowned with the characteristic parapet.

Little more building was undertaken at Lamphey until the early sixteenth century. At that time, it was probably Bishop Edward Vaughan (1509–22) who was responsible for the chapel constructed against the northern face of the early hall. A third floor was also inserted under the existing roof of the *camera*. The tall thirteenth-century windows were partly blocked, and were reformed as rectangular openings. It has been suggested that these modifications represent a certain measure of economy, a concentration of the essential life of the household in one comprehensive block. The Tudor bishops may well have found the earlier medieval layout costly and unmanageable.

Late in the reign of King Henry VIII, Bishop William Barlow (1536–48) surrendered the ownership of Lamphey in favour of the powerful Devereux family. Barlow was intent upon removing the centre of the diocese to Carmarthen, and had consequently tended to neglect the estates in the west. Richard Devereux acquired the palace in 1546 and began adapting the buildings to more secular needs. The circular chimneys above the *camera* and great hall belong to this period. His grandson Robert Devereux, later earl of Essex, and a favourite of Queen Elizabeth I, spent much of his boyhood at Lamphey.

Laugharne Castle

The pretty little seaside town of Laugharne is probably best known for its associations with Dylan Thomas. It was here, from 1949 until his death in 1953, that the greatest of modern Welsh poets lived and worked at the 'Boathouse'. The Georgian fronted main street, the inns, the cottages, the breaking waves and the people he knew are believed by many to have provided the inspiration for Dylan's masterpiece, *Under Milk Wood*. Surprisingly, the picturesque remains of the substantial medieval stronghold at the southern end of the old town are far less well known. Yet over the past 15 years, the 'romantic' ruins of Laugharne Castle have been the subject of a painstaking programme of consolidation and archaeological investigation. Gradually, a complex sequence of building development has been uncovered, a sequence which extended throughout much of the Middle Ages and well into the Tudor period. The castle stands at a point where the small Coran stream enters the estuary of the River Taf. A fine late medieval gatehouse leads

Best known for its associations with the poet Dylan Thomas, Laugharne has a superb castle with origins in the early twelfth century. In the earlier Middle Ages it was held by the de Brian family, and was extensively remodelled in the late Tudor period.

into the diamond-shaped outer ward, with parts of the original curtain wall surviving on the western side. Much of the inner ward still rises to the full height of its battlements.

Laugharne may have been the site of Robert Courtemain's Norman outpost of Abercorram, mentioned in the early twelfth century, though at present the archaeological evidence cannot be pushed back this far. None the less, an earthen 'ringwork' castle had certainly been established here before the end of the twelfth century. Documentary evidence suggests that the castle was captured from the Anglo-Normans by the Welsh in 1215, and again in 1257. It was probably the first stone castle of Sir Guy de Brian IV which was destroyed by fire during the 1257 attack. Following its recovery, the de Brians strengthened Laugharne with the addition of a new gatehouse to the inner ward. The de Brian family, who were also lords of Okehampton in Devon, continued to hold the castle through until 1390. From them it passed to various descendants until, in 1488, the inheritance came to the fourth earl of Northumberland.

Parts of the site appear to have fallen into ruin in this period, but at the end of the sixteenth century it was to see a further change of fortune. In 1584, Elizabeth I granted Laugharne to Sir John Perrot, who has been called a 'tempestuous and choleric character of Shakesperian proportions'. He is said to have been the illegitimate son of Henry VIII and was perhaps, therefore, half-brother to the queen. Sir John lost all in 1592 when he was found guilty of high treason. He was fortunate enough to escape the executioner, dying of natural causes in the Tower of London.

A full analysis of the buildings must await the completion of the archaeological study, although certain details seem clear. The two large round towers of the inner ward form part of the de Brian castle, and their gatehouse was unusual in having a basement below the gate-passage. A hall block, which still stands between the towers, was added in the Tudor period. There is a large semicircular stair turret on its outer wall. However, as at nearby Carew Castle, under Sir John Perrot, Laugharne was converted into a veritable mansion with a second hall constructed against the south curtain. Only the outer wall remains, but this reveals evidence of

fireplaces and grand windows. The excavations have also recovered the pitched stone floor of the kitchen basement. It seems the courtyard and entrance passage of Sir John's castle were paved with a decorative arrangement of cobblestones.

During the Civil War Laugharne Castle was initially held by the Parliamentarians, but was captured by Royalists in 1644. It was retaken later in the year following a fierce week-long siege. Musket shot and cannon balls dating to the siege have been found embedded in the castle walls. Following this episode, parts of the site were systematically demolished, and the castle was never reoccupied. It gradually fell into decay, becoming the ivy-clad ruin captured on canvas by Turner. Now as a monument in the care of the State, the programme of consolidation work nears completion, and the site should be fully open to visitors within the next few years.

Llansteffan Castle

Llansteffan was never one of the greatest castles of Wales, but it provides the visitor with noteworthy insights into the development of medieval fortifications. Like many thirteenth-century Marcher families, the de Camvilles spent large sums on the latest architectural innovations. In a period of Welsh resurgence and threat, they were seeking to defend and consolidate the often precarious hold on their coastal lordship. The castle itself stands on an abrupt headland overlooking the sandy Tywi estuary, a site in fact of great antiquity. Long before the castle was raised, this bluff was occupied by an Iron Age promontory fort as early as the sixth century BC. It was probably refortified as a Norman stronghold in the opening years of the twelfth century, when the Iron Age ditches were recut and a castle of earth and timber constructed within.

The first positive documentary reference to the site is for 1146 when it was taken by a group of Welsh princelings. By 1158 the area was reappropriated and Llansteffan was generally in English hands thereafter, though not without the occasional struggle. From the end of the

The de Camville castle at Llansteffan, overlooking the Tywi estuary.

twelfth century until 1338 the castle was held by William de Camville and his descendants; apparently five lords in all, alternatively named William and Geoffrey. It was clearly something of a chequered period in the history of the lordship, with the family briefly ousted by the Welsh on three separate occasions. However, each time the de Camvilles recovered the castle, greater effort and investment went into the successive stages of stone fortification.

To begin with, shortly before the end of the twelfth century, the upper ward was surrounded with a slender stone wall. About 1225 this area was strengthened by the addition of the inner gatehouse, with its passage defended by a portcullis and doors. Excavations in this area have revealed the foundations of several buildings, including a round tower situated along the line of the inner curtain wall. At this time the defences of the lower ward were probably still of earth and timber.

By the mid thirteenth century the Welsh had found a new leader in Prince Llywelyn ap Gruffudd of Gwynedd. Everywhere they were turning the tide against English control. In 1257

Stephen Bauzan was heading an expedition in the Tywi valley, and was utterly overwhelmed in one of the most devastating defeats ever inflicted on an English army in Wales. That army contained the garrisons of the castles nearby, and the Welsh pushing home their advantage soon captured the defenceless Llansteffan. When the de Camvilles recovered the castle they set about a major programme of improvement, walling the lower ward and flanking it with large D-shaped towers. The north tower in particular dominates the defences on the landward side. It would also have provided a considerable degree of comfort as the private quarters of the castle's lord.

Llansteffan's most imposing feature is the massive twin-towered gatehouse added to the outer curtain wall about 1280. It was to become the main living quarters at the castle, and in the Tudor period was converted into a 'house' by walling up both ends of the gate-passage. Inside, various features of the original arrangement can still be seen, including grooves for the portcullises and 'murder-holes' overhead. The overall design is remarkably similar to Gilbert de Clare's east gatehouse at Caerphilly, and the master mason must clearly have been familiar with that great work. The similarity extends to the unusual slot-shaped chute over the front arch, through which boiling liquids could be poured on attackers.

During the fourteenth and fifteenth centuries Llansteffan was held by various lords, and was sometimes in Crown hands. Henry VII granted the castle to his uncle, Jasper Tudor, who held it until his death in 1495. It was perhaps at this time that the gatehouse was converted to a 'house', and the large barn was added to the lower ward. In military terms the site passed into obscurity, gradually being occupied by farm buildings.

Llawhaden Castle

Llawhaden lay at the centre of a particularly rich group of manorial estates belonging to the bishops of St Davids. The site was already of great importance when, in about 1175, Gerald of Wales visited his uncle Bishop David fitz Gerald here. At the time, Gerald described the earth and timber construction he must have seen as a 'castle'. However, the later stone buildings show few obvious signs of serious defensive planning. The main emphasis is undoubtedly upon household comfort, and Llawhaden is perhaps best described as a fortified palace. It was clearly a favourite episcopal residence, and in 1287 the charitable Bishop Thomas Bek (1280–93) founded a hospital hereabouts for pilgrims, poor orphans, the aged infirm, the sick and other feeble people.

The extensive remains stand in attractive wooded countryside, on a commanding spur above the Eastern Cleddau river. The great oval dry ditch survives from the early stronghold visited by Gerald. Originally, a bank on the edge of the inner 'ringwork' was probably crowned with a wooden stockade, and various timber buildings provided the internal accommodation. In 1192, Llawhaden was taken by the Welsh prince, Rhys ap Gruffudd, and the defences were apparently destroyed. Following its recovery by the bishops, work may have begun on a stone curtain wall and towers. The

foundations of two circular towers along the western edge of the site may date from the early thirteenth century.

But it was under Bishop David Martin (1293–1328) that Llawhaden was totally transformed. A new palatial residence was designed, with its own individual household requirements. Thereafter Llawhaden provided the comfort required by a wealthy prelate, quarters for a permanent garrison, and lodging for estate officials and important guests. Great emphasis was placed on the standard of accommodation, and all earlier work on the site was cleared to make the necessary room. The new buildings were arranged to look out on a no doubt attractive pentagonal courtyard, with several towers and extensions projecting out over the earlier ditch.

Inside, opposite the gatehouse, the two-storey block contained the great hall at the centre, originally entered by a stair covered by a wooden porch. The kitchen and service rooms were in the wing at the western end. The bishop had his own very substantial private apartment in the wing at the opposite (upper) end of the hall. The vaulted rooms on the ground floor of this range provided storage space.

The outer wall and towers of the range to the south-east still stand almost to their full height. The bishop's private chamber was once linked to the one end of this block, providing him with a private entrance to the chapel of the Blessed Virgin. A chamber, with a latrine and fireplace, situated in the adjacent angle tower, was clearly designed for the chaplain. Small isolated rooms over the chapel porch probably housed an archive store and perhaps a finance or estate office. This range also contained a series of very comfortable guest apartments. There were four sets in all, two on either floor, each with an attached bedchamber and latrine. These lodgings may also have been used by more important members of the household staff.

It has been suggested that from time to time, in a fortified palace such as this, the bishop may have kept a body of armed retainers or mercenaries. They would certainly have been housed in separate accommodation, and a two-storey block just inside the gatehouse could have provided a small barracks. The adjacent building was perhaps their kitchen, and beyond this lay a large bakehouse which retains evidence of its ovens.

The imposing facade of the late fourteenth-century gatehouse at Llawhaden.

The gatehouse was rebuilt as a more imposing structure in the later fourteenth century, and its front facade remains standing to parapet level. Llawhaden continued to be used as a residence by the bishops of St Davids through to the Reformation. It was perhaps during the episcopate of William Barlow (1536–48), the first Protestant bishop, that the site was abandoned. It was at this time that Abergwili, outside Carmarthen, became the chief residence of the bishops.

itself, and may date back as far as 3500 BC. It is of the form archaeologists call 'portal dolmen', with the front of the tomb defined by three uprights set in an H-shaped formation. Pentre Ifan, however, is somewhat unique in Wales since the 'portal' stands at the centre of a curving facade of slabs, and resembles a family

Pentre Ifan – one of the most impressive Neolithic tombs in Wales.

Pentre Ifan Burial Chamber

Lying on the northern footslopes of the Preseli Hills, and commanding a wide view over the Nevern valley, this is without doubt one of the most impressive megalithic monuments in Wales. Pentre Ifan has long attracted attention due to its unusually high great capstone, and various early pictures show that a horseman could pass underneath. It is hardly surprising then, that along with Arthur's Stone on the Gower peninsula, it was the first burial chamber to be conserved under the Ancient Monuments Protection Act of 1882.

The most prominent feature is the chamber

of tombs called 'court cairns', better known in northern Ireland. The huge capstone, some 16 feet long, tips back from the 'portal' and at the rear of the chamber it rests on a single pointed upright.

The site was excavated in 1936–37 and again in 1958–59, and the central tomb was found to lie in a large oval pit. The long sides of the chamber are thought to have been constructed of dry-stone walling, together with a few larger slabs. In fact, the chamber lay at the southern end of a wedge-shaped cairn which extended back some 120 feet from the forecourt formed by the facade. Finds from the excavation were meagre but included Neolithic pottery and a few flint tools. Since these excavations, it has been suggested that Pentre Ifan represents two phases of building. Beginning with the chamber and a small cairn, the facade and extension of the cairn could have followed at a later date. Such developments would not be unusual, but this theory cannot be pursued without further excavation at the site.

St Davids Bishop's Palace

There were few landowners in medieval Wales wealthier or more powerful than the bishops of St Davids. As well as being princes of the church, with considerable influence in religious affairs, they also controlled huge estates in the largest of the four Welsh dioceses. A survey made in 1326, known as the *Black Book of St Davids*, reveals that the bishop's holdings rendered an income of some £333 in that year. With these landed possessions and wealth came great temporal power. The bishops were Marcher lords in their own right, owing allegiance only to the Crown. They had their own prison, gallows, and the right to hold courts.

It is scarcely surprising, therefore, that within their cathedral city these mighty prelates created a group of medieval buildings unsurpassed throughout the principality. Even in ruin, the beauty of the magnificent palace is unquestioned. It represents the physical expression of men rich in experience of both church and state affairs. The entire close was surrounded by a precinct wall, pierced by four gates. Only one

of these – Porth y Twr – now survives, and probably dates to the late thirteenth century. From this gate, visitors can gaze down past the cathedral towards the palace. At a distance it appears to be one harmonious architectural whole, an impression created by the superb arcaded parapet which crowns the southern and eastern ranges. In fact, the palace was largely the work of a succession of 'builder bishops' in the later thirteenth and fourteenth centuries.

The story of St Davids, however, begins long before the thirteenth century. This spot on the banks of the River Alun is generally believed to be the *Vallis Rosina*, the 'valley of the little marsh', chosen during the sixth century as the site of a monastic foundation by St David. The location became famous, and by the eve of the Norman conquest the bishopric and its cathedral were already well established. In 1115, Bernard, chaplain to Queen Matilda, became the first Norman bishop of the diocese. His efforts were concentrated on building a new cathedral, and we can say nothing of the episcopal residence at this time. King Henry II came to St Davids on pilgrimage in 1171 and was entertained in a hall, but once again the nature of the building is unknown. In 1182, Bernard's church was destroyed by fire, and it was Bishop Peter de Leia (1179–98) who began the work of reconstruction. In particular, he was responsible for the striking arcades which can be seen in the nave today.

The earliest surviving part of the palace, the western range, could date from the end of the twelfth century, though it retains no original details. Indeed, it is difficult to be certain about any of the buildings before the time of Bishop Thomas Bek (1280–93), the first in a line of distinguished ecclesiastics and statesmen who held the see over the next century. Bek had been a trusted servant of Edward I, serving as keeper of the Wardrobe and Chancellor of the University of Oxford. It seems unlikely that such an active reformer and powerful magnate would be content with the scale of the early medieval palace buildings for very long, and it was perhaps the pilgrimage to the shrine of St David by King Edward and his queen, in November 1284, which drew attention to the various inadequacies. In any case, Bek soon began work on a major programme of reconstruction. He raised the spacious rectangular hall and chamber

An aerial view of the magnificent bishop's palace and cathedral city of St Davids.

block, which now forms the centre of the eastern range. The principal rooms were on the first floor, and were carried on great barrel vaults set transversely across the building. Two fine lofty windows looked out from the bishop's hall over the courtyard, and visitors will notice the superb series of corbels carved as human heads which carried the roof trusses in both the hall and the adjacent private chamber. Bishop Bek also built the chapel in the south-west corner of the complex. This, too, has a vaulted basement, and there is a square bellcot with an octagonal spire at one corner.

The greatest of the St Davids 'builder bishops' was without doubt Henry de Gower (1328–47), the man who more than any other left his imprint so decisively and characteristi-cally on the palace. In addition to significant works in the cathedral, notably the imposing rood screen, it was de Gower who was respon-sible for the magnificent great hall. Moreover,

The great hall porch at the bishop's palace.

71

A detail of the richly decorative arcaded parapet added to the bishop's palace by Henry de Gower (1328–47). Bishop Gower is also associated with similar parapets at the palace of Lamphey and at Swansea Castle.

he brought a graceful unity to the palace as a whole with the distinct arcaded parapet which crowns the top of the great hall and extends to the earlier buildings. As with Bek's constructions, the hall was raised over a barrel vaulted basement. It was entered via an elaborately decorated porch, with grand steps leading up from the courtyard. The hall proper was more than 80 feet long, with three handsome windows overlooking the courtyard, and an attractive wheel window in the gable of the eastern end. The size of this great hall, together with the absence of any domestic buildings, suggests it was used for state occasions and feast days, rather than as the normal residence of the bishop.

The richly decorative details of the parapets are best viewed from the courtyard. Essentially, this cunning architectural device carried a battlemented wall-walk, and also allowed water to drain freely from the roofs. Heavy rain would run down through the arcades, flushing out well clear of the wall faces. But not only was

the design highly practical, it was also intended to create a striking impact. The arcades were supported on carved corbels, and the battlements, the gables and the turrets of both the great hall and the earlier eastern range were all ornamented with a chequered veneer of local Caerbwdi purple sandstone, white spar, and a pale freestone. Although similar parapets are associated with de Gower at Lamphey Palace and at Swansea Castle, they are of altogether cruder workmanship, and lack the decorative veneer of St Davids.

The scheme of work begun by Henry de Gower may well have been completed with slight modifications under his immediate successors. In the main, a new vaulted kitchen was added to the southern end of the earlier bishop's hall. A covered passageway was extended to link both halls, and this was again surmounted with a parapet. The northern end of this passage provided a porch to the main entrance of the bishop's hall, with steps leading up from the

courtyard. The building generally attributed as the bishop's private chapel also belongs to this period.

With the exception of Adam de Houghton (1362–89), the later medieval bishops of St Davids were men of lesser note, and do not appear to have added much to the palace. In 1536, William Barlow became the first Protestant bishop, and with the Reformation the story of decay and destruction begins. Barlow himself seems to have begun the process by unroofing the great hall, and transferring his chief residence to Carmarthen. Although bishops continued to occupy parts of the site in the later sixteenth century, the trend towards decay continued. The palace was finally abandoned around the mid-seventeenth century.

St Dogmaels Abbey

The cult of St David was widespread throughout south Wales in the medieval period. This rare survival of a fourteenth-century 'antiphoner' represents the office for the saint's day.

Founded for a community of Tironian monks, this site is of great interest as one of the very few houses of the order established anywhere in medieval England and Wales. Although the

St Dogmaels Abbey, founded for Tironian monks by Robert fitz Martin about 1115.

ruins are not particularly extensive, they span four centuries of monastic life and reveal several phases of modification and rebuilding.

It was around the year 1115 that the Norman lord of Cemais, Robert fitz Martin, decided to establish a new monastic house on the site of the ancient *clas* church of Llandudoch. Like his Marcher colleagues he showed scant respect for the traditions and customs of the pre-Conquest native church. Instead, fitz Martin brought 13 monks from the French house of Tiron to introduce Benedictine monasticism to this distant part of west Wales. He later obtained a further 13 monks and raised the house to the status of an abbey. St Dogmaels, as it came to be known, held estates in the lordship of Cemais, and Robert also granted the abbey lands in Devon. His mother, meanwhile, gave the monks the island of Caldey, where they established a small dependent priory cell. We know little of the internal history of St Dogmaels, though the ideals and austere life style of the Tironians had much in common with the Cistercian order.

The buildings were initially laid out on a fairly grand scale in the early 1100s, but the work stopped short of completion and much was added and reconstructed in later centuries. Within the church, the crossing piers survive from the original arrangement. The nave, however, where the west and north walls stand almost to their full height, was not completed until the thirteenth century. There is a fine north doorway carved with ball-flower ornament, dating to about 1330, and there are areas of later medieval floor tiles. The east end of the church, including the presbytery and the once vaulted crypt, formed part of the thirteenth-century rebuilding. In the Tudor period, not long before the suppression of the abbey, the north transept was reconstructed to provide elaborate chapel space, probably for the commemoration of the lords of Cemais. Several corbels which once carried the vault can be seen, and these are finely carved with figures: an angel for St Matthew, a lion for St Mark, and the Archangel Michael.

The cloister lay to the south of the church, and again the basic arrangement dates to the twelfth century. A new chapter house was added in an odd position beyond the east range in the fourteenth century. Soon afterwards an

A corbel carved with the eagle of St John, from the north transept at St Dogmaels.

abbot's house or guest lodging was constructed outside the west range. The monks' infirmary survives particularly well, and houses a collection of carved stones found around the site.

The abbot and eight monks were present at the dissolution of St Dogmaels in 1536. The church was saved from immediate destruction and continued to be used by the parish for a time. The south-west corner of the cloister may well have been developed as a house for the rector. Many alterations were made to this area of the buildings during the sixteenth and seventeenth centuries.

St Non's Chapel

Perched above the waves, overlooking St Non's Bay, are the ruins of a small medieval chapel dedicated to St Non (Nonnita), traditionally the mother of St David. The chapel is said to be built over the spot where she gave birth to David. There are few distinguishing features in the building, though unlike the majority of Christian churches it is aligned north and south,

The small medieval chapel dedicated to St Non, the mother of St David.

probably due to the steep fall in the ground. Inside, resting against the south-east corner, there is an early Christian cross slab, dating from between the seventh and ninth centuries, but the chapel itself is unlikely to be this early. It is first mentioned in a document of 1335, and during the Middle Ages was reckoned as the 'chief and principal' of the many pilgrimage chapels situated throughout the diocese of St Davids. In the early sixteenth century, offerings from St Non's and the other chapels were brought every Saturday to the cathedral chapter house, and were divided among the canons 'by the dishful'.

The chapel passed out of use at the Reformation, and later appears to have been converted to a dwelling house. Near the site there is a 'holy well', visited as a place of pilgrimage through to the eighteenth century.

Strata Florida Abbey

It was in June 1164 that the Norman baron Robert fitz Stephen, who held the district of Pennardd in the Marcher lordship of Ceredigion, drew a colony of 13 monks from the Cistercian abbey at Whitland to found a new house on the banks of the Fflur brook. Strata Florida ('vale of flowers'), as it became known, was a comparatively modest foundation, and traces of the early church have been uncovered at a site called 'yr hen fynachlog'. Political events, however, were soon to change the tide of fortunes for the infant community. The following year, Rhys ap Gruffudd – 'the Lord Rhys' – overran fitz Stephen's estates, and in due course assumed the patronage of the abbey. He became a munificent benefactor, granting the monks vast tracts of upland grazing land, as well as arable holdings in the Teifi valley. Rhys undoubtedly took great pride in this monastery he is said to have 'loved and cherished', and by 1184 had begun to build a brand new church on a site almost two miles from the original location. The work was sufficiently advanced in 1201 for the monks to make use of the choir, though construction of the nave and the monastic buildings around the cloister must have continued well into the thirteenth century.

The new abbey retained the name Strata Florida, and even today the location continues to echo the ideals of the early Cistercians. Deep in the green and tranquil heart of Wales, it is a very lonely setting, typical of those sought by this most austere of orders. In fact, it was just this puritan austerity which caught the imagination of the Welsh princes and led to the great success of the Cistercians in Wales. Strata Florida, in particular, became a great focus of

Strata Florida – a typical Cistercian site in the heart of mid Wales.

native culture and influence. Much of this was fostered by the Lord Rhys himself, and the abbey church became virtually the mausoleum for members of his Deheubarth dynasty of princes. An interesting collection of grave slabs can be seen on the eastern side of the abbey church, and hereabouts lie two of Rhys's sons. Such was the loyalty of the monks to their Welsh benefactors, that in 1212 King John ordered the destruction of the house 'which harbours our enemies'. The abbot appears to have prevented this, but only through payment of a massive fine. The spirit of the monks was far from dampened. Indeed, it was in the scriptorium at Strata Florida that the lost Latin chronicle which forms the basis of the *Brut y Tywysogyon* (Chronicle of the Princes) was compiled in the late thirteenth century, and it was there also that at least one Welsh translation of the chronicle was produced. In 1238 the abbey was the venue for a major assembly of Welsh princes who were summoned by Llywelyn the Great to swear allegiance to his son and heir, Dafydd. There is a strong tradition, too, that the greatest poet ever to have written in the Welsh language, Dafydd ap Gwilym, was buried within the precinct walls in the late fourteenth century.

This fourteenth-century effigy in St Davids Cathedral is generally believed to be a memorial to Rhys ap Gruffudd – the Lord Rhys (d. 1197). Strata Florida was virtually his foundation, and many of his dynasty of princes were buried there.

The early thirteenth-century west doorway at Strata Florida.

Against this background, the monks were also engaged in a thriving agricultural and commercial economy. As well as the original endowments granted by the Lord Rhys, they built up other holdings which included several considerable coastal granges. Together, the enormous upland sheep ranches and lowland estates added up to many thousands of acres. At the dissolution of the abbey in 1539 the community had dwindled to about eight monks, with an assessed income of some £118 a year.

Dating from the early thirteenth century, the west doorway into the abbey church is an attractive and most unusual construction. Inside, the columns of the nave arcades stood on solid screen walls, an arrangement found in some Irish churches. In turn, the monks' choir was separated from the nave and transepts by further screen walls. Set into the floor at the centre of the choir is a particularly interesting 'basin', with steps at either side. This may have been for a ritual ceremony at which the abbot washed the feet of his brethren. Three chapels, with their altar bases, can be seen in each transept. The south transept chapels are roofed over for protection, and there are very attractive

areas of decorated paving tiles.

The cloister, rebuilt in stone at the end of the fifteenth century, lay to the south of the church. Here, along the northern side, an alcove marks the position of a lectern for the Collation, or reading before the monks' evening service of

Decorative medieval floor tiles in the south transept at Strata Florida.

Compline. The remains of the chapter house can be seen to the east, but the site of the southern range and monks' dining hall now lies under the farmhouse adjacent to the site. There is a small exhibition at Strata Florida, with details of the abbey and its history, as well as an interesting collection of carved stones.

Talley Abbey

Talley, or Talyllychau in Welsh, literally means 'the head of the lakes'. Set in beautiful hills, the abbey of the Blessed Virgin Mary and St John the Baptist was founded about 1184–89 by Rhys ap Gruffudd, prince of Deheubarth, and takes its name from its situation at the head of two lakes. Talley was established for Premonstratensian – 'white' – canons, and was to remain the only monastery of this order in Wales. The Lord Rhys may well have been influenced in his choice of the canons through links with the court of King Henry II, particularly his connections with the justiciar, Ranulf de Glanville, who was a great patron of the Premonstratensians in England.

Rhys endowed the abbey with the core of its estates, and by 1250 the canons held extensive tracts of upland pasture, together with smaller holdings along the river valleys of the Teifi and Towy. It is also interesting to note that Rhys's eldest son had married a daughter of the powerful William de Braose, who granted the canons property as far afield as Abergavenny. Despite such gifts, Talley's economic affairs were rarely in good order. In 1278 the house was taken into the hands of Edward I in view of its impoverishment in the war of the previous year. Edward, too, was suspicious of the Welsh sympathies of the canons and proposed to replace certain members 'by others of English tongue who were able and willing to observe the religious life'.

Today, the remains of the central tower beckon the visitor from the road which passes by. Little survives beyond the abbey church itself, and this reveals a much modified and marked reduction in the initial architectural ambitions of the community. As planned, the church was intended to be some 240 feet long. The presbytery, crossing, transepts and nave were laid out in the late twelfth century, and work focused upon the completion of the east

The Premonstratensian abbey of Talley, founded about 1184–89 by the Lord Rhys.

The central crossing and remains of the tower at Talley. The abbey church was planned on a large scale, though lack of funds eventually led to a reduction in the overall scheme.

end where the canons' choir would have been located. The nave, however, was never finished as planned, and in the early thirteenth century the west wall and door were eventually built halfway along its proposed length. The planned aisle on the north side, and four western bays were totally abandoned. A long and costly quarrel with the neighbouring Cistercian abbey of Whitland may have been in part responsible for this early setback, but the canons were clearly never able to muster sufficient funds to progress further. Two arches of the central crossing survive, and two walls of the tower rise up to 95 feet above. The north and south transepts each had three chapels on their eastern

side. The base of the night stair to the canons' dormitory can be seen in the south transept. No doubt the original cloister on the southern side was planned to match the church, but in due course a smaller one was built alongside the reduced nave.

Financial problems again led to the abbey being taken into the king's hands in 1381, and it further suffered damage in the Glyndŵr rebellion 20 years later. The assessed income of the house at its suppression in 1536 was £136, when there were still eight resident canons. Following the Dissolution of the Monasteries, the presbytery continued in use as a parish church until 1772.

GLAMORGAN
Upland and Lowland Contrasts in the South

The historic shire of Glamorgan was created under King Henry VIII's Act of Union (1536–43), which united the medieval Marcher lordship of Glamorgan with that of Gower. It is a region of profound contrasts, stemming largely from major differences in upland and lowland topography. The southern half of the county – *Bro Morgannwg* – includes the rich agricultural lowlands of the Vale of Glamorgan and the Gower peninsula. These areas are fringed in the north by mountain moorland – the *Blaenau* – as bleak as anything in the highest of mid Wales hills. It is scarcely surprising that such differences have influenced patterns of settlement since earliest times.

Under the Romans, for example, it was indeed the Vale of Glamorgan that proved the most attractive area. Nowhere else in Wales has produced such a concentration of Romanized villas and farmsteads. The life and economy of the Vale were more akin to those of south-west England than to those in the poorer Welsh uplands. Again, the pattern is even clearer for the Middle Ages. The Normans swept quickly into the fertile coastal lowlands, and under their rule an 'English' manorial economy soon emerged. The *Blaenau*, however, was to remain essentially Welsh in character, controlled by native rulers who held their lands under the chief Marcher lords. Nothing emphasizes these medieval differences more than the distribution of castles.

Wales, we are so often told, is a land of castles, but even in this context Glamorgan is quite exceptional. Only four counties in England, and none in the principality, exceed the total figure of 85 known castles in the historic county. This concentration is yet more striking when we appreciate that virtually all of them lie in the southern coastal regions, with very few in the Welsh areas to the north. Many of these strongholds, it must be said, survive merely as earthworks, though some of the finest masonry examples are now cared for by Cadw. Coity and Ogmore, Swansea and Weobley, all have their points of interest, and Caerphilly stands as one of the most magnificent strongholds in the entire British Isles. Nor should visitors overlook other extensive castle ruins at Cardiff, and at Oystermouth and Pennard on the Gower peninsula.

Moreover, Glamorgan has a great deal of historic interest besides its castles. Cadw looks after three major Neolithic burial chambers, the superb Cistercian abbey at Neath, an important collection of early Christian stones at Margam, and the fairytale creation of William Burges at Castell Coch.

Since 1974, the historic shire of Glamorgan has been divided into the three new counties of Mid, South and West Glamorgan. It is the most heavily populated region of Wales with some of the largest towns, including Bridgend, Swansea and the national capital, Cardiff. This, too, was one of the areas at the very heart of the Industrial Revolution in Wales. Recently, as the upland landscape has gradually been healed of its nineteenth-century industrial wounds and scars, we have become aware of the great need to preserve examples of buildings and sites associated with this highly significant episode in our history. Some of the main attractions include the somewhat earlier Aberdulais Falls, the Cefn Coed Colliery Museum, the Welsh Miners' Museum at Afan Argoed and the Welsh Industrial and Maritime Museum at Cardiff.

Cardigan Bay

GLAMORGAN

Bristol Channel

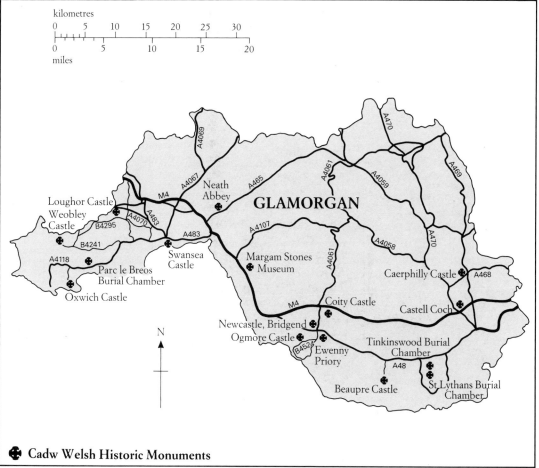

kilometres

0 5 10 15 20 25 30

0 5 10 15 20

miles

A4069

A4067

M4

Neath Abbey

A465

A4061

A470

A4059

A4069

Loughor Castle

Weobley Castle

A4070

A483

GLAMORGAN

B4295

B4241

A483

A4107

A4058

A470

A4118

Swansea Castle

Parc le Breos Burial Chamber

Margam Stones Museum

A4061

Caerphilly Castle

A468

Oxwich Castle

N

M4

Coity Castle

Castell Coch

Newcastle, Bridgend

Ogmore Castle

B4524

Ewenny Priory

Tinkinswood Burial Chamber

A48

Beaupre Castle

St Lythans Burial Chamber

✤ **Cadw Welsh Historic Monuments**

Beaupre Castle, in the heart of the pastoral Vale of Glamorgan.

Beaupre Castle

The name Beaupre is derived from the old French *beau-repaire*, beautiful retreat, which is a perfect description for this secluded spot in the heart of the rural Vale of Glamorgan. Sometimes known as Old Beaupre, the 'castle' is approached along a footpath which shadows the banks of the meandering River Thaw. Despite its location just a few miles west of Cardiff, Beaupre remains relatively undiscovered, and yet within its principal courtyard there is a magnificent Renaissance porch.

The first recorded mention of Beaupre is in 1376 when it was held by a John Basset. The Bassets had, none the less, been there for some time and were almost certainly responsible for the initial early fourteenth-century buildings. At the time, the house – for that is how it should be described – was grouped around an open courtyard with few indications of serious defence, not unlike Weobley Castle on the Gower peninsula. This courtyard, the focus of

medieval Beaupre, lay to the south of the hall, and is now in the grounds of a private house. The hall range itself, however, preserves much of its fourteenth-century core. There is, for example, evidence for a blocked gateway into the inner courtyard, and next to this a tall gabled structure not unlike a 'tower house'. The hall is at the centre, and although much modified it appears to have had a gallery at the east end.

In the early sixteenth century Beaupre passed in marriage to Rice Mansel of Oxwich, and although his wife died childless he was entitled to hold the house until his death in 1559. In turn, Sir Rice's daughter – by his second marriage – was betrothed to the new heir, William Basset. Indeed, it was under Sir Rice that the Tudor transformation of Beaupre began. Over the next half century the plan of the house was to change dramatically, with the present courtyard becoming the focal showpiece. The work culminated in the outer gatehouse and inner porch, completed under William Basset's son, Richard.

The courtyard is entered through the showy outer gate, with a Basset shield of arms above the door bearing the motto 'Better death than dishonour'. The numerous windows to the large upper room of the gate are very suggestive of attempts to emulate a 'long gallery', supplemented no doubt by the wall-walk on the adjacent curtain wall. It may well have been an ingenious solution to introduce 'status' features of the more grandiose Elizabethan houses. On the west side of the courtyard there is a three-storeyed block of accommodation, which once contained a particularly impressive stair around a central pillar. Each of the rooms was provided with a fireplace and window, and each had access to a latrine.

The undoubted glory of Beaupre is the inner porch, raised in 1600 by Richard Basset as a grand entrance to the much altered medieval hall. Its three stages demonstrate an ostentation and flamboyance typical of the late Elizabethan and Jacobean period. The detail includes the three orders of Classical architecture: Doric columns at the base, Ionic at the centre, and Corinthian in the top stage. The central panel bears an elaborate heraldic shield, and below this three small panels carry an inscription which includes 'Rycharde Bassett, having t[o w]yf Katherine dovght[e]r to Sir Thomas Iohns knight, built this porche . . . 1600. His yeres 65,

Sir Rice Mansel, who held Beaupre in the early sixteenth century.

The glorious Renaissance porch at Beaupre.

his wife 55'. The windows of the porch, unlike earlier examples in the house, were rebated internally for glass. The plaster in the room on the first floor carries some interesting seventeenth-century graffiti, including a ship of about 200 tons, bedecked with the flag of St George.

Beaupre certainly appears to have been occupied into the early eighteenth century, with blocked fireplaces and windows suggesting avoidance of hearth and window tax. But later in the century, apart from the one medieval wing occupied as a farmhouse, the site gradually became ruinous.

Caerphilly Castle

Caerphilly was the greatest of all the Marcher fortresses of south Wales, if not one of the most remarkable defensive complexes ever completed by an individual patron in the Middle Ages. The interest and extraordinary impact of the castle derive from its enormous size. In all, it covers some 30 acres, and illustrates the might of medieval military architecture on a majestic scale. Seen mirrored in the waters of its great lakes, or rising evocatively through a morning mist, Caerphilly Castle presents a prospect only rarely surpassed in these islands. It is the more impressive as the work not of an English king, but of a major Marcher lord, Gilbert de Clare (d. 1295) – called 'the Red'.

Not surprisingly, the strategic importance of the site for such a major stronghold had first been recognized by the Romans. During its military conquest of south-east Wales, the Second Augustan Legion established a fort for some 500 auxiliary soldiers here about AD 75. Situated beside the road from Cardiff to Gelligaer, it was abandoned under more peaceful conditions some 50 years later. The fort occupied the tree-covered hill to the immediate north-west of the castle.

As the Norman conquerors swept into Glamorgan in the closing years of the eleventh century, however, this upland region was largely ignored. Robert fitz Hamon and his followers chose to concentrate their efforts on the fertile coastal plain, leaving the higher areas to the north largely to the Welsh. Indeed, Caerphilly Mountain effectively formed a geographical barrier between Welsh and Anglo-Norman for almost 200 years. All this was to change in the political climate of the 1260s.

Llywelyn ap Gruffudd had gradually been building up his power base in Wales, and by 1262 he had moved into Brecon. There is little doubt that the frontier of his ambitions lay still further south. Moreover, he seized the opportunities raised by the growing baronial opposition to the government of Henry III, and allied himself to the rebel leader, Simon de Montfort. Despite de Montfort's death at the battle of Evesham, Llywelyn was at the height of his power and the king was forced to recognize him as prince of Wales under the

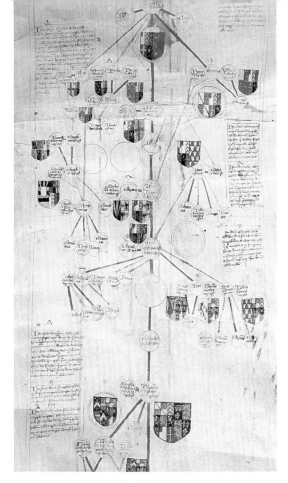

Part of a late medieval armorial roll of the patrons of Tewkesbury Abbey. It includes several lords of Caerphilly, with Gilbert de Clare at the top and the Despensers below.

Treaty of Montgomery in 1267. Meanwhile, Gilbert de Clare had succeeded to the vast earldom of Gloucester – including the lordship of Glamorgan. Earl Gilbert had led the royal forces at Evesham, and his fears for the safety of Glamorgan soon encouraged him to push forward on the offensive. In January 1267 he arrested Gruffudd ap Rhys, the Welsh ruler of upland Senghenydd and a would-be supporter of the prince. In the following year de Clare took the opportunity to begin the construction of Caerphilly itself. Confrontation with Llywelyn was inevitable, with raids and counter-raids to follow, and to begin with the outcome was by no means certain.

Construction of the formidable defences progressed with speed, but in October 1270 Llywelyn's forces burnt some at least of the fortifications. Earl Gilbert began work again the following summer and the prince prepared for outright war. It was only through the intervention of the king that this was avoided. A truce

Begun in 1268, Gilbert de Clare's Caerphilly is one of the largest castles in Britain.

was agreed, and a neutral force held the castle pending the result of negotiations. The earl was not prepared to accept this for long, and soon afterwards his constable of Cardiff Castle arrived at the gates and requested permission to check the armoury. Once inside, the gates were thrown open and 40 men at arms retook the castle for de Clare. He was never again to lose possession, and building probably progressed through until his death in 1295. The work continued under his son, another Gilbert de Clare, who died at the battle of Bannockburn in 1314.

Caerphilly is a superb example of land and water defences built to a 'concentric' plan, with successive lines of fortification set one inside the other. If an attacker stormed through one line he would find himself face to face with a second. This system of defence was to be refined in Edward I's great castles of north Wales, though none had the overall scale of Caerphilly. It is the vast lakes which give de Clare's masterpiece such a distinct character. They are comparable to the water defences at Simon de Montfort's castle at Kenilworth, where Gilbert himself had been present at the siege in 1266. He was clearly greatly impressed with their strength, and Kenilworth must have been at the forefront of his mind when planning here at Caerphilly. As a whole, the defensive principles of the site can only be understood, in their totality, from the air. A seemingly impregnable series of concentric lines of water and stone radiates, in a succession of larger and larger circles, from the central inner ward.

The first line of defence against any attack

The inner ward and main east gatehouse.

gatehouse here set a pattern later adopted by Edward I at Harlech and Beaumaris.

We should remember that by the later 1270s Caerphilly was not only exceptional in its architecture, but also in the circumstances that brought it into being. Gilbert the Red was no ordinary magnate. His vast Gloucester inheritance provided one of the largest fortunes in the kingdom and, as a Marcher lord, he had the freedom to build castles without royal licence. In these somewhat unique circumstances, rare in medieval Britain, the result was a showpiece of military might. Whatever else Edward I thought of de Clare on coming to the throne in 1272, he could only have viewed the building of Caerphilly with grave suspicion.

From the de Clares, the castle passed to the Despensers, and in 1316 it was attacked by some 10,000 men during the revolt of Llywelyn Bren. Although the town was burnt, the defences remained intact. Hugh le Despenser the younger earned the hatred of the Welsh by putting Llywelyn to death in 1318. Unpopular with all save King Edward II, Despenser was none the less responsible for rebuilding the great hall at Caerphilly. The work was of exceptional quality, with the king lending his carpenter William de Hurley, and his master mason Thomas de la Bataille. The beams of the roof came down to rest on finely-carved capitals with portrait busts, possibly representing Edward II, his queen – Isabella, and the young prince – the future Edward III. The tall windows and the doors were decorated with fashionable ball-flower ornament. Since its restoration, the hall is certainly one of the highlights of a visit to Caerphilly.

The ill-fated Edward II fled to the castle in 1326, and left much of his treasure with the constable and one of the Despenser brood. He went on to Margam and Neath, and was eventually captured and imprisoned, only to be barbarously murdered at Berkeley Castle in 1327. Hugh le Despenser was also captured and was hung from a gallows 50 feet high. After this time, Caerphilly gradually lost both its military and stately value and by the middle of the sixteenth century it had already fallen into decay. The castle probably saw some further action in the Civil War, but the details are not clear. The famous 'leaning tower', however, was probably not the result of Cromwell's

was the outer moat, spanned by two drawbridges, and backed by a huge curtain wall and gatehouse, through which the visitor enters the castle today. The walls here provided a fortified fighting platform, and stand on great earthen banks, which are in effect the dams holding back the northern and southern lakes. The lakes themselves made it impossible to use many of the normal methods of siege warfare. Stone-firing catapults could not be brought within range; siege ladders were virtually useless, and it was totally unfeasible to tunnel below the waters to undermine the walls.

The inner moat and the gatehouses of the outer ward formed the second line of defence. Finally, there stands the very heart of the castle, the inner ward. This is a large quadrangle enclosed by a curtain wall, with hefty round towers at each corner and yet more gatehouses on the east and west sides. These two gatehouses protect the points of entry and could be shut off and held separately should the remainder of the castle fall. That on the east side is by far the most impressive, with an entrance passage closed at either end by a portcullis and door. It was probably intended as the quarters of the constable, and includes a very fine hall and its own private chapel. In design, de Clare's great gunpowder. It is more likely due to ground subsidence following the drainage of the lakes. Whatever the case, this south Wales answer to Pisa adds an unexpected and fascinating touch of interest.

Restoration of the castle began under the third marquess of Bute, and was continued by the fourth marquess between 1928 and 1939. At present, a major programme of works is planned, and includes a scheme to open the inner rooms of the great east gatehouse to visitors. Meanwhile, an exhibition in the outer gate tells more of the story of Caerphilly, and the site also houses an exhibition on the castles of Wales.

Castell Coch

As though in some alpine setting, the sharp pointed turrets of Castell Coch peep above the beech woodland on a steep hillside overlooking a gorge in the Taff valley. It is a truly astonishing construction, a combination of Victorian Gothic fantasy and timeless fairytale, one of the most romantic – if equally unexpected – buildings in Wales. As it stands, the castle is the product of two fellow enthusiasts hopelessly in love with the Middle Ages. Beginning as patron and architect, Lord Bute and William Burges were eventually cast more in the role of friends. Even before they turned their attention to Castell Coch, Bute and Burges were already engaged in an extensive programme of work at Cardiff Castle, where they were busy creating a yet more fantastic vision of the medieval past.

The nineteenth century had, of course, been an age of industrial opportunity. In Wales, as in England, vast fortunes had been made from the profits of coal, copper, iron and slate. Encouraged by architects, many of the new 'barons' of industry still saw the castle as the ultimate expression of wealth and status, resulting in buildings such as Cyfarthfa in Merthyr Tydfil and Penrhyn near Bangor. Indeed, such an idealized picture of the feudal past is a thread which can be traced widely through Victorian literature, art and architecture. Bute and Burges were thoroughly caught up in this mood, and together they produced easily the most remark-

able expressions of its romantic escapism. Brimming with imagery, Castell Coch and Cardiff were reactions against the squalor to be seen in the smoke-ridden towns that everywhere accompanied the sources of industrial wealth.

John Patrick Crichton Stuart (1847–1900), third marquess of Bute, was reputed to be the richest man in the world, with a fortune yielded from the expanding coal port at Cardiff. He was a particularly intriguing man, a scholar with wide interests. He studied history, archaeology, heraldry, mysticism, and mastered 21 languages. On coming of age, Bute shocked the establishment by becoming a convert to Roman Catholicism. Whilst at Oxford he met William Burges, a kindred spirit who could rebuild the imagery and symbolism he dreamt of.

William Burges (1827–81), 'Billy' as he was always known to his friends, was a boyish and playful eccentric who not only studied the earlier Middle Ages, he did his best to live them. His sketch books were of vellum, he wore medieval clothes at home, and his house in London had a working portcullis. Burges was also a highly professional architect, the son of a successful civil engineer. Gradually he gained a profound knowledge of medieval architecture, from books, manuscripts and extensive travels throughout Europe. Burges was a Pre-Raphaelite in all but name, with Pugin as his greatest hero.

In 1865, Bute commissioned Burges to advise on the restoration of Cardiff Castle, where work began in 1868. The young architect was soon creating highly original compositions, based on his beloved medieval themes, inspired at times by the opium pipe! With the work in hand, in 1871 the marquess asked 'Billy' to consider what could be done to Castell Coch – the 'Red Castle' – a thirteenth-century ruin on the Bute estates. Burges produced the *Castell Coch Report*, a work of art in itself, in which he recommended restoration as 'a country residence for occasional occupation in the summer'. Building began in 1875 and continued through to Burges's death in 1881, with the interior decoration completed over the next 10 years from his drawings and models. The design was clearly influenced by continental sites, such as Chillon Castle on Lake Geneva, and by the work of the contemporary French architect Viollet-le-Duc at Carcassonne.

Castell Coch – William Burges's Victorian Gothic fantasy, begun in 1875.

As the visitor approaches Castell Coch through the beech wood, there is a smell of wild garlic. Lord Bute had vineyards here, and the best of the product went for use as communion wine. In the gatehouse there is attention to every detail, with a working drawbridge and portcullis, as well as 'murder holes' overhead. Inside the courtyard a staircase leads up to an encircling gallery and the decorative extravaganza of the interior.

The first of what Burges called the Castellan's rooms is the banqueting hall – perhaps the least exciting. The theme is a religious one, with St Lucius – the mythical bringer of Christianity to Roman Wales – sculpted by Thomas Nicholls standing over the chimney-piece. The roof is of timber, and the end walls decorated with scenes of obscure saints and martyrs. A doorway leads on to the drawing room, where the design, colours and themes show Burges and Bute at their most exuberant. It was originally planned as two rooms, one above the other, but the two were thrown into one with magnificent effect. The stone ribs of the glorious vault appear to fall from a sky full of stars and birds. On the walls, portraits of members of the Bute family hang from the decorative vegetation on painted ribbons. There are scenes from Aesop's Fables –

the Hare and the Tortoise, the Fox and the Crow, all complete with Burges touches. A frog holds a bottle of medicine for the frog in his throat, and a monkey has Victorian side whiskers. Even the door surrounds have moulded caterpillars and snails. Finally, above the chimney-piece are the carved figures of the 'Three Fates', resting above the 'Three Ages of Man':

Detail from Aesop's Fables in the drawing room.

The drawing room ceiling at Castell Coch, completed in 1887. Here, Burges explained in his Report, 'I have ventured to indulge in a little more ornament'.

Lady Bute's bedroom (1879–91), where the decoration is pure Burges.

Clotho spins the thread of life, Lachesis measures its length, and Atrepos cuts it at death.

In contrast to this opulence, up the spiral staircase Lord Bute's bedroom is somewhat restrained. The bed looks particularly uncomfortable, and there is a rather spartan looking hip bath. Moving on to the top of the tower the visitor arrives at Lady Bute's bedroom, altogether the most imaginative and fanciful apartment, with French Gothic and even Moorish influences. In the panels of the domed ceiling, monkeys and squirrels cavort among bunches of grapes and foliage. The brambles and thorns appear to represent the Sleeping Beauty motif. Above the chimney-piece the winged figure of Psyche – a lover of Cupid – probably represents the soul. At the centre is a splendid bed, scarlet and gold with crystal-ball bedknobs. The hand basin with its turrets for hot and cold water tanks adds one further touch of colour.

Back outside, the gallery leads to a large and functional kitchen in the tower which bears its name. In the final tower there is a well, and a long narrow flight of steps leads down to a gloomy dungeon. Burges's designs for this tower included a chapel projecting from the roof, and although this was built it had been removed before 1898. Indeed, 20 stained glass windows were made for the chapel, and eight of these have recently been acquired for display at Castell Coch. A further ten can be seen at Cardiff Castle.

An exhibition at the site tells more of Lord Bute, of William Burges, and of the two timeless buildings they created. Surprisingly, Castell Coch was never greatly used by the Bute family, but it remains a wonderful tribute to Burges's genius, the man of whom Lady Bute said: 'ugly Burges who designs lovely things. Isn't he a duck'.

Coity Castle

In 1833 the topographical writer Samuel Lewis described Coity as 'extensive and magnificent even in its ruins', and more than 150 years later these words still ring true. It is a particularly fine castle, all too little appreciated and greatly overshadowed by its more celebrated neighbours in the southern Marches. Serving as the *caput* – the administrative and military centre – of the important lordship of Coity, it had a long and complex structural development spanning much of the Middle Ages.

The initial stronghold was almost certainly a 'ringwork' and bailey, and was raised by Payn de Turberville – 'the Demon' – soon after 1100. Along with Robert fitz Hamon's Newcastle and the de Londres castle at Ogmore, Coity marked the western limits of the early Norman advance into Glamorgan. The circular earthen bank of Payn's 'ringwork' would have been crowned by a timber palisade, and the exterior was further protected by a surrounding ditch. The bailey probably lay in the area of the later outer ward. Through much of the twelfth century, as far as we can tell, the de Turbervilles were content with these timber defences and continued to occupy wooden domestic buildings.

Then, in the 1180s, at the same time as major building was in progress at nearby Newcastle, Gilbert de Turberville replaced the timber palisade with a hefty stone curtain wall and a powerful square keep. The keep was heavily altered in later centuries, but survives on the north side of the middle gatehouse. Gilbert's curtain wall was typical of the period, laid out in a series of short straight lengths, and can still be seen surrounding much of the inner ward.

Coity continued to pass to various de Turberville lords throughout the thirteenth century, but none of them appears to have left any significant stone building. Much of what we now see was added in the fourteenth century, when the castle was extensively rebuilt and remodelled as a residence of some comfort. The works, begun soon after 1300, reflect not only the changing times, but also the wealth and influence of the later Turbervilles. The defences of the inner ward were improved by the construction of the middle gatehouse, while the adjacent keep was rebuilt internally with stone-vaulted floors. An annexe was added to the north side of the keep, improving the provision of domestic accommodation. Meanwhile, a well-appointed hall block and service rooms were built along the south side of the ward. The hall itself stood above an elaborate vaulted basement, and the entire block was served by a round latrine tower raised against the outer face

Coity – one of the finest castles of the southern March.

of the curtain. It was in this phase, too, that the outer ward was first surrounded by a stone wall, with three square projecting towers, and a gate on the west side.

Part of this rebuilding probably continued under Sir Lawrence Berkerolles who inherited Coity from the Turbervilles in 1384. Under Sir Lawrence the defences were put to serious test, when the castle was closely besieged by the rebel forces of Owain Glyndŵr in 1404–05. Indeed, the Commons in Parliament petitioned Henry IV to send a relief force. This assembled under Prince Henry at Hereford in November 1404, and may have achieved its objective. But Coity was again in danger by September 1405, and this time the king himself led a second expedition. This failed miserably, its baggage train plundered and the confusion made complete by autumn storms and flood. We can be left in no doubt as to the ferocity of the Welsh assault. A large breach in the northern inner curtain wall had to be completely rebuilt, and a

section of the outer ward wall also required extensive repairs. About the same time, a well defended gatehouse was added to the north-east corner of the inner ward, providing a more prestigious entry facing the church.

Sir Lawrence Berkerolles died in 1411, and the castle passed to the Gamage family. They continued to make further additions to Coity through the fifteenth century, including the first-floor chapel next to the earlier hall. A large barn was built in the outer ward, and the southern tower there was converted to a gate-house.

Finally, in the Tudor period, the castle was again altered and modified with considerable improvements to the domestic arrangements. A new floor was added to the keep and also to its northern annexe, and up-to-date windows and fireplaces were inserted in most areas. In 1584, however, Coity passed to Robert Sydney, earl of Leicester, who showed little interest in the site and it gradually fell into decline.

Ewenny Priory

There was a strong colonist flavour to the early Norman ecclesiastical settlement of Wales. Monasteries of the Benedictine order in particular were rarely sited out of the shadow of the new castles. 'Strengthen the locks of your doors and surround your house with a good ditch and an impregnable wall', wrote Gilbert Foliot, later bishop of Hereford, to the prior of one of these houses in the 1140s. Ewenny's rural location, divorced from borough and castle, was far and away an exception to this pattern, but there is clearly a distinct echo of Foliot's advice in the fortress-like architecture of the priory church, and in the somewhat remarkable curtain wall which eventually surrounded it.

The church of St Michael at Ewenny was part of a package of gifts given by the lord of Ogmore, William de Londres, to the Benedictine abbey of St Peter's, Gloucester – now Gloucester Cathedral. In 1141, his son Maurice, who 'excelled all other Barons of Wales in valiantness and liberality', converted the church to a full Benedictine priory of 12 monks with their prior. It was not only an act of piety on the part of Maurice, but also an indication that he had arrived socially and territorially in the higher ranks of Norman aristocracy in the southern March. His gifts to the priory were enriched by neighbouring families, including the Turbervilles of Coity, but it was Maurice who was undoubtedly regarded as founder. His unusual tomb slab, carved about 1200, can be seen in the south transept, inscribed 'Here lies Maurice de Londres, the founder. God reward him for his labour. Amen'. Ewenny was never a particularly wealthy house, though conventual life continued through to its suppression in 1539 when there were just two monks present.

The nave may date from the early twelfth century, and still serves as the parish church. The massive circular pillars and north aisle belong to a remodelling at the end of the century. The cavernous eastern sections of the church – the monastic choir and chancel – display some of the finest Norman architecture in Glamorgan, if not in Wales. The walls were raised in two stages, and the break is marked by the heavy band of chevron, or zigzag, decoration. The lower sections were built soon after the foundation of the priory, but the upper parts of the walls, the eastern vault and the tower were all added about 1200. The original stone altar table can still be seen below the east windows. A doorway leads out to the ruins of the south transept chapels, and it was on this

One of the gates through the precinct wall at Ewenny.

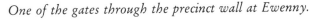

The stone tomb slab of Ewenny's founder: 'Here lies Maurice de Londres, the founder. God reward him for his labour. Amen'.

side of the church – now a private house and gardens – where the monastic cloister and domestic buildings lay. The north transept has been in ruins since 1800, but parts of the walls still survive. Strange sculptured beasts form the finials of an arch, giving insights into the mythical and fantastic beliefs which inspired the medieval stone mason's craft.

Often of more surprise to visitors are the towers and gatehouses of the fortified perimeter wall, giving the priory more the appearance of one of Gilbert Foliot's strongholds than a house of religion. We cannot be certain why these walls were built, and there is some dispute as to their true defensive capabilities – they may have been intended merely for show. The north and south gates do, none the less, go back to the late twelfth century, and were remodelled around 1300. In places the enclosure is finished with wall-walks and battlements.

Loughor Castle

To the Romans this place was *Leucarum* – named after the river nearby. Here, during the conquest of south Wales by the Second Augustan Legion, an auxiliary fort was established about 75 AD. Just over 1,000 years later, the Normans – under Henry de Beaumont, earl of Warwick – swept into the Welsh commote of *Gŵyr*, and were quick to realize the strategic importance of the site. Loughor controlled the western approaches to de Beaumont's new lordship of Gower. By 1116, an oval enclosure, or 'ringwork' castle of earth and timber had been thrown up on the crest of a natural spur, directly over a corner turret of the Roman fort.

Entrusted to Earl Henry's steward, Henry de Villers, the castle afforded protection to a small borough. In 1151, however, the Welsh laid siege and burnt the castle and town. Norman authority was restored, and Loughor passed with the lordship into the hands of John de Braose. Fragments of the curtain wall, probably built by de Braose, can be seen just beneath the turf. The single surviving tower appears to date to a later thirteenth-century strengthening of the castle. It reveals evidence of a comfortable residence – windows, fireplaces and latrines – in both standing and fallen masonry.

Laughor Castle, raised over a Roman fort.

Margam Stones Museum

Situated just to the north of the church and monastic ruins of the once large Cistercian abbey, the Margam lapidary museum houses a very fine collection of inscribed and sculptured stones found in the surrounding neighbourhood. They have been brought together in a charming little building which was once the village school. Indeed, as one of the earliest church schools in Wales, this is of particular interest in its own right. There are around 25 stones in the museum, ranging in date from the sixth century to a few post-Reformation grave slabs of the late 1500s. The jewels of the collection are with little doubt the 15 or so early Christian memorials, slabs and crosses.

One of the earliest pieces originally served as a Roman milestone, and was recut in the sixth century to mark the resting place of 'Cantusus'. There are two other sixth-century grave-markers, one of which is inscribed 'Pumpeius Carantorius', and the other 'Of Bodvocus – he lies here, the son of Catotigirnus and great-grandson of Eternalis Vedomavus'. These stones provide some of the very earliest evidence for Christianity in post-Roman Wales. The most impressive group, however, comprises the once free-standing large cross slabs, dating from between the late ninth and early eleventh centuries. We cannot be certain of their purpose, though some probably commemorated people or events, and others could have been territorial markers or even preaching points. One example, the so-called 'Ilquici' stone, stands over six feet high and was first noted in 1698, in use as a footbridge!

Five of these great crosses come from Margam itself, and although only two were certainly there in great antiquity, they have long been taken to indicate the presence of a pre-Norman religious foundation on the site of the later Cistercian abbey. They include the 'Grunte' slab, with its inscription 'In the name of God Most High. The cross of Christ [which] Grunte prepared for the soul of Anest'. Pride of place goes to the celebrated tenth-century 'Conbelin' cross, a rich votive gift which may well have stood in the enclosure of the pre-Conquest church. It has a large disc head, carved with plait and knot patterns, with the figures of St John and the Blessed Virgin below the cross. The slab stands on a heavy base which is also intricately carved.

Among the later stones, there are two thirteenth-century grave slabs of abbots of Margam. Another is inscribed, 'Faithful and true here lies concealed Robert, Abbot of Rievaulx, to whom God be merciful, Amen'. Rievaulx was, of course, situated many miles away in north Yorkshire, and it is just possible that Abbot Robert died here whilst on a visitation. There is also a sadly weathered fourteenth-century effigy of a knight, perhaps a patron buried at the abbey.

The collection of inscribed and sculptured stones in the lapidary museum at Margam.

Neath Abbey

Today, it is perhaps a little difficult to appreciate the once glorious features of the Cistercian abbey at Neath. Shortly before its dissolution in 1539, it was described by John Leland as 'the fairest abbey in all Wales'. Sadly it was forced to bear the scars of the Industrial Revolution, and a nineteenth-century gentleman traveller was to lament: 'Neglected Neath, once the ornament of a lovely vale, looms up through its dense veil of smoke, like the skeleton of a stranded ship crumbling piecemeal to decay under the influence of almost perpetual rain'. Despite such sufferance, the site is one of the most intriguing historic monuments in the principality, with the remains of not just one, but two major buildings: a medieval abbey and a substantial Tudor mansion.

Neath Abbey was founded on 25 October 1130 by Richard de Granville as a daughter house of Savigny near Avranches in Normandy. The abbot and 12 monks were given almost 8,000 acres of 'waste' between the Neath and Tawe rivers, and gradually other powerful landowners added further property to the initial grant. In 1147, in common with all other Savigniac monasteries, it was absorbed into the Cistercian order. Initially, however, the monks appear to have found some difficulty in running their estates efficiently. The abbey's lands were widely scattered, and included holdings across the channel in Devon and Somerset. Management and expansion of its Glamorgan property led to a bitter dispute with the neighbouring abbey at Margam, flaring into contested cases on at least five occasions. Searching for a way to improve the situation, serious thought was given to transferring the house to the site of its grange at Exford in Somerset. The plan was only finally scotched by the foundation of nearby Cleeve Abbey in 1198.

The situation improved as the monks began to consolidate their possessions. Neath's farms or granges, such as Monknash in the Vale of Glamorgan (still with impressive remains), gradually became profitable estate centres. By 1235 we know of an abbey ship, the *Hulc*, which was trading with English ports, and towards the end of the century the monks owned some 220 cattle and almost 5,000 sheep.

The rib-vaulted dormitory undercroft at the Cistercian abbey of Neath.

Indeed, with the steady economic expansion the monastic community itself soon began to outgrow the initial twelfth-century buildings. Major programmes of reconstruction spanned the thirteenth and fourteenth centuries.

The very complete remains of the west range, dating from 1170–1220, now form the earliest surviving part of the abbey. This block was originally occupied by the lay brothers, with their common room and dining hall on the ground floor, and their dormitory above. In the early Middle Ages the lay brothers did much of the manual work on the outlying estates. The buildings on the eastern and southern sides of the cloister were completely rebuilt in the mid thirteenth century. The monks' dining hall ran off to the south, and there are traces of the recesses where they washed before going into meals. Their dormitory occupied the entire upper floor of the east range, and was linked by a bridge to a large adjacent latrine block. The superb rib-vaulted dormitory undercroft is undoubtedly the finest part of the abbey structure to remain intact.

North of the cloister stand the ruins of the abbey church, rebuilt on a grand scale between 1280 and 1330. The twelfth-century building had been a relatively small Norman structure,

Following the Dissolution of the Monasteries, Neath Abbey was transformed into a country house.

adhering to the Cistercian ideals of plainness and austerity. But in the mood of the late thirteenth century, with peace and prosperity, the monks began work on an ambitious and decorative cruciform church, very similar in scale to that begun at Tintern just a few years earlier. It seems Edward I approved of the scheme, and a consecration ceremony may have been conducted in his presence in 1284, when he presented the abbot with a beautiful cope or canopy. Enough of this new church survives for us to appreciate the quality of the architecture. The columns of the nave, choir and presbytery were richly clustered, and the floors were decorated with attractive areas of tile paving. Some of the finest of these tiles can now be seen at the National Museum of Wales. The high altar stood on a stone plinth near the east end, and in the south transept the night stair down from the monks' dormitory is well preserved.

The conventual life at Neath reached new heights under its last abbot, Leyshon Thomas. He was a powerful figure in local politics, and raised the scholastic reputation of the house, winning great praise from the poet Lewis Morgannwg. Already, by his time, the southern end of the dormitory range had been developed for the abbot's personal use. When Neath was finally dissolved in 1539 there was clearly a

comfortable residence here with an attractive and sunny southern aspect.

In 1542 the abbey was purchased by Sir Richard Williams who was to give the site a new lease of life. It was almost certainly Williams or his son who began to raise an impressive Tudor mansion in the south-east corner of the cloister. Skilfully raised over the dormitory undercroft and the monks' latrine, it also incorporated the later abbot's house. By 1600 the house had passed to Sir John Herbert, who probably continued the building programme. Built with materials from the abbey, it eventually included a grand hall and long gallery, and is easily recognized today by the large rectangular windows of dressed stone. Occupied throughout the seventeenth century, the house may have been totally abandoned in the early 1700s.

Copper smelting was introduced to the area about this time, and spread to the very precinct of the once proud abbey. Furnaces were set up in the west range, and workers were accommodated in lodgings hacked out of the derelict mansion. The monastic kitchen was to become a casting workshop, and the entire site smothered in industrial waste. Encircled by canal and railway, it was not until the early part of this century that the abbey was gradually cleared of debris, in places up to 17 feet deep.

Newcastle, Bridgend

Having passed through the rather unpromising streets of modern Bridgend, Newcastle Hill comes as a pleasant surprise. Crowning the scarp which overlooks the Ogmore river is Newcastle itself, an early Norman castle which guarded a ford where the later medieval market town of Bridgend would develop. The site is especially notable for its fine twelfth-century curtain wall and superb gateway, recently attributed to royal intervention and the hand of King Henry II.

The earliest stronghold on the site was established by Robert fitz Hamon in about 1100, and for a short while during the Norman conquest of Glamorgan it was the only castle to the west of the Ogmore. At the time, it was probably an earth and timber 'ringwork' enclosure, but there are several hints of early stone buildings. A round-cornered structure in the south-east corner of the later curtain wall could well be a twelfth-century hall. Moreover, about 1835, the antiquarian scholar G. T. Clark recorded a substantial building at the centre of the ward which he noted as 'once a keep' – perhaps an early detached stone keep at the centre of the essentially timber defences.

Newcastle remained in the hands of the chief lords of Glamorgan until the death of William, earl of Gloucester in 1183. In that year the Welsh rose in serious revolt under the lord of nearby Afan. So serious was the blow, that King Henry II chose to retain Glamorgan in his possession. Between then and his death, in 1189, he seems to have been responsible for the complete reconstruction of the Newcastle defences in stone. The lavish quality of the masonry is otherwise unknown at this period in the area. In particular, the gateway with its twin columns, decorated capitals and panel and pellet ornament, is quite exceptional and argues strongly for royal involvement. The curtain wall is laid out in a series of short straight lengths, typical of the twelfth century. There is a strong external battered plinth, and two powerful towers straddle the wall on the southern and western sides.

In 1217 the site passed to Gilbert de Turberville, lord of Coity. The major castle-building of the de Turbervilles, and that of their successors, focused upon Coity itself. Little further building appears to have been undertaken at Newcastle, though in the sixteenth century the southern tower, at least, was remodelled by John Gamage, lord at the time. There is clear evidence of this work in the typically Elizabethan windows on the first and second floors.

The late twelfth-century gateway and curtain wall at Newcastle, Bridgend.

Ogmore Castle continues to overlook a fording place across the Ewenny river.

Ogmore Castle

As the Norman *conquistadores* swept into the lowland plain of Glamorgan during the closing years of the eleventh century, Robert fitz Hamon and his followers may have been forced to halt for a while at the Ogmore river. The higher inland fords were soon fortified and protected with strongholds at Coity and Newcastle. Downstream, near the confluence with the smaller River Ewenny, a castle was set up to guard an important lower bridgehead. The ruins of Ogmore Castle continue to overlook this fording place across the Ewenny, now marked by a line of picturesque stepping stones.

It was William de Londres – a household knight in the service of fitz Hamon – who threw up the earliest earth and timber castle at Ogmore. Although first mentioned in 1116, it was perhaps raised soon after 1100. Despite the later masonry additions, visitors should have little difficulty in identifying the form of the initial 'ringwork' and bailey defences. At the time, the prominent earthen banks were no doubt surmounted by stout wooden palisades, with a cluster of timber buildings huddled inside. However, as at most important Norman castles in the area, Ogmore soon acquired a hefty stone keep. This could have been built by William de Londres himself, though he was dead by 1126. If not, it was the work of his son, Maurice – the founder of nearby Ewenny Priory. It is the finest twelfth-century keep to survive in Glamorgan, standing up to 40 feet

high. The ground floor served as a basement, and was originally reached from a trap door in the floor above. The first floor itself must have been entered via an external stair. There were two rooms here, providing comfortable accommodation for the lord. Two round-headed windows survive, and there is evidence of a particularly fine fireplace with a projecting hood supported on round columns. A stairway in the thickness of the wall led up to a second floor, added slightly later.

The building identified as the 'cellar' was also built in the twelfth century, and may have had a timber superstructure. Here, during clearance work in 1929, a pre-Norman cross slab was discovered quite by chance. This is now at the National Museum of Wales and a cast stands at Ogmore. The inscription reads: 'Be it [known to all men] that Arthmail gave (this) estate to God and Glywys and Nertat and his daughter'. It provides evidence of a grant of land to a local church long before the construction of the castle. Just behind the 'cellar', a further exciting discovery has been made in a recent detailed study of the castle. Two reused dressed stones have been identified in a later wall. They are dated to about 1180, and clearly come from a now lost doorway, perhaps similar to the elaborate gate which survives at Newcastle.

In the early thirteenth century, while still in the hands of the de Londres family, a stone curtain wall was erected on the line of the timber defences. As at Coity and Newcastle, the wall is laid out in a series of straight lengths, but with no mural towers. A simple gateway, secured by double doors, was built next to the keep. A bridge crossed the moat in front of this gate, and was presumably raised into a now vanished superstructure on the inner abutment. Where the curtain joined the other corner of the keep, a latrine turret was built projecting out over the moat and serving each of the upper chambers. Two smaller latrine turrets were built into the wall on the eastern side of the ward. This period also saw the addition of a large new hall block along the north side of the curtain, and a smaller suite of accommodation in the southern part of the ward. Only the basement of the hall block survives, though the hall itself was probably on the upper floor, and may have been reached by an external staircase.

By the later thirteenth century Ogmore had passed by marriage to the de Chaworth family whose efforts were concentrated on an extensive rebuilding of Kidwelly Castle. In 1298 the de Chaworth heiress married Henry of Lancaster, carrying both Ogmore and Kidwelly to her husband. This established a connection with the duchy of Lancaster which endures to the present day. In the later Middle Ages Ogmore Castle declined to the status of a purely administrative and manorial centre for its large and important lordship. In the outer ward for example, although the defences were never replaced in stone, there are the remains of a substantial fourteenth-century building which probably housed the manorial court of the dukes of Lancaster. Documentary evidence suggests that this was largely rebuilt in 1454–55, and was still in good repair as late as 1631.

Oxwich Castle

Oxwich 'Castle' is in fact a sumptuous courtyard-house built by the powerful Mansel family during the sixteenth century. This once very handsome building stands proudly on a headland above Oxwich Bay, in one of the loveliest locations on the Gower peninsula. The Mansels themselves can be traced in Gower as early as 1310, and by the fifteenth century a series of shrewd and judicious marriages had brought them an enviable group of manorial estates. Even so, they remained a relatively obscure brood, with their influence largely restricted to the western part of the peninsula. All this was to change under the brilliant Rice (Rhys) Mansel (1487–1559) who began building Oxwich Castle as it survives today.

Rice Mansel was undoubtedly one of the

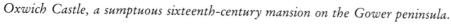

Oxwich Castle, a sumptuous sixteenth-century mansion on the Gower peninsula.

more enterprising men of his day; an able soldier, sailor and administrator, he served Henry VIII in Ireland and elsewhere. Between 1540 and 1557 he purchased the bulk of the former estates of Margam Abbey, an investment which in due course placed the Mansel family in the front rank of county gentry. Sir Rice's fortunes grew still further under Queen Mary, culminating with his appointments as chamberlain and chancellor of south Wales. But by this time he had made Margam his chief residence and Oxwich had passed to his son, Edward (d. 1595). Unfortunately, Sir Edward inherited little of his father's talent. Even so, we cannot deny his ambitions for Oxwich.

As completed, the house was arranged around an enclosed courtyard of mock military design. It was a building appropriate to the Mansel dignity, representing the new and powerful Tudor gentry class whose lifestyle resembled that of earlier feudal lords. The courtyard was approached through an imposing gateway bearing Sir Rice's arms. Within, the two adjacent ranges appear to have been designed independently of each other, and each could have accommodated its own household.

The smaller two-storey block was occupied until recent years as a farmhouse. Here, the architectural detail suggests that it was the work of Sir Rice, about 1520–38. It is worth remembering that at this time he also had a life interest, through marriage, in the delightful house at

The arms of Sir Rice Mansel at Oxwich.

The celebrated Oxwich brooch.

Beaupre near Cowbridge. Later still he was to put considerable investment into Margam. In this context, his work at Oxwich is comparatively modest and reflects an early phase in the career of the great man. He may already have been thinking of his descendants, and making the necessary provision. The circular dovecot at the northern end of the site could also have been raised in Sir Rice's time.

In contrast, the larger east range is an independent great house of remarkable and complex design. Conceived as a whole by Sir Edward Mansel, about 1559–80, its construction must have stretched all available funds, and may well have led to his financial difficulties in the 1560s. Steps led up from a projecting porch to a large first-floor hall, and the windows of an elegant long gallery can be seen above. Numerous chambers in the three tower-like projections at the back would have provided lavish suites of family accommodation, as well as housing a large body of retainers.

Oxwich Castle is also famed as the site where a superb medieval gold ring-brooch was found in 1968. Its presence here naturally implies that it was a Mansel family heirloom. It has, however, been suggested that it was originally part of Edward II's treasure, some of which was dispersed from Swansea Castle in the years after 1326. The brooch can now be seen at the National Museum of Wales.

A long programme of conservation works is currently nearing completion at Oxwich. It can, none the less, be viewed from the surrounding area, and a footpath to the coastal headland passes the western side of the site.

Parc le Breos Burial Chamber

The lane which leads to Parc le Breos is wooded and dark. It suddenly opens into a peaceful glade – a narrow dry valley floor, with a distinctly eerie atmosphere, somehow echoing the rituals of the ancient past. The tomb was first partially explored by Sir John Lubbock in 1869, the man whose book *Prehistoric Times* (1865) introduced the word Neolithic – New Stone Age – to the English language. Lubbock, however, thought the cairn was virtually circular, and it was not until 1937 that the late Professor Glyn Daniel demonstrated its elongated form. Daniel linked it to similar tombs he had been studying, and he baptized them 'Severn-Cotswold', after the area in which they chiefly occur. Parc le Breos was excavated more extensively in 1960–61, at which time it was consolidated and laid out for display.

The tomb was indeed raised in the Neolithic period – the age of the 'first farmers' – probably around 4000–3500 BC. It was undoubtedly of great symbolic meaning to its builders, if only in terms of the man-hours involved in construction. Characteristic of the 'Severn-Cotswold' group, it consists of a wedge-shaped cairn about 70 feet long, surrounded by a double revetment wall. At the wider end, two rounded 'horns' flank a recessed funnel or forecourt. This leads to a central passage with two 'transeptal' chambers at either side. A similar arrangement of chambers can be seen, for example, at Notgrove in Gloucestershire, or at West Kennet, Wiltshire. At Parc le Breos the side chambers were separated from the passage by low sill slabs, but all four have lost their capstones.

The excavations recovered fragments of human bone representing some 25 to 40 individuals. Here, as elsewhere, archaeologists now believe that before final entombment, bodies may have been exposed to the elements while the flesh decomposed – 'excarnation' as it is called. It is also likely that during the several hundred years the tomb was in use, skeletons were ritually moved about, or dismembered, so as to accommodate further burials.

The Neolithic burial chamber at Parc le Breos on the Gower peninsula.

The chambered tomb at St Lythans.

St Lythans Burial Chamber

Just a mile from the larger tomb at Tinkinswood, St Lythans is also known as Gwal y Filiast – 'Kennel of the Greyhound Bitch' – a folk name possibly allusive to a variant of the Arthurian legend of Kilhwch and Olwen. Today, almost all of the surrounding cairn has disappeared, but this means that the single rectangular chamber stands impressive and conspicuous. In fact, to be precise, the chamber is trapezoid in plan, and three surviving upright slabs support a single great capstone, all of which are locally derived Triassic mudstones. The tomb again belongs to the 'Severn-Cotswold' family, and its overall shape must have been similar to that of Tinkinswood. Slight traces of the much denuded cairn can be seen extending for about 80 to 90 feet to the west of the chamber.

Swansea Castle

Henry de Beaumont, earl of Warwick, enjoyed a position of great trust and favour under King Henry I. About 1106, the king granted him permission to conquer the Welsh commote of *Gŵyr*, and it was at Swansea that he chose to raise his chief castle, the *caput* (capital) of the new lordship of Gower. This initial stronghold – an earth and timber motte and bailey – stood a little to the north of the surviving remains. With something of a chequered history throughout the twelfth century, Swansea was attacked by the Welsh in 1116, and was again besieged in 1192. During the anarchy which prevailed in the reign of King Stephen (1135–54), Henry of Newburgh struck silver pennies here to pay his soldiers. Then, in the early thirteenth century the site was refortified in stone, probably under the de Braose lords of Gower. This was to become known as the 'old castle', since it was eventually replaced by the handsome block which survives today.

The 'new castle' was originally part of a much larger complex. However, about 1300, under William de Braose II or his son, these apartments appear to have developed into a self-contained castle. The remains include a spacious

The 'new castle' at Swansea.

The chambered tomb at Tinkinswood, with its great capstone weighing over 40 tons.

hall, solar and service rooms on the first floor, with a series of vaulted basements below. The crowning glory of the block is the magnificent arcaded parapet. This is clearly an addition, and undoubtedly a work in some way inspired by Henry de Gower, bishop of St Davids (1328–47). It is very similar to those parapets raised on his unfortified palaces at Lamphey and at St Davids itself.

Alas, in the later Middle Ages, decay gradually set in. A survey of Gower taken in 1650 referred to 'an Ancient decayed Buildinge called the new Castle' and 'a piece of ruinous buildinge called the old Castle'. By 1686 a glassworks had been established within the ruins. In the late eighteenth century the surviving northern block was remodelled as a debtors' prison, the conditions of which became a Victorian scandal until it was closed in 1858.

Tinkinswood Burial Chamber

Situated in pleasant countryside, close to Dyffryn Gardens, a path winds its way across several fields to this striking Neolithic burial chamber, probably raised around 4000–3500 BC. First impressions are dominated by the huge capstone, weighing over 40 tons, and one of the largest in Britain. It has been estimated that to move the stone from the nearby 'quarry', and to erect it on the site, would have involved the labour of at least 200 people. In addition, the stone cairn is about 130 feet long, and its construction would have involved further labours.

The tomb was carefully excavated in 1914 when the remains of at least 50 individuals – men, women and children – were found in the rectangular chamber at the eastern end of the cairn. Like Parc le Breos and nearby St Lythans, Tinkinswood belongs to the family of tombs archaeologists call 'Severn-Cotswold'. In particular, the 'horns' and forecourt are quite distinct, though the herringbone walling represents modern reconstruction. Recent research has shown that the neat revetment walls seen in such tombs were rarely left exposed, but were for the most part masked by heaped stone slabs. Here at Tinkinswood, the excavations also recovered fragments of 'Beaker'-style pottery, which suggests that the monument was reopened or reused in the very late Neolithic or the earlier Bronze Age. Indeed, finds of

'Beaker' material are not uncommon in megalithic tombs, and perhaps indicate the lingering influence of a tradition which had lasted for some 2,000 years.

Weobley Castle

Weobley sits precipitously above the stark northern shore of the Gower peninsula, just where the scarp gives way to Llanrhidian marsh and the sandy Loughor estuary. It is an attractive site, best regarded as a later-medieval fortified manor house, and is described as just this in a document of 1410: *manerium batellatum vocatum Webley*. The buildings reveal an emphasis upon gracious living and domestic comfort, though this is combined with a degree of much needed security.

The origins of the small lordship of Weobley are obscure, though it was probably among the earliest Norman holdings in Gower. Nor can we be absolutely sure of the builder of the initial castle on this site. Nevertheless, it seems that by the early fourteenth century it was held by a branch of the widespread de la Bere family. Firm evidence comes from a document of 1397, which records that Sir John de la Bere had died

possessed of the castle. In fact his kin had long held lands in the area. Around 1300, David de la Bere was steward to William de Braose, lord of Gower, and is known to have acquired property just to the east of the site. Moreover, in 1318, Adam de la Bere witnessed a deed signed at Weobley itself, which confirms the castle's existence by this time. Another John de la Bere held Weobley in 1432, but he may have been the last of that name associated with it.

The substantial remains of the castle buildings are grouped around a small courtyard, with few indications of serious fortification. The chief exception is the south-west tower, which could date to the mid thirteenth century and perhaps served as a defensible 'tower house'. The remaining apartments were put up between the late thirteenth and early fourteenth centuries, with all the main rooms at first-floor level. On the north side is the hall, situated above the castle kitchens. From a modern wooden gallery the visitor will notice the great fireplace at the far end, and opposite this the window which lit the high table. Again it is a modern staircase which leads up to the solar – the lord's private chamber – set over a deep cellar. With its spacious window seats, this was clearly a comfortable room, and now houses a comprehensive and colourful exhibition covering the castle, together with details of various other

Weobley Castle, perched above the northern shore of the Gower peninsula.

The hall range at Weobley, with the porch added by Sir Rhys ap Thomas.

ancient and historic sites in the Gower area. On the other side of the courtyard, the east range may have provided accommodation for guests or other members of the family. There are, however, clear indications that the southern end of this range was never completed. It may well be that the initial design for the buildings as a whole was not matched by the size of the de la Bere purse.

Weobley was one of the many castles which suffered substantial damage during the Owain Glyndŵr uprising in the early 1400s, but by the end of the century it had passed to Sir Rhys ap Thomas – the most powerful Welshman of his day. Henry VII had granted him estates and offices in south Wales as a reward for his support at the battle of Bosworth in 1485. Weobley was a relatively minor item among these estates, but even here Sir Rhys initiated the construction of a stately entrance porch on the south side of the hall, befitting his position as a major early Tudor magnate. In 1560 the lordship was sold to Sir William Herbert, earl of Pembroke, but by this time the medieval role of the castle as a home for its lord was long over. It

was gradually leased out and served as a farmhouse. A 1666 survey shows that the tenants occupied farm buildings by the 'decayed castle'.

Sir Rhys ap Thomas (d. 1525), from his tomb in St Peter's Church, Carmarthen.

GWENT
The Southern Border

Today, the beautiful wooded slopes of the lower Wye valley mark the border between Wales and England, but for centuries this south-eastern corner of the principality has been unsure as to its true allegiance. Under the influence of Rome, for example, with the vast legionary fortress situated at Caerleon (*Isca*), lowland Gwent became fully absorbed into the heavily Romanized economy of southern England. With the exception of the Vale of Glamorgan, nowhere else in Wales has produced quite such a pattern of Roman occupation; nowhere else were the native peoples quite so ready to embrace the benefits of the *pax Romana*. As the centuries progressed, legionary veterans retired to civilian settlements in the shadow of the Caerleon fortress, or to farms in the surrounding countryside. Moreover, at Caerwent (*Venta Silurum*) there emerged a substantial town with many of the trappings of the Mediterranean world, including large public buildings, temples, and courtyard houses complete with mosaics and underfloor heating.

In the years before the Norman Conquest, Gwent stood rather apart from the rest of Wales politically, and in 1065 the Saxon Earl Harold Godwinson annexed much of the area to the earldom of Hereford. He held it under his direct lordship, and ordered a fine hunting lodge to be built at Portskewett. Thus, even before the arrival of the ruthless and land-hungry Norman barons, the rich agricultural lands of the southern border had become a natural target for invaders and colonists. William fitz Osbern, a trusted confidant of the Conqueror himself, was another who was quick to appreciate the opportunities offered in this area. From his castles at Chepstow and Monmouth, he swiftly laid the foundations for the complete conquest and subjugation of south-east Wales. It was fitz Osbern, too, who probably established the earliest strongholds at Grosmont, Skenfrith and White Castle. By the 1080s, Norman lordship was more firmly established here than virtually anywhere else in Wales, a position that was to go largely unchallenged throughout the Middle Ages.

During the medieval period, the area which is now Gwent was divided into several chief Marcher lordships. It was in the reign of Henry VIII that these were merged into the new shire of Monmouth under the Act of Union (1536–43), and since 1974 this historic county has become Gwent.

In the west of the county are the industrialized valleys of the Ebbw and Sirhowy, and hereabouts Cadw now looks after the important eighteenth-century ironworks at Blaenavon. The central part of Gwent varies from the coastal flatlands of the Caldicot Levels, to the gently undulating farmlands either side of the River Usk, and climbs to the fringes of the Black Mountains in the north. Finally, in the east of the county is the glorious Wye valley, an 'area of outstanding natural beauty'. Within this attractive landscape, Cadw maintains a selection of superb monuments. The Roman remains at Caerleon are of international significance, whereas the castles at Chepstow and Raglan, and the magnificent Cistercian abbey at Tintern, are among the most impressive medieval sites in Britain. There is also much of interest at the 'Three Castles' of Grosmont, Skenfrith and White Castle, and there is scarcely a more impressive setting for a monastic ruin than Llanthony in the lovely vale of Ewais.

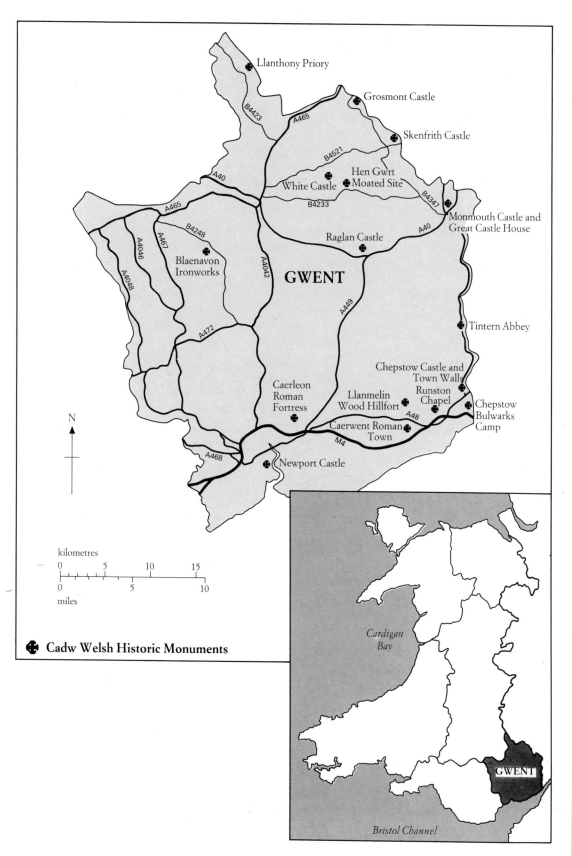

Llanthony Priory

Grosmont Castle

Skenfrith Castle

B4423

A465

B4521

Hen Gwrt
Moated Site

White Castle

B4233

B4347

Monmouth Castle and
Great Castle House

A40

A465

B4248

A467

A4046

A4048

A40

A4042

Raglan Castle

Blaenavon
Ironworks

GWENT

A472

A449

Tintern Abbey

Chepstow Castle and
Town Walls

Caerleon
Roman
Fortress

Llanmelin
Wood Hillfort

Runston
Chapel

Chepstow
Bulwarks
Camp

Caerwent Roman
Town

A48

M4

N

A468

Newport Castle

kilometres

0   5   10   15

0   5   10

miles

✤ **Cadw Welsh Historic Monuments**

*Cardigan
Bay*

GWENT

Bristol Channel

Blaenavon Ironworks

Wales played a key role in the events of the Industrial Revolution. This period of late eighteenth and early nineteenth century technological change resulted in an unprecedented economic boom, and was accompanied by an enormous expansion in the population of the Principality. Much of the Welsh landscape was radically transformed as pioneering industrialists set up their works and began to take advantage of a largely untapped supply of natural resources. Until recent years, however, the built heritage of these events – houses, chapels, factories, mines and works of all kinds – had been virtually overlooked. It is only over the past few decades that a growing interest in 'industrial archaeology' has led to a change of

heart. Gradually, the State and local authorities have extended levels of protection, hitherto reserved for castles and other more ancient monuments, to a growing number of the many fascinating buildings which survive from this highly significant episode in our history.

Blaenavon, of course, is just one site associated with the Industrial Revolution in Wales, one of a string of ironworks set up along the northern rim of the south Wales coalfield in the late eighteenth century. Nevertheless, it belongs to the period when Welsh ironworking dominated the trade in Britain and Europe, and is one of the most complete works to survive anywhere in the country. The full importance of this industrial monument was recognized in 1974 when not only the ironworks, but also an associated group of workers' houses, passed into the care of the State.

The origins of ironmaking in this area go back to at least the Middle Ages, and in the seven-

An engraving of Blaenavon Ironworks, from a drawing by Sir Richard Colt Hoare, 1798.

teenth and eighteenth centuries the Hanbury ironmasters of Pontypool built up a small-scale, but flourishing business. Their lease lapsed in 1787, and by November of that year a new draft lease on some 12,000 acres of mineral ground around Blaenavon and Nantyglo had been drawn up between three entrepreneurs from the English midlands and the earl of Abergavenny. Thomas Hill and Benjamin Pratt – joined soon afterwards by Thomas Hopkins – intended to exploit the local resources of coal, ironstone and limestone, and to take advantage of the latest developments in ironmaking technology. By 1789 they had erected three coke-fired blast furnaces terraced into a hillside here at Blaenavon. These were accompanied by casthouses and a steam-blowing engine, and a start was quickly made on housing for the key workers. Within ten years the ironworks was employing 350 people. Transport of the finished iron was greatly aided by the opening of the Monmouthshire Canal in 1796, thus linking Blaenavon with the docks at Newport.

The Blaenavon ironworks prospered during the Napoleonic Wars with France, and about 1810 another two furnaces were put into blast – completing the early bank of five, the remains of which can be seen today. By this stage Blaenavon was producing some 10,000 tons of 'pig' iron per year. Around 1815, control passed to Thomas Hill II, the son of one of the original partners. He devised an ambitious scheme to exploit the cheaper freight costs of the Brecon and Abergavenny Canal. New forges – producing wrought ('worked') iron – were established at Garnddyrys, and a tunnel one and a quarter miles long was dug through the Blorenge mountain to link the two operations by tramway. From Garnddyrys trams descended to meet the Brecon and Abergavenny at Llanfoist.

Unfortunately, in the 1820s production began to stagnate, and Hill was unable to raise the capital required for investment in new plant. In 1836, Thomas Hill III sold the entire concern to a newly-formed joint stock company – the Blaenavon Iron and Coal Company. James Ashwell, an ambitious new managing director, began to make various improvements, including the addition of the water balance tower which is now so much a dominant feature of the site. But lack of adequate capital for investment continued to hamper plans for expansion and the

Company was eventually forced into liquidation in 1864. By this time, a new works had been set up on the other side of the Afon Lwyd valley, at a site to be known as Forgeside, though it was not until 1868 – after many delays – that the first furnace there came on blast. The transfer of activity to Forgeside, with steel rather than iron production becoming ever more important, inevitably led to the decline of the old works. When the last blast furnace was blown out in 1904, ironmaking on the site finally came to an end.

The row of furnaces are now in varying states of preservation, and can be viewed across the furnace yard. The raw materials were weighed and 'charged' into the top of the furnaces from the high ground behind. The molten iron was run off into channels in a sandfloor within the casthouses, two of which also survive. The central channel and the rows of 'pig' moulds leading off were thought to resemble a sow with her piglets – hence the name 'pig' iron. To the right of the furnaces is the water balance tower, a counterbalance lift used to raise material from the furnace yard to the upper level.

Most of the rows of industrial housing linked with the ironworks have now disappeared. The notable exception is Stack Square – literally next door to the works – which is now being conserved. The square was built between 1788 and 1792 and takes its name from the large chimney stack, connected to a later steam blast engine, which stood in the central courtyard. In the early days of the Blaenavon works, these houses were probably for the skilled workers brought in from the English midlands, though there was no plumbing or sanitation. The middle row may have housed the company offices during the early years, and at one corner is the company 'truck shop' where employees could obtain goods on credit against an advance on their wages. The 1851 Census returns show there were some 84 people living in the square.

The extensive programme of conservation at Blaenavon has already involved huge labours, and much remains to be done before it is fully open to the public. Even so, visitors can already view and appreciate much of the layout of Stack Square and the furnace yard. There are regular guided tours, and an exhibition deals with the processes of ironmaking and its growth and development at this highly significant site.

An aerial view of Caerleon, showing the extent of the 50 acre legionary fortress.

Caerleon Roman Fortress

The superb remains of the legionary fortress at the small Gwent town of Caerleon lay just claim to being one of the largest and most important Roman military sites in Europe. The amphitheatre, barracks, defences, and particularly the fortress baths, are of truly international significance. The Romans named their fortress on this site *Isca*, taken from the river on which it stood, now the Usk. It was established about AD 75 as the headquarters of the Second Augustan Legion – *Legio II Augusta* – one of about 30 legions whose fortresses guarded the frontiers of the empire from Scotland to the Arabian desert. To the Welsh it was the 'City of the Legions', and in later translation became Caerleon. The twelfth-century scholar, Geoffrey of Monmouth, in his *History of the Kings of Britain* located the crowning of King Arthur at this place, and in legend the remains of the great Roman amphitheatre were 'King Arthur's Round Table'. Indeed, in 1405, a French expeditionary force in support of Owain Glyndŵr took time off to inspect the already famous ruins.

The Second Augustan Legion was named after the emperor Augustus who raised it. Like other legions it was a division of some 5,500 heavily armed infantry, who were all Roman citizens. Under a new governor, Sextus Julius Frontinus (AD 74–8), *II Augusta* was moved into south Wales and set out to crush finally the troublesome native tribe – the *Silures*. The site chosen for the new fortress was a large area of flat land at a good bridging point on the River Usk, and close enough to the estuary to be readily supplied by sea-going ships. With characteristic Roman efficiency *Isca* was laid out to a remarkably uniform plan. The defences enclosed an area of some 50 acres, shaped rather like a playing-card. With rare exceptions – notably the fortress baths – both the defences and internal buildings were first constructed of timber. Only later, from about AD 100-10, were they gradually replaced in stone. At the centre of the fortress, under the present church, was the *principia* or headquarters where the legionary eagle and standards were kept. Across the main street there were officers' houses, a hospital and the fortress baths. The front and rear ranges and the areas flanking the *principia* held the barrack-blocks, housing the ten cohorts into which the legion was divided. Finally there were storerooms and workshops providing the essential back-up services for a fighting force of 5,500 men.

Today, the streets of modern Caerleon overlie many of the buildings of the mighty fortress, and much of our knowledge comes from archaeological excavations undertaken almost every year (save during the war) since 1926. Visitors will find the buildings on display are all within a few minutes walk of the church at the centre of the town. From this point, a road still known as Broadway follows one of the major streets of the fortress towards the south-west gate. To the right, in an area known as Prysg Field, are the only legionary barrack blocks now visible in Europe. The fortress originally contained about 60 blocks, and four of these can now be seen. Each block housed a centurion with his century of men. At one time a century was made up of 100 soldiers, as the name implies, but by the time *Isca* was established the complement had become 80. The centurion – sometimes compared to a modern sergeant major – occupied the slightly broader range of rooms to one end of each block, with his men in the double cubicles at the narrower part. Eight soldiers were allocated to each pair of cubicles, the larger room providing sleeping accommodation and the smaller served as a kit store. Also visible in the Prysg Field are examples of early cooking ovens, later cookhouses, and there is a latrine in the far corner.

On the opposite side of Broadway a path leads to a surviving section of the fortress defences. These originally comprised a turf and clay bank, with a timber palisade and interval towers. About AD 100–10, a stone wall was added to the front of the bank and was surmounted with a series of stone turrets. The wall still stands up to 12 feet high, though much of its dressed stone facework has been robbed. One of the interval turrets and the southern corner turret can also be seen.

Just outside the line of these defences, the

The amphitheatre at Caerleon.

large oval amphitheatre is one of the best surviving features of *Isca*. The legionary soldiers were originally recruited from Italy, southern France and Spain, and would expect to be provided with some of the amenities of home. About AD 90 it was decided to provide *II Augusta* with their own amphitheatre. It was designed to seat some 6,000 spectators, and played host to a variety of events and special festivals. The lower part was built of stone, much as we see it today. The superstructure and seating were built as a timber openwork grandstand, perhaps intended as a temporary measure though never completed in stone. Nevertheless, from the outset, it seems certain that the central arena was the scene of the grim blood sports so common to Imperial Rome. On occasions like

This inscription, found at the amphitheatre, records the building of a particular wall by soldiers of the 'III cohort, century of Rufinus Primus'.

the emperor's birthday, expensive gladiatorial combats and animal baiting with bears, wild boars, wolves or bulls could well have taken place here. The amphitheatre was also used for a degree of basic troop training and weapon demonstrations. One of the entrances to the arena, below the 'president's box', was later converted to a small shrine of Nemesis, the goddess of fate and divine vengeance, who punished crime.

Impressive though these monuments are, the centrepiece of a visit to Roman Caerleon is without doubt the magnificent Fortress Baths complex. Discovered and excavated as recently as 1964–81, a spacious cover-building now

The excavated remains of the Fortress Baths.

protects the long open-air swimming pool (*natatio*), a heated changing room (*apodyterium*) and part of the cold bath hall (*frigidarium*). The baths were an essential amenity of Roman life, and at Caerleon they served as a leisure and social centre for the soldiers. In their off-duty hours they would come to gamble, or perhaps to play ball games, meet friends, take a massage, and even to buy a pasty, a roast duck or a mutton chop. A soldier coming to the baths might begin with a cold dip, move on to the warm and hot rooms, scraping oil and sweat from his body with a metal scraper or strigil. Finally the bather might return to the cold hall where attendants would have thrown buckets of water over him to cool him off. Items of jewellery, and even a number of milk teeth, found during the excavations reveal that the baths were also used by women and children.

The baths were built about AD 80 by an unusually innovative architect, and would have towered above the remainder of the fortress. The vast construction of stone and concrete was clearly meant as a showpiece, not just to the *Silures*, but for the new province of *Britannia* as a whole. In sheer mass, with their adjacent exercise hall, the complex would have equalled a medieval cathedral as large as Wells. Indeed, the design seems to have anticipated that of the great Imperial Baths of Rome itself. The buildings were much altered and repaired during their history, but were maintained by the legion until about AD 230–40. About 50 years later all hope of reopening the baths was given up.

It is interesting to note that apart from the initial campaign against the *Silures*, the whole force of the Second Legion was rarely present at Caerleon as a complete unit. A number of inscriptions and other archaeological evidence reveals how various buildings were constructed and reconstructed through the second and third centuries, but the fortress seems to have been finally abandoned by about AD 290.

Displays in the Fortress Baths cover-building explain and illuminate the visible remains there. Visitors should also make time to see the new Roman Legionary Museum at the centre of the town. It contains many of the intriguing and precious artefacts excavated in and around the fortress, including a collection of 88 gemstones from the drain of the Fortress Baths.

The fourth-century town walls at the Roman town of Caerwent.

Caerwent Roman Town

The traveller who comes to modern Caerwent will find no more than a sleepy rural Gwent village, but to the Romans this was *Venta Silurum* – 'the market town of the *Silures*'. The site is now largely greensward, though archaeologists have long been drawn to the well-preserved remains below. Indeed, almost two-thirds of the entire town were explored between 1899 and 1913. A more recent programme of excavations has begun to paint a much fuller picture of this important Romano-British settlement. The work has also led to the conservation and presentation of further structures for public display.

The *Silures* themselves had been a warlike tribe, and their conquest cost the legions many years of hard fighting. Even so, they gradually adopted Romanized ways under the shadow of the Second Augustan Legion, whose base was established at nearby Caerleon around AD 75. The archaeological evidence points to the foundation of a settlement at Caerwent soon after this date. We know little of its early character, but it would not have been defended, and most of the buildings were probably of wood. This settlement was eventually to become the regional centre of self-government, the capital of

the *civitas Silurum*, perhaps by the early second century. Direct evidence comes from a somewhat rare inscription carved on a statue-pedestal, now to be seen in the porch of the village church. The statue honoured Tiberius Claudius Paulinus, commander of the Second Legion in the early third century. However, the really significant point is that it was set up 'by decree of the council, the community of the state of the *Silures*'.

The initial timber structures were replaced piecemeal in stone, and the town grew to cover

The statue-pedestal in Caerwent Church.

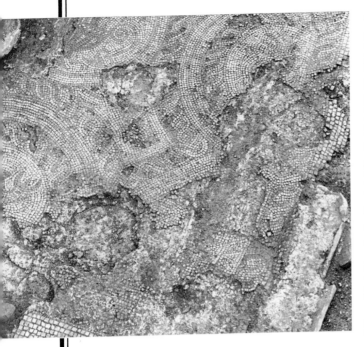

Detail of a mosaic floor excavated at Caerwent.

some 45 acres. The streets were laid out in a regular grid pattern, with houses, shops and public buildings located along the frontages. Although other Roman towns in Britain grew rapidly, the process of urbanization at Caerwent may have been long and drawn out. The recent excavations in the north-west corner have led to suggestions that parts of the town may have remained undeveloped until the late second century.

At the centre of the town, just to the north of the present main street, lay the *basilica* (town hall) and *forum* (market place). The *basilica* was a large and imposing building, with a central hall, offices, a council chamber and tribunals where the local magistrates sat whilst hearing cases. It is currently under excavation, with walls still standing more than six feet high, and will in due course be conserved for display. The market place was surrounded by ranges of shops and taverns, many with open fronts. Just to the south, on the opposite side of the road, lay the public bath house.

On arriving at Caerwent, the massive town walls are the most obvious sign of its ancient past, rising up to 17 feet tall on the southern side of the site. The modern road through the village enters and leaves on the line of the Roman east and west gates. Earthen defences were first raised in the late second century, but about AD 340 these were replaced in stone. Little more than ten years later, projecting bastions were added along the northern and southern stretches. Inside, near the middle of the village, there are the foundations of a Romano-Celtic temple complex. Probably built in the early fourth century, there is a central shrine or *cella* with an entrance hall to the south. In Pound Lane the remains of two houses are displayed. That to the south appears to have been owned by a blacksmith and was much altered through its history. The adjacent courtyard house was built in the early fourth century, doubtless by a prosperous family. Another large fourth-century courtyard house has recently been excavated and consolidated just to the north-west of these two.

Although many Roman settlements in the surrounding countryside had been abandoned by about AD 350, Caerwent was occupied through to the end of the century, and possibly into the fifth. In the early Christian period there may have been a church or monastic foundation established here by the sixth century. A number of likely Christian burials have been excavated both within and outside the walls, and are dated by the radiocarbon method over a wide period between the fifth and ninth centuries.

Chepstow Bulwarks Camp

This is a small Iron Age promontory fort standing above Hardwick Cliffs, and overlooking the River Wye. The double bank and ditch defences are of considerable size, but enclose an area of less than two acres. The fort was probably constructed in the period immediately before the Roman conquest, and is likely to have been a strongly defended homestead. Similar sized camps can be seen elsewhere in south-east Wales, including an interesting group – with less prominent ramparts – along the southern coast of the Gower peninsula. Today, the interior of the fort is quite flat, and is used as a playing field and playground.

Chepstow Castle and Town Walls

Chepstow Castle is magnificently sited high upon a river cliff above the swirling waters of the Wye. Throughout the Middle Ages it was situated at the centre of a major Marcher lordship, guarding one of the principal river crossings from southern England into Wales. Few sites in the whole of the British Isles tell the story of medieval fortification, let alone the changing role of the castle, as does this mighty border stronghold. Beginning as one of the earliest stone-built castles in the entire country, Chepstow was to be modified and developed in successive stages right through to the Civil War of the seventeenth century. Today, its pictur-

esque silhouette continues to hug the cliffline, and remains a familiar and engaging sight for travellers taking this ancient route into south Wales.

Just a few months after the battle of Hastings, William fitz Osbern, lord of Breteuil in Calvados, was created earl of Hereford by William the Conqueror. He was among the most trusted, experienced and ruthless of the new king's companions, and had already played a key part in the subjugation of England. Before his death in 1071, Earl William built the rectangular stone keep which still forms the core of Chepstow to this day. From this secure base he laid the strategy for the conquest of Gwent. The keep remains the earliest dateable secular stone building in Britain, though it is very similar to other eleventh-century hall-keeps in Normandy and the Loire valley. The builders used several

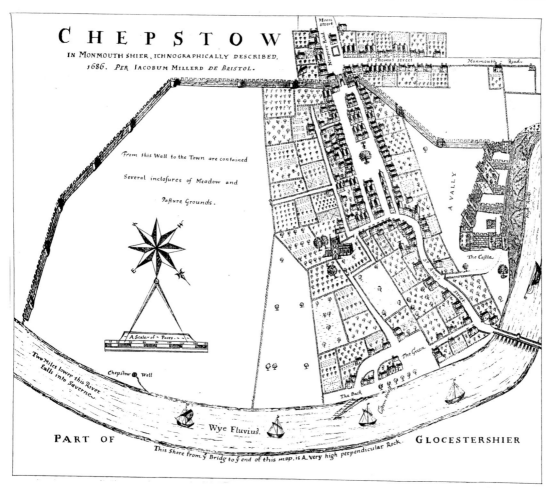

A map of Chepstow in 1686, with the castle to the right, and the full extent of Roger Bigod III's town walls enclosing the borough.

115

First raised by 1071, Chepstow Castle stands on a river cliff high above the Wye.

bands of red Roman tile in its construction, probably robbed from the ruins at Caerwent. The hall was situated on the first floor, with a basement below. Although modified in later centuries, the original round-headed Norman arches can still be identified. Interestingly, there were no openings in the more exposed southern wall, which from the outside appears as a blank buttressed face.

Henry I granted Chepstow to the de Clare family, and in 1189 it passed to the dashing William Marshall (d. 1219), a formidable soldier of fortune. He had won the esteem of Richard I who married him to the de Clare heiress, *la pucelle d'Estriguil* – 'the maid of Chepstow'. In one stroke he became one of the major barons of the March, with the lordships of Usk and Chepstow, as well as the earldom of Pembroke.

Marshall had considerable experience of military architecture in France, and set about bringing the eleventh-century castle up to date. He rebuilt the east curtain wall, with two round towers projecting outwards, in order to protect this vulnerable flank. His gateway, however,

was a simple arched entrance, tucked in beside one of the towers and the river cliff. Banks of arrowslits in the towers were designed to give covering fire to the ground in front of the curtain. As such, this was one of the earliest examples of the new defensive mode which was to become characteristic of the medieval castle.

Before 1245, William Marshall's five sons went on to greatly extend Chepstow's defences and improve the internal accommodation. They added a new lower bailey, with an impressive twin-towered gatehouse, which far outmatched their father's earlier gate. Moreover, they also added the strongly defended barbican to the upper end of the castle. But at least as important as this work on the defences was the extensive rebuilding of the domestic accommodation. The younger Marshalls completely transformed fitz Osbern's hall-keep, inserting large new windows at first-floor level on the more secure northern face, and adding a second storey over the western side, again with further large windows. By the time they had finished, the austere keep had become a hall and chamber block of

The hall-keep at Chepstow, seen through the entrance of the middle bailey.

palatial dimensions. It was under the Marshalls too, that the square tower between the upper bailey and the barbican was added. This contained further rooms of high quality, and in the ruins there are still traces of original painted decoration.

In 1270 Chepstow was inherited by Roger Bigod III, earl of Norfolk and one of the greatest magnates at the court of King Edward I. Despite the comfort and security already offered at the castle, the arrangements were simply not adequate enough for this exceptionally powerful man. He required accommodation for himself, for his personal army and retinue, and for the administrators of his Marcher lands. Evidently, between about 1272 and 1278, Earl Roger was also responsible for building the town wall. His work on the castle began with the splendid new hall block around 1278. Situated on the north side of the lower bailey, the range includes a two-tier group of service rooms, a large kitchen, domestic accommodation, and of course the great hall itself, entered by a grand porch. There is also a deep vaulted cellar where food and drink could be hauled up from the river and stored. Nearby a double-seater latrine is set spectacularly high over the river cliff.

Work on the hall range was followed almost immediately by the complete rebuilding of the tower on the crucial south-east angle of the lower bailey. Situated away from the noise of the hall and kitchen, the tower was built around 1287–93, and provided a lavish suite of rooms undoubtedly intended for Earl Roger himself. The entrance was protected by its own portcullis, and the spacious rooms were served with fireplaces and large windows. The tower also housed a private chapel, with richly carved decoration and a seat at either side for the priest. Unusually, when raised, the portcullis closing off the wall-walk below would have stood in front of the altar.

By Tudor times Chepstow had passed to the hands of the Herberts of Raglan, and further modifications were made at this time. Large rectangular mullioned windows were inserted in various apartments, and lodgings were built against the curtain walls. At the outbreak of the Civil War, Henry, earl of Worcester, garrisoned the castle for the king. It was twice besieged, first in 1645 and again in 1648. On both occasions its defences, designed against medieval attack, rapidly fell to Parliamentary cannon. Following the war, the castle was granted to Cromwell and the whole southern face was reinforced with earth and stone to absorb the shock of any future cannon fire. The parapets of the walls were remodelled with openings for musket loops. Even after the Restoration of Charles II, a military garrison was maintained at Chepstow, and it served as a place of detention for political prisoners. Henry Marten, a committed republican who was one of those to sign the death warrant of Charles I, was imprisoned in the tower which bears his name for almost 20 years.

The town wall – known locally as the 'Port Wall' – was built, as stated, by Roger Bigod III. It was equipped with a series of semi-circular projecting towers, and the remains of several of these can still be seen along the surviving stretches. The recently restored town gate continues to span the main road into the centre of Chepstow. It may date back to the time of Earl Roger but was much altered in the later Middle Ages. Recently, the porch and service area of Roger Bigod's hall complex have been carefully restored, and the area now houses a new exhibition. It covers the buildings and history of this fascinating castle, and also focuses upon the all too neglected aspects of Chepstow's major role in the Civil War.

Grosmont Castle

Grosmont stands on the very border of Wales, separated from the modern county of Hereford and Worcester by no more than the Monnow river. The village is particularly attractive and especially large for the area: due to the fact that until the 1850s Grosmont had borough status, with its own mayor and corporation. The importance of the place undoubtedly sprang from the presence of the castle, and is again reflected in the remarkable size of the church of St Nicholas. For this was a garrison church, extended and embellished under the patronage of the castellans. The nave now stands disused, far too large for the needs of parish worship.

The earliest castle here was probably raised by William fitz Osbern, who overran much of central and eastern Gwent from his strongholds at Chepstow and Monmouth. Along with Skenfrith and White Castle, Grosmont was eventually part of the lordship of 'Three Castles', a defensive and by no means unprofitable block of territory on the line of the major routeways between Herefordshire and the Usk valley. The Norman castle would have been thrown up at great speed and was constructed of earth and timber. Indeed, the name is derived from the French *gros mont* – 'big mound' – which aptly describes the great earthwork on which the later buildings stand.

In 1201 King John granted the 'Three Castles' to Hubert de Burgh, a politician and soldier of fortune who eventually rose to the ranks of justiciar of England and earl of Kent. Much of what we see at Grosmont today was the work of Earl Hubert. Between 1201 and 1204 he almost certainly built the impressive rectangular hall block overlooking the valley below. The comfortable first-floor apartments – great hall and private chamber – were approached by an external timber stair. The hall was fitted with a large fireplace and there were handsome windows on all sides. The basement served for storage space and was originally reached by a circular stair from the first floor.

Earl Hubert lost the 'Three Castles' in 1205, when he was taken prisoner of war in France. It was not until 1219 that he regained them, but thereafter he soon began rebuilding Grosmont in the up-to-date defensive style of the period.

A stone curtain wall was built around the western edge of the mound, with three strong half-round towers protecting the angles on the north and west sides, and a two-storey gatehouse fortifying the entrance. All three towers had deep circular basements, and the upper rooms were equipped with sets of arrowslits.

In the uncertain world of medieval politics, de Burgh was again to fall from power in 1232, and although he regained the king's favour for a short while, in 1239 he was finally forced to surrender his lands and castles to the Crown. King Henry III had in fact used Grosmont as an emergency base in 1233. He had come to the Marches to scotch a revolt led by Earl Richard Marshall of Pembroke, but met with little success. Marshall's forces made a daring night attack on the castle, routing the royal army and forcing the king to retreat to Gloucester.

In 1267 the 'Three Castles' passed to Henry III's second son, Edmund 'Crouchback', earl of Lancaster. Grosmont was to become a favourite residence of his son Henry of Lancaster, and his grandson Henry of Grosmont who was born at the castle. The Lancasters were engaged in an extensive rebuilding of Kidwelly Castle in the early fourteenth century, but they also remodelled Grosmont to provide a suite of apartments for a noble household. The rear face of the south-west tower dates to this time. The northern block of rooms, dominated by a fine octagonal chimney, was also built over one of de Burgh's towers.

Grosmont saw action for the last time during the Owain Glyndŵr uprising, when it was attacked by the Welsh in 1404. It was relieved by a force sent by Prince Henry, later Henry V.

Hen Gwrt Moated Site

Although little now survives above the turf at this tranquil location deep in rural Gwent, the archaeologist's spade has recovered some of its hidden secrets. Hen Gwrt, or Old Court, was probably the centre of a manor belonging to the bishops of Llandaff in the thirteenth and fourteenth centuries. Soon after 1300, along with

Grosmont Castle, a residence of the house of Lancaster in the fourteenth century.

Hen Gwrt (Old Court), a medieval moated manor of the bishops of Llandaff.

many sites where owners had similar social aspirations in both Wales and England, the manor was surrounded with a substantial moat. This moat is still filled with water today, and is up to 30 feet wide in places.

Although abandoned for a period, in the later fifteenth century it may have become a hunting lodge. It was situated at the edge of a newly created deer park, probably established by Sir William Herbert of Raglan Castle. It continued to serve this purpose for the lords of Raglan through until the seventeenth century.

Llanmelin Wood Hillfort

In the last four to five centuries before the arrival of the Roman legions, Wales had become divided into several main tribal areas. The south-east was occupied by the *Silures*, described by the Roman historian, Tacitus, as a powerful, warlike, valiant, savage and stubborn people. Almost all of their known settlements throughout Glamorgan and Gwent are fortified enclosures, often on coastal or inland promontories, or on the tops of hills. Llanmelin is one such settlement, or hillfort, and occupies a wooded spur overlooking the Gwent levels, just over a mile to the north-west of the later Roman town at Caerwent.

The site is one of considerable strength, now partly disguised by the tree cover. The principal enclosure occupies little more than five acres, but with its defences and outlying earthworks the fort covers more than 10 acres. Llanmelin was excavated in 1930–32, and may have had three main phases of development. At first, there are hints that the spur was defended with a single rampart, though none of the excavated finds can be assigned to this stage. In the second century BC, the defences were constructed on much more elaborate lines. Two or three banks and ditches culminated with a massive inner

bank which was revetted in stone on both sides. In the third phase, shortly before the Roman conquest, the gateway was rebuilt with an inturned entrance of much greater strength. At this stage, too, curious rectangular annexes were added on the south-eastern side.

The interior of the fort was not fully explored, but would probably have been densely occupied with circular wooden huts and storage buildings. The annexe area may have served as stock enclosures. A few finds of pottery suggest sporadic occupation during the Roman period, but the site – like other hillforts – was largely abandoned after the military conquest by the legions.

Llanthony Priory

Set in the lovely Vale of Ewais, 'no more than three arrow-shots in width', the ruins of Llanthony lie amid the rugged grandeur of the Black Mountains. Contemplating the priory towards the end of the twelfth century, Gerald of Wales recognized 'a religious site truly suited to the monastic life ... in a wilderness far removed from the bustle of mankind'. Earlier in the century, Gerald informs us, Bishop Roger of Salisbury had been moved to say: 'the entire treasury of the king and his realm is not sufficient to build such a cloister'. Even 800 years later, few visitors to this beautiful location

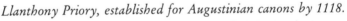

Llanthony Priory, established for Augustinian canons by 1118.

The pointed arches of Llanthony Priory, an early experiment in the new Gothic style.

can fail to appreciate the significance of these remarks.

The very foundation, recorded in a chronicle of about 1200, is a romantic tale of men in search of religious solitude. For it was here that William, a knight in the service of Hugh de Lacy, stumbled upon a ruined chapel dedicated to St David. Thereafter he resolved to abandon his profession of arms and chose to establish a hermitage. In 1103 William was joined by Ernisius, who had formerly been chaplain to Queen Matilda, and gradually they attracted a group of like-minded followers whose church was consecrated in 1108. Hugh de Lacy became the patron, and by 1118 the community had been reorganized as a priory of Augustinian canons – one of the earliest in Britain and the first in Wales. Henry I and Queen Matilda were benefactors, and the priory was to achieve considerable wealth and importance, with as many as 40 canons in these opening years.

We know virtually nothing of the buildings occupied in this early period, though recent archaeological excavations have offered one or two clues. It seems almost certain that the little church built 'after a homely manner' in 1108 would have been far too small for the growing Augustinian community. It was replaced by a much larger building, traces of which have been found beneath the present remains. But the death of Henry I in 1135 signalled disaster for both the canons and their prestigious new priory church.

The Welsh rose in revolt forcing most of the community to flee, and in 1136 they were given a new site just outside the thriving borough of Gloucester. When peace was restored, however, the canons proved reluctant to return to Wales, and stripped the mother house of its books, ornaments, and even the bells. Although the Welsh priory was far from abandoned, it probably fell into a state of neglect; so much so that the church was clearly beyond saving. Thus, with a notable upturn in fortunes at the end of the twelfth century, a completely new church was begun about 1175. The cash came from lands and churches granted by the de Lacy family from their recent conquests in Ireland. Indeed, these were to provide Llanthony with a comfortable income for much of the Middle Ages.

Work on the church began with the choir and transepts at the east end, and about 1200 it progressed to the nave. The surviving north arcade of the nave is particularly lovely, where the pointed arches represent an early experiment in the new Gothic style. The west front must also have been greatly impressive when its vast window was in place. The courtyard in front of the modern hotel preserves the form of the canons' cloister, the hotel itself occupying much of the west range. On the east side, the unusual chapter house was built in the mid thirteenth century. Further to the south, the present parish church formed part of the priory infirmary. One further intriguing feature, discovered during the recent excavations, was the drastic transformation of the north transept during the fourteenth century. It was blocked off from the remainder of the church and converted to domestic use, with a kitchen, a chamber and even a privy!

As well as its Irish property, Llanthony of course held estates in south-east Wales, and also controlled important manorial possessions in Herefordshire. The house was finally suppressed in 1539, when there were just four canons with their prior in residence.

121

The hall-keep at Monmouth Castle.

Monmouth Castle and Great Castle House

Monmouth Castle is perhaps best known as the birthplace of one of our most celebrated monarchs, King Henry V. As a son of the house of Lancaster, the future victor of Agincourt, Shakespeare's 'Harry Monmouth', was born here on 16 September 1387, probably within the 'Great Tower'. The original stronghold, however, was established by William fitz Osbern, one of William the Conqueror's most trusted barons. It was fitz Osbern who built the mighty Chepstow to control the lower crossing of the Wye, and here at Monmouth his castle commanded a double crossing of both the Wye and the Monnow rivers. An infant borough grew up on the sloping ground running down to the Wye from the castle and the Benedictine priory, and in the later Middle Ages was fortified with walls and gates. The western approaches were further strengthened by the gate tower which still stands on the Monnow bridge.

The oldest surviving building is the twelfth-century 'Great Tower', a hall-keep similar to that built by fitz Osbern at Chepstow. A row of Norman slit windows can be seen on the ground floor, and the hall itself was on the upper storey. About 1270 a new great hall was built at right-angles to the keep, probably when the castle and lordship were held by Edmund 'Crouchback', earl of Lancaster. This single-storey building was used for feasting and for holding lordship courts. In the next century, under Henry of Grosmont, duke of Lancaster (d. 1361), the earlier keep was remodelled on a princely scale. Some of the windows of this period can still be seen.

We know, too, from the writings of a local diarist, that the castle had a round tower, similar no doubt to that at nearby Skenfrith. This was pulled down in 1647, following the Civil War. It was not long after this that the site passed to Henry Somerset, grandson of the marquess of Worcester who had defended Raglan for King Charles I. Henry had proved a skilful politician, and recovered many of the family possessions even before the Restoration of Charles II in 1660. He eventually became the first duke of Beaufort in 1682. Indeed, it was Henry who was responsible for the construction of Great Castle House, completed in 1673, to replace Raglan as the Somersets' residence in the county.

Great Castle House is a superb Renaissance construction, with a Classical front, and 'hipped' roofs. Inside there are panelled rooms, a fine staircase and exquisite plaster ceilings. In 1875 the house became the official headquarters of the Royal Monmouthshire Royal Engineers (Militia), and as such it remains one of the few British castles still in military occupation.

Great Castle House, Monmouth.

Newport Castle

Standing hard by the muddy banks of the River Usk, surrounded by modern roads and bridges, this once handsome nobleman's residence is all too often overlooked. The surviving towers are the work of the earls of Stafford – later dukes of Buckingham – in the fourteenth and fifteenth centuries, but this was not the earliest castle at Newport. An earth and timber Norman stronghold stood at the top of Stow Hill, close to what is now St Woolos Cathedral. The remains of the mound were visible until covered with the spoil from a Great Western Railway tunnel in the 1840s.

In the early Middle Ages Newport was part of the lordship of Glamorgan, but in 1314 it passed in marriage to Hugh d'Audele – a knight of the royal household – and soon afterwards it appears to have become a separate lordship. Following an early setback, d'Audele held Newport continually from 1326 until his death

in 1347, and it may have been at this time that a new site was chosen for the castle. The lordship again passed in marriage to Ralph, earl of Stafford, who could have begun building the present structure. It seems more likely, however, that his son Earl Hugh was responsible for the core of the work, probably around 1372–86. The curious plan with three towers on the river front, with no substantial landward defences, suggests the castle was left unfinished when Hugh died suddenly in 1386. Then, in 1405, at the height of the Owain Glyndŵr revolt, large numbers of masons were working here on what must have been an emergency building programme, perhaps putting the site in a defensible state with a curtain wall on the western (land) side.

Earl Hugh's grandson, Humphrey Stafford, came of age in 1424 and quickly seems to have taken a great personal interest in all his estates. Under King Henry VI he rose to the leading ranks of the aristocracy and became duke of Buckingham in 1444. Surviving building ac-

Newport Castle from a painting by J. M. W. Turner (1775–1851).

counts reveal that he spent considerable sums in rebuilding Newport Castle as a residence commensurate with the rank of a powerful grandee. Construction may have begun as early as 1427, and was largely finished by 1450. As completed, the buildings would have been spacious and comfortable enough to accommodate the duke and his large retinue when resident on an estate tour or executing official business.

The base of the central tower formed a substantial vaulted dock or water gate. Above this was a grand state apartment, again vaulted, and no doubt the scene of courts, hearings, and ceremonial occasions under Duke Humphrey. There was a chapel above this chamber. To one side lay a first-floor hall, and the smaller north tower. At the southern end the tower near the bridge provided a richly adorned set of private lodgings for the duke himself.

In later centuries the castle fell into decline, and was probably already ruined at the time of the Civil War. By the 1820s the buildings were used for a brewery, the castle well providing an excellent supply of water.

Raglan Castle

In the half century after the rebellion of Owain Glyndŵr, Wales was in a state of uneasy calm. Soldiers returning from the French wars of King Henry V found a restless, and frequently lawless and violent, countryside. From 1437, when the young Henry VI came of age, the situation deteriorated still more markedly. The great noblemen who now owned the Marcher lordships of the south and east were mostly absentees, and the real power fell to the hands of local agents. Moreover, the outbreak of bloody civil war in 1455 – the Wars of the Roses – was a further opportunity for these men to exploit the vacuum left by the non-resident magnates. In such conditions, the castle had far from lost its place. It was precisely this situation which gave rise to one of the most glorious and chivalrous castles of the fifteenth century – Raglan. Nothing short of exotic in the context of Wales, Raglan continues to stand proud and handsome. Its superb façades might have remained yet more intact had it not been for Parliamentary

cannon during the Civil War of the 1640s. The knarred walls of the Great Tower, brought down by Cromwell's demolition engineers, bear witness to the last phase in this superb castle's history.

Raglan was begun by William ap Thomas, a veteran of the French wars, who gained possession of the site through marriage. Knighted in 1426, Sir William began to exploit his local position as an agent of both the Crown and leading magnates. He was a prominent member of the duke of York's council, and became chief steward of his estates in Wales. About 1435, now as a person of some status, ap Thomas started to build the Great Tower, perhaps on the site of an earlier motte and bailey castle. Subsequently known as the 'Yellow Tower of Gwent' – Twr Melyn Gwent – it is a remarkable structure, more easily paralleled in France than in England. Virtually a self-contained fortress in its own right, the hexagonal Great Tower is surrounded by a water-filled moat. Details such as the elaborate drawbridge arrangement are particularly French, and must surely have been influenced by Sir William's military experience in that country. Inside, the tower contained a spacious room on each floor. The basement served as a kitchen, with a great chamber above, and private rooms with larger windows on the upper floors. Apart from the 'Yellow Tower', the South Gate and parts of the hall also formed part of ap Thomas's castle.

Following his death in 1445, the wily ap Thomas was succeeded by his eldest son, William, who took the surname Herbert. The new heir was soon to become involved in the affairs of state, eventually holding a position of immense power in Wales. Herbert was a premier supporter of the Yorkist cause in the Wars of the Roses, and played a major role in the defeat of Henry VI's Lancastrian forces at Mortimer's Cross in 1461. Edward IV was acclaimed king, and a few months later Sir William was raised to the peerage as Baron Herbert of Raglan. As a trusted friend and advisor to the young King Edward, he became effective ruler of south Wales. In 1468, as a reward for the capture of the Lancastrian-held Harlech Castle, the king created him earl of Pembroke. He was thus one of the earliest members of the Welsh gentry to enter the ranks of the English aristocracy.

William Herbert's meteoric rise to power is

The handsome fifteenth-century castle at Raglan, seen from the air.

'The Yellow Tower of Gwent', begun about 1435 by Sir William ap Thomas. The details give Raglan a particularly French appearance.

reflected in his sumptuous building at Raglan. Between about 1460 and his death in 1469, he created a veritable palace, quite unmatched in the fifteenth-century southern March. In fact, most of what we see today is the work of Sir William. Next to his father's Great Tower, he developed lavish suites of state apartments around the Fountain Court – so named after a 'pleasant marble fountain in the midst thereof, called the White Horse, continually running with clear Water'. The remains of the chapel can be seen at one side of the court, and opposite is the Grand Stair.

Sir William also added the Pitched Stone Court with its gatehouse. The service rooms were situated around this second courtyard, and the ovens and huge fireplaces can still be seen in the Kitchen Tower. The gatehouse itself is vast and imposing. Much of its character comes from the prominent 'machicolations' at the top

125

of the towers. Through these arched openings, suitable missiles could be dropped on a besieging enemy. But even here the masons could not resist carving humorous gargoyle faces, some serving as rainwater spouts. At the base of the gatehouse, the circular openings – also to be seen in other parts of the castle – mount up to an impressive array of gunloops, largely intended for the use of handguns. To one side of the gate is the Closet Tower, probably providing accommodation for the household steward. From here he could run the estate office, with a strongroom for documents and valuables, and a deep prison for poachers, trespassers and other criminals.

William Herbert was beheaded following his defeat at the battle of Edgecote in 1469, and by the end of the century Raglan passed by marriage to the Somersets, earls of Worcester. It was William Somerset, the third earl, who was responsible for the last major phase of building at the castle, in the period 1549–89. In the main, Earl William was responsible for remodelling the hall range which separates the Fountain and Pitched Stone courts. It remains the finest and most complete of all apartments at Raglan. It was here that this powerful Elizabethan gentleman would have dined in state. At the upper end is the great oriel window which lit the high table. Also at this end is a carved stone shield, bearing the arms of the earl as a Knight of the Garter. From a surviving description, we know that the elaborate hammer-beam roof was of Irish oak.

William Somerset also added an extremely elegant long gallery to Raglan, without which

The oriel window in the hall at Raglan.

no Elizabethan house of any pretension was complete. Little of this survives today, though the large end windows which look out towards the Gwent countryside give some idea of its grandeur. Finally, the earl rebuilt much of the Pitched Stone Court, including an office wing.

In the following century, at the outbreak of the Civil War, Raglan was garrisoned for the king by Henry Somerset, the fifth earl. He was a staunch Royalist and was created marquess of Worcester by Charles I in 1643. He is said to have poured a vast fortune into the monarch's cause, and Charles was certainly entertained at Raglan on more than one occasion during the war. Indeed, following the crushing Royalist defeat at Naseby in 1645, the unhappy king sought some tranquility in playing bowls on the terrace outside the Fountain Court.

By June 1646, Raglan itself was under siege. Heavy cannon and mortar fire pounded the walls throughout the summer months. Sir Thomas Fairfax – the commander of the New Model Army – arrived at the scene in August, and realizing that further resistance was futile, the old marquess finally surrendered. The fall of Raglan effectively marked the end of the first Civil War. Henry Somerset was taken prisoner to London, but was dead by December of that year. As for the castle, deliberate destruction was added to the damage already sustained in the siege. Remarkably, the strength of Sir William ap Thomas's Great Tower almost defied the demolition gangs. Only 'after tedious battering the top thereof with pickaxes' were the walls undermined, bringing two of its six sides crashing down.

Arms of the third earl of Worcester at Raglan.

Runston Chapel

The little chapel of St Keyna's, Runston, is virtually all that remains of a once sizeable medieval village. To the south and east, earthen banks spread over the hilltop and mark the position of perhaps 15–20 houses long since deserted. The chapel itself dates back to the early twelfth century, soon after the Norman settlement of southern Gwent. It is only 50 feet from end to end, but apart from its roof it survives largely intact. A doorway leads into the nave from the south, and inside the fine chancel arch is a notable feature. A later medieval font from St Keyna's is now at the National Museum of Wales.

It is known that the chapel was used for burials into the early eighteenth century, but by 1772 the village had shrunk to just six houses. A few years later both St Keyna's and the village had been completely abandoned, probably the result of a powerful landowner intent upon change.

On his fall from power in 1232, Hubert de Burgh took sanctuary at Merton Priory, Surrey – an illustration of about 1250.

Skenfrith Castle

Skenfrith is a pretty little village on the banks of the River Monnow in the heart of rural Gwent. It boasts an attractive church, famed for its possession of a fine fifteenth-century cope. There was a timber castle here from soon after the Norman Conquest, but all that survives is due solely to the work of Hubert de Burgh (d. 1243), justiciar of England and earl of Kent, a soldier of wide experience and considerable skill. Throughout the Middle Ages, Skenfrith was held in common ownership with its neighbouring strongholds at Grosmont and White Castle – the 'Three Castles' as they became known. Together, they controlled the routes from England into Wales in the gap of fairly open country between the cliffs of the Wye valley to the south and the Black Mountains to the north-west.

In 1201 King John granted the 'Three Castles' to de Burgh, as a reward for faithful service. Just four years later, fighting for the king, the seemingly luckless Hubert was taken prisoner in France. The castles were made over to the avaricious William de Braose, who in turn quickly fell victim to the suspicion and spleen of John. The tide was again to turn and at the court of the young King Henry III, de Burgh rose to the height of his power and influence. He recovered the 'Three Castles' in January 1219, and by 1232 – when he again fell from power – he replaced the earth and timber castle at Skenfrith with an up-to-date stone building.

The defences of the Norman stronghold were completely levelled to make way for a bold new design. Earl Hubert's plan for the castle was straightforward, distinctly military and heavily influenced by his years of warfare against King Philip Augustus of France. A circular keep dominates a rectangular ward, with a round tower at each of the angles. The keep was originally entered at first-floor level, by way of an external timber stair. There was evidently a comfortable chamber on the second floor, with two large windows, a fireplace and a latrine. The top of the tower was probably surrounded with a projecting wooden gallery, or *hourd*, allowing archers to cover the ground on all sides. The castle's principal accommodation was provided in the ward below, particularly in the well-built western range, the lower floor of which is now exposed. The corner towers have deep circular basements for storage, and their doorways were raised above ground level for security. Each was equipped with batteries of arrowslits, providing covering crossfire to the ground in front of the walls. A moat fed by the Monnow surrounded the walls, and a bridge crossed to a simple raised entrance on the north side.

In many ways the design stands at a point of transition from the keep-based castles of the twelfth century, to the curtain wall strongholds of the later thirteenth century. A major round keep was also built, for example, by de Burgh's ally William Marshall at Pembroke, and neighbouring Marcher lords followed suit. The detached round keep was certainly a novel introduction to the southern March at this time, but it represents the end of a fading tradition, not the beginning of a new one. The chief strength of Skenfrith lay not in the keep but in the curtain, a trend which was to become ever more apparent as the century progressed, culminating of course in the supreme achievements of Edward I in north Wales.

Tintern Abbey

'The way to enjoy Tintern Abbey properly, and at leisure,' suggested the Honourable John Byng in 1781, 'is to bring wines, cold meat, with corn for the horses; (bread, beer, cyder and commonly salmon, may be had at the Beaufort Arms;) Spread your table in the ruins; and possibly a Welsh harper may be procured at Chepstow'. Tourists have indeed been visiting this romantic site for more than two centuries, and it remains one of the loveliest and most impressive of all the ruined British monasteries. The graceful walls and arches rise from a narrow valley floor, surrounded by a tree-covered land-

Hubert de Burgh's Skenfrith, raised largely between 1219 and 1232.

Tintern Abbey, founded in 1131 and set amid the wooded slopes of the Wye valley.

scape of wild natural beauty. Seen against the reds and golds of a dying autumn foliage, Tintern is truly breathtaking, and justly world famous. Moreover the Wye valley itself, with its 'steep and lofty cliffs', has become immortalized through Wordsworth's *Lines Composed a Few Miles above Tintern Abbey.*

This was a Cistercian abbey founded in 1131 by Walter fitz Richard de Clare, the Norman lord of Chepstow. Walter drew the first colony of monks from the Norman house of L'Aumone in the diocese of Chartres. The fledgling community was only the second of the order to be established in Britain, but Tintern's remote setting 'far from the habitations of men' was to become typical of the 'white monks' – a name derived from their habits of undyed wool.

A Cistercian lay brother at work reaping corn, from an early twelfth-century manuscript.

129

The Cistercians placed great emphasis upon manual labour, as well as the spiritual life, cultivating their own lands with the help of a special class of monks, the *conversi* or lay brothers. Tintern soon built up extensive estates on both sides of the River Wye, and these were organized into compact farms, known as granges. In 1270 Roger Bigod III became the new lord of Chepstow and was a generous patron of the abbey. Eventually hailed as the 'second founder', he gave the monks the valuable Norfolk manor of Acle. In fact, by the end of the thirteenth century the monks were working well over 3,000 acres of arable land in the present counties of Gwent and Gloucestershire alone. Their ships were trading with Bristol, and up the river to Monmouth, they also had important fishing rights on the Wye, the Usk and the Severn.

The original stone church may have been completed by 1150 and was a simple Romanesque construction, no doubt with very plain and austere furnishings to suit the early ideals of the Cistercian order. The initial monastic buildings, arranged around a cloister to the north of the church, were also relatively small. For a community growing in both size and status, these twelfth-century constructions soon proved rather too small. They were gradually replaced in frequent rounds of rebuilding in the years after 1200; so much so, that it appears few monks could have spent their entire lives at Tintern free of avoiding masons' scaffolding in one or other part of the abbey complex.

The centre of daily life was of course the great abbey church, rebuilt in the late thirteenth century under the patronage of Roger Bigod III, and still gloriously intact. Gone now were the Cistercian standards of austerity, in a building which was richly carved and decorated with painted glass and patterned floor tiles. It dwarfed the earlier Romanesque edifice, whose foundations can be seen marked out in the turf. Few visitors entering by the superb west front will fail to appreciate why in 1801 Archdeacon William Coxe was filled with delight in 'an

The crossing and nave of the great abbey church at Tintern, built between 1269 and 1301.

instantaneous burst of admiration'. The clustered columns of the aisle arcades support bold arches, between which delicate triple shafts rise to the 'springers' which once took the weight of the stone vault. Along the full length of the church, the stubs of stone screen walls between the columns show that it was originally divided up to suit the ritual arrangements of the monks.

The nave was occupied by the lay brothers, who entered the church to attend services via a doorway in the north-west corner. Moving eastwards, beyond a now lost stone screen known as the *pulpitum*, lay the monks' choir and presbytery. Their choir stalls stood in the crossing under the central tower, and it was here that the brothers gathered for the seven major services of the day. The high altar stood on a raised plinth below the huge east window. This window has sadly now lost its stone tracery, but we know when the church was completed it was filled with painted glass, some bearing the arms of Roger Bigod. The steps in the north transept mark the position where the monks came down from their dormitory to attend services at night.

We should also remember that, by the end of the Middle Ages, many of the more important benefactors would have been buried throughout the abbey church. The founder himself was laid to rest in the first church, as were several members of the powerful Marshall family, lords of Chepstow, in the first half of the thirteenth century. In the fifteenth century, William Herbert of Raglan was buried at Tintern, and in turn he was followed by his son. The tombs and memorials doubtless matched those of many a cathedral.

The cloister was, as stated, on the north side of the church; an unusual arrangement perhaps necessitated by the need for an adequate water supply and drainage. Covered passageways ran around the four sides of this open court, linking the monastic buildings which were arranged in a distinct Cistercian plan. The remains of the chapter house can be seen in the east range. The monks met here each day to hear a chapter of their *Rule* (hence the name 'chapter house'), to correct faults, and to transact various business. North of this lies the large novices' lodging, and the entire first floor of the east range was occupied by the monks' dormitory. In the northern range of the cloister the warming

The full extent of Tintern seen from the air.

house survives particularly well, the only place in the abbey – apart from the kitchens – where a fire was allowed. The Cistercians also used this room for periodic blood letting, for health reasons! Nearby, the dining hall retains evidence of a pulpit where one of the brothers read during meals. In early centuries the monks would have eaten eggs, fish, fruit or potage, but not meat.

The lay brothers were accommodated in the west range, with their dining hall on the ground floor and their dormitory above. On this side too was the outer parlour where the monks could meet and converse with tradesmen and other visitors. Elsewhere in the complex, to the north and west of the main cloister, there are the remains of the infirmary and the abbot's private apartments. The infirmary housed both the sick and elderly brethren, whereas the scale of the fourteenth-century abbot's hall speaks more of a wealthy landed magnate than a man of God.

Indeed, in the later Middle Ages many of the initial ideals of the order were abandoned. Lands were leased out for hard cash, and we cannot escape the view that the entire spiritual

'White' monks seen in their choir stalls, from a fifteenth-century manuscript.

and economic sides of abbey life were very different from those of the twelfth century. Tintern was finally dissolved in 1536, at which time it was the richest abbey in Wales. Abbot Richard Wyche and 12 monks surrendered the house to Henry VIII's visitors, and thus ended a way of life that had endured for 400 years. The silver and plate were sent to the king's treasury; the roofs were stripped of lead; the windows smashed, and soon the shell of the buildings fell into decay.

Today, there is a specially designed exhibition at the site, telling more of the Cistercians, the monastic life at Tintern, and of its resurrection when first 'rediscovered' by tourists in the late eighteenth century. Tintern's beauty remains timeless. Standing amid the peaceful ruins, one can perhaps still sense the spirit which greeted that very first community of monks over 850 years ago.

White Castle

The earliest Norman castle here was known as Llantilio, after the manor in which it lay. It is not until the thirteenth century that documents refer to 'White Castle' – a name which can only be derived from the plaster rendering which once covered its walls and towers, traces of which can still be seen. Together with Grosmont and Skenfrith, the 'Three Castles' formed an important strategic triangle controlling this area of the southern March, and at times they provided a significant foothold for the expansion of Crown authority in Wales. Today it is a tranquil setting, and the wall tops offer fine views of the surrounding countryside.

The extensive earthwork defences at the site go back, in part at least, to the initial Norman stronghold. In the later twelfth century the 'Three Castles' were in royal hands, and expenditure accounts of 1184–86 reveal that Henry II spent £128 16s. at Llantilio. The work was directed by Ralph of Grosmont, and is represented by the curtain wall which now surrounds the inner ward. A small square keep, whose foundations still survive, was linked to this curtain, but its construction may have begun a little earlier in the century. As completed, the entrance to this castle was probably adjacent to the keep. It was at this stage of development that, in 1201, White Castle was granted to Hubert de Burgh. At the sister castles of Skenfrith and Grosmont, de Burgh spent large sums on bringing the sites right up to date, employing some of the most advanced military characteristics of the period. Here at White Castle, however, he appears to have been content to accept the garrison outpost as he found it.

On Earl Hubert's final fall from power in 1239 the 'Three Castles' reverted to the Crown, becoming an important base in Henry III's efforts against the expansionist policies of the princes of Gwynedd. In 1254 the king granted them to his eldest son, the Lord Edward – later King Edward I. In 1267 they passed to his younger brother, Edmund 'Crouchback', earl of Lancaster. At this time, the threatening power of Llywelyn ap Gruffudd was at its height, and White Castle stood dangerously near the frontier of his conquests. Consequent-

The garrison fortress of White Castle – one of the 'Three Castles' of Gwent.

ly, under the Lord Edward or his brother – probably between 1263–77 – Henry II's simple curtain at White Castle was completely transformed into a powerful front-line fortress, giving the site the appearance much as we see it today. The remodelling involved turning the inner ward back to front, with a new gatehouse on the northern side and the addition of four projecting towers around the curtain wall.

The visitor enters the outer ward through an outer gatehouse, where the groove for the portcullis can still be seen. The wall which surrounds the ward is covered by one rectangular and three rounded towers. This great open space was doubtless used as a defended camp and base for the royal army. Today, a modern bridge spans the deeply-sunk water filled moat to the inner ward. The twin towers of the inner gatehouse loom ahead, originally defended by a drawbridge, a portcullis and gates at the inner and outer ends. All six towers were equipped with cruciform arrowslits, covering the moat and adjacent stretches of wall. Within the ward are the slight remains of a small hall and various domestic buildings which were probably half-timbered. The second storey of the tower in the south-east corner served as the castle chapel.

The course of its history, together with the character of the buildings, gives the distinct impression that White Castle never really functioned as a nobleman's residence. Unlike its fellows at Grosmont and Skenfrith, it remained distinctly military, perhaps more familiar to a garrison commander than a noble lord.

King Henry II and his queen, from a stained glass window at Poitiers Cathedral.

133

GWYNEDD
Snowdonia and the Mountain Fastness

The mountain peaks, lakes and forests of Snowdonia undoubtedly present the most dramatic and spectacular scenery in the whole of the principality. Snowdon itself, Eryi – 'the haunt of the Eagles' – in Welsh, rises 3,560 feet above the Llanberis Pass and is the highest mountain in England and Wales. This region has always been a natural stronghold and remains at the very heart of the country. Until the Welsh wars of King Edward I in 1276–77 and 1282–83, its early medieval independence was maintained with great tenacity by a series of gifted native princes. King Edward's conquests divided the area into the shire counties of Anglesey, Caernarfon and Merioneth, but since 1974 these have once more been united in the new county of Gwynedd – itself with a legacy firmly rooted in the ancient past.

In fact, Gwynedd was one of the kingdoms which emerged in the fifth and sixth centuries out of the wreckage of the Roman province of *Britannia*. Gradually the strength and influence of its dynasty expanded, and on occasions its rulers exercised overlordship of the greater part of Wales. Notably this occurred under Rhodri Mawr (844–78) and the brilliant Gruffudd ap Llywelyn (1039–63). Gruffudd in particular not only imposed unity upon much of Wales, but also extended its bounds and stemmed the tide of English advance on the eastern borders.

Following the Norman conquest, the power of the Gwynedd dynasty was eclipsed until the rise of Owain Gwynedd (1137–70). His reign marks the start of what has been called the golden age of Welsh independence. He recovered the north-east of the country from the Normans, pushing the frontier of his principality to its natural borders, stretching between the Dyfi and the Dee estuaries. Owain was praised by the poets as 'the destroyer of our bondage'. Indeed, his statecraft laid the foundations for the success in the following century of Gwynedd's two greatest princes: Llywelyn ab Iorwerth – 'the Great' (1173–1240), and his grandson Llywelyn ap Gruffudd – 'the Last' (d. 1282). The course of political development and the progress of thirteenth-century castle-building can be charted mainly by reference to their dazzling achievements.

Under the Treaty of Montgomery (1267), King Henry III was forced to acknowledge Llywelyn the Last's proud title as prince of Wales. In the event, it was a temporary taste of power lasting only a decade. The final demise of Welsh independence began late in 1276 when King Henry's son, Edward I, announced that he would go against the recalcitrant prince as a rebel and disturber of the peace. It was war; Edward conducted two campaigns against Prince Llywelyn. The first was in 1276–77, and the second followed a co-ordinated Welsh revolt in 1282–83. Llywelyn was killed near Builth Wells in December 1282, and with him died all hopes of an independent state. The breathtaking strongholds at Caernarfon, Conwy and Harlech bear witness to the king's determination to finally break the spirit of the Welsh.

Today, as well as the enormous Edwardian fortresses, Cadw maintains three important Gwynedd castles originally raised by the native princes – Criccieth, Dolbadarn and Dolwyddelan. Nor are the sites described here restricted merely to the Middle Ages. There are two intriguing Neolithic chambered tombs, the Roman fort at *Segontium*, and the charming post-medieval chapel at Gwydir Uchaf.

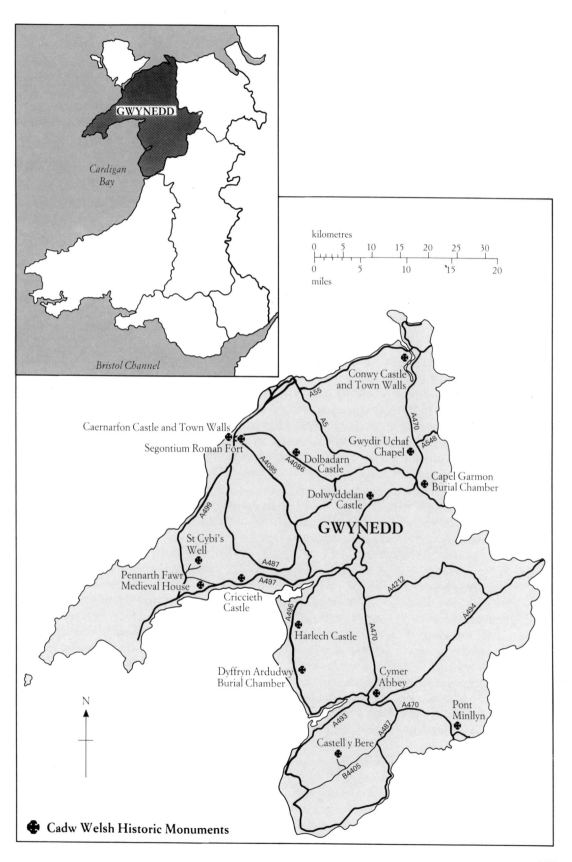

GWYNEDD

Cardigan
Bay

Bristol Channel

kilometres
0   5   10   15   20   25   30
0   5   10   15   20
miles

Conwy Castle
and Town Walls

Caernarfon Castle and Town Walls
Segontium Roman Fort

Gwydir Uchaf
Chapel

Dolbadarn
Castle

Capel Garmon
Burial Chamber

Dolwyddelan
Castle

GWYNEDD

St Cybi's
Well

Pennarth Fawr
Medieval House

Criccieth
Castle

Harlech Castle

N

Dyffryn Ardudwy
Burial Chamber

Cymer
Abbey

Pont
Minllyn

Castell y Bere

✠ **Cadw Welsh Historic Monuments**

Caernarfon Castle and Town Walls

For any visitor who has travelled to see the great castles of King Edward I in north Wales, Caernarfon immediately stands out from the remainder of the group. Quite apart from its enormous size, the outward appearance of Caernarfon's angular walls and towers is quite unique. At Conwy and Harlech, Flint and Rhuddlan, or even at the somewhat later Beaumaris, the curtain walls are punctuated by stout circular drum towers, giving them all a distinct family resemblance. Caernarfon, however, is plainly a building bearing an aspect of nobility all of its own. Edward's castles, of course, were all to serve roles beyond that of military subjugation. They were to be more, acting for instance as seats of civilian governance and as the headquarters of a new administrative, financial, and judicial dispensation. But at Caernarfon the king encouraged his architect, Master James of St George, to create a fortress of some special purpose, a structure of immense symbolic significance, with all the appearance of a regal palace.

Indeed, Edward seems to have gone to considerable lengths to give substance to the tradition linking Caernarfon with imperial Rome. He must have been well aware that the Roman fort of *Segontium*, lying just above the modern town, was inseparably associated in legend with Magnus Maximus, the usurper emperor. In fact, in 1283 what was believed to be the body of Maximus, or his alleged son the 'noble emperor Constantine', was found at Caernarfon and was reburied in the church on the king's orders. The same Maximus appears as the Macsen Wledig of the *Mabinogion*, and it is *Segontium* which provides the background to his dream of journeying from Rome into a land of high mountains facing an island. There he saw a great defended city at the mouth of a river, with a fort strengthened by great towers of many colours; and in its hall a chair of ivory with two eagles fashioned out of gold thereon.

So it was that at Caernarfon the walls and polygonal towers were given a prominent patterning with bands of different coloured stone. It is difficult to escape the conclusion that Edward I was drawing upon symbolism, and that for inspiration he almost certainly turned to the famous city of Constantinople. There, in the eastern successor to Rome and one of the wonders of the ancient world, stood the massive fifth-century Theodosian walls, which the king and his advisers would undoubtedly have attributed to the Emperor Constantine the Great (AD 306–37). With their alternating coloured bands of tile and masonry, these celebrated walls bear a striking resemblance to the southern facade at Caernarfon.

In all, even before the birth within its precincts of the first English prince of Wales – Edward of Caernarfon – King Edward must surely have planned that this castle would serve a special purpose. It was to be a fitting building for his representative in the principality, a major official residence, and the principal seat of government for the newly-formed shire counties of north Wales. Everywhere strength and majesty are evident in the walls and turrets. Even in decay, when visited by John Taylor in the middle of the seventeenth century, he commented that 'if it be well manned, victualled, and ammunitioned, it is invincible'.

Construction began in June 1283, soon after the final defeat and death of Llywelyn ap Gruffudd, prince of Wales. Over the next decade a sum totalling approximately £12,000 was spent on the castle, town walls and related works. This was a huge figure, totalling many millions at today's values, but was by no means disproportionate to the achievement. The town walls had been completed, and the whole of the southern and eastern faces of the castle stood to a good height. At this stage, however, in October 1284 the Welsh rose in general revolt under Madog ap Llywelyn. The revolt took Edward I completely by surprise, as well as the garrisons of the new royal castles in north Wales. Caernarfon was captured and sacked, and very heavy damage was inflicted on the town walls. When order was restored in the following year, a further massive programme of works was initiated, and another £4,500 had been spent at Caernarfon by 1301. In fact, it was the rebuilding at Caernarfon and the brand new castle at Beaumaris which contributed to the financial crisis which overwhelmed the king in the late 1290s. During the early 1300s the work progressed steadily, and under King

An aerial view of King Edward I's castle at Caernarfon.

Edward II the programme of finishing and fitting out continued. By 1330 the total outlay must have been in the region of between £20,000 and £25,000.

As at Conwy, Master James planned a single curtain wall, albeit an immensely powerful one. To compensate for the lack of outer defences, the wall is honeycombed by continuous wall-passages at two separate levels. These are all particularly well equipped with arrowloops and, on the town side, there are lethal multiple embrasures which would have allowed cross-bow men to spread their firepower to awesome effect. The circuit is broken by no fewer than nine polygonal towers and two vast gatehouses, though neither of the two gates was ever fully completed. Nevertheless, the visitor who looks carefully at the arrangements of the King's Gate will be left in no doubt as to why it has been described as the mightiest in the land. Built after the uprising of 1294–95, it seems almost an over-reaction, the product of a designer deter-mined that a similar catastrophe should never be

The King's Gate, Caernarfon.

137

allowed to happen again. An attacker would have needed to cross a drawbridge, spanning a ditch the full width of the modern road, then to pass through no fewer than five hefty wooden doors and six portcullises, negotiating a right-angled turn before entering the lower ward over a second drawbridge! The Queen's Gate lay outside the circumference of the town walls, and was approached by a great stone-built ramp. The high level of the gate-passage is explained by the fact that this end of the castle – the upper ward – was raised around the substantial mound of an earlier motte and bailey castle, thrown up around 1090 by Earl Hugh of Chester during the initial Norman advance into north Wales.

Inside, the plan of Caernarfon is somewhat unusual, being shaped rather like an hour glass, originally divided into two wards by a cross wall at the narrowest point. Much of the upper ward was, as outlined, occupied by the Norman motte. This could be seen until the nineteenth century, though it has been levelled more recently. Its presence accounts for the difference in height between the two wards. The lower ward was originally lined with timber-framed buildings, and the foundations of these can still be seen. To the south was the great hall, with the kitchens on the opposite side of the courtyard. But it is the provision of private accommodation in the towers which demands our greatest attention.

Most impressive of all is the Eagle Tower, crowned by its triple cluster of turrets. From the outset, this was probably intended as the residential quarters of Sir Otto de Grandison (d. 1328), one of the king's most loyal friends, and of whom he said 'there was no one about him who could do his will better'. Sir Otto was appointed the first justiciar of north Wales, a post equivalent to that of a viceroy and carrying an annual income of £1,000. Everything about the tower is on a regal scale, each of the turrets once bearing a stone eagle as further symbolic evidence of links with imperial power. The basement of the tower served as an ante-chamber, through which anyone coming to Caernarfon by water would enter the castle. Above this are three floors, each with a large central chamber, and there are further rooms – including small chapels – within the thickness of the walls. In addition to the accommodation

Accounts of payments to building workers who were finishing and fitting out the castle.

here, the Queen's Tower is almost as spacious, and there must have been many more private suites in the Chamberlain, Black, North-East and Granary Towers.

It was on 25 April 1284 that Queen Eleanor gave birth to a son within temporary wooden apartments in the lower ward of the rising castle. Not until 1301, however, was Edward of Caernarfon – so named after his birthplace – formally created prince of Wales. Henceforward Caernarfon Castle was undoubtedly seen as the capital of a new dominion, and the palace of a new dynasty of princes. With this in mind, the majestic architecture, together with the extent and scale of rooms, falls into perspective. It had to be capable, when occasion required, of accommodating the household of the king's eldest son, with his council, his family, his guests and all who attended them. Ironically, this high role was seldom if ever fulfilled for the castle. As an adult, Prince Edward – later King Edward II – never returned to its walls, though a statue of him was erected above the King's Gate in 1321.

By the mid fourteenth century, Caernarfon had become little more than a depot for the armament and building maintenance of the other north Wales castles. Even so, it continued to be maintained and garrisoned, and successfully withstood sieges by Owain Glyndŵr in 1403 and 1404. During the Civil War, it was finally surrendered to Parliamentary forces in 1646.

The massive interior of the castle is divided into upper and lower wards.

Centuries of neglect were halted by extensive repairs and restoration undertaken in the late nineteenth century, under the direction of the deputy constable, Sir Llewelyn Turner. In the early years of this century, David Lloyd George was able to suggest that the young Prince Edward be invested as prince of Wales at Caernarfon. The ceremony took place in 1911, and since then the castle has become an almost obligatory venue for royal tours in Wales. It was, of course, again the venue for the Investiture of Prince Charles in July 1969, when Her Majesty the Queen conferred the title and status of Royal Borough upon Caernarfon.

Visitors to Caernarfon should not overlook the remains of the town walls, the circuit of which survives unbroken. Built at the same time as the castle to protect the English inhabitants of an infant borough established by King Edward, the walls extend for a distance of about 800 yards, and include eight towers and two twin-towered gateways. In places the wall stands to the full height of its battlements, and the towers are also well preserved. On the eastern side, the rooms above the main east gateway served from the first to accommodate the Exchequer, the administrative and financial centre of the new counties of Caernarfon, Anglesey and Merioneth. The long stretch of wall facing the Menai Strait stood next to the quay. Crucial to the commerce of the new borough, the quay was originally constructed of wood, but it was burnt in the uprising of 1294–95, and was rebuilt in stone in the early fourteenth century.

Few castles can claim such a rich heritage as Caernarfon, and today a visit is made yet more interesting by a number of exhibitions and displays situated throughout the towers. The Eagle Tower houses both an exhibition and an audio-visual presentation. All three floors in the Queen's Tower are occupied by the Regimental Museum of the Royal Welsh Fusiliers, and there are further exhibitions in the Chamberlain and North-East Towers.

A section of the town walls at Caernarfon, built in the same period as the castle.

Capel Garmon Burial Chamber

The walk to this comparatively humble monument is a joy in itself. In spring and early summer, the visitor's path winds through flocks of young lambs, along the farm track, through several fields, all of which is enhanced by superb views over the upper Conwy valley. The tomb is of considerable interest, and is a far-flung member of the family archaeologists call 'Severn-Cotswold', named after the area where they chiefly occur.

Capel Garmon was first cleared in 1853, and was further excavated in 1924. It has been laid out to show the principal elements of the plan. The tomb was enclosed in a wedge-shaped cairn, some 94 feet long, with 'horns' extending either side of a false 'portal' or entrance at the east end. This cairn was surrounded by a neat revetment wall, whose position is now marked by a line of small stones. The true entrance was on the south side of the tomb, from which a passage, 16 feet long, led to a rectangular area, with two roughly circular chambers opening to the east and west. The westernmost chamber, which provides access today, still preserves its capstone.

The form of the tomb, particularly the false entrance and the side passage leading to the chambers, is very similar to long cairns in the Black Mountains of Breconshire. We can only speculate on why this should be the case, but it has been suggested that the spread of architectural ideas may have been associated with the Neolithic trade in polished stone axes from Penmaenmawr, further to the north, and accessible via the Conwy valley. Capel Garmon may thus have been constructed sometime before 3000 BC.

The chambered tomb at Capel Garmon.

Castell y Bere

An entry in the Welsh Chronicle of the Princes, the *Brut y Tywysogyon*, records that in 1221 Llywelyn ab Iorwerth took the territories of Meirionnydd and Ardudwy from his son, Gruffudd, and 'he began to build a castle there for himself'. This is generally taken to refer to Castell y Bere, but is the only documentary reference to the site until its conquest by the forces of Edward I in 1283.

In the early years of the thirteenth century, Llywelyn had relentlessly built up his power base in Gwynedd, and by 1218 the English government was driven to acknowledge his overall supremacy. He had become *de facto* prince of native Wales. He was not about to let the actions of an impetuous youth undermine this achievement, and expelling Gruffudd from his lands in 1221 was a cautionary, but necessary, discipline. In addition, this was perhaps just the incentive for Llywelyn to begin work on an ambitious new castle. It would guard the vulnerable southern flank of the principality, and would again proclaim his overall strength and authority.

Today, the ruins of Castell y Bere are a little off the beaten track, deep in the mountainous

Castell y Bere, begun in 1221 by Prince Llyweln ab Iorwerth of Gwynedd.

heart of mid Wales, but a visit is well rewarded. Situated on an isolated rock outcrop commanding the upper Dysynni valley, the site is in turn overshadowed by the sombre Cader Idris range to the north-east. It is soon clear that the plan of the castle was tailored to fit the uneven rocky spur on which it was placed. The entrance was heavily defended by a formidable arrangement of two gates, deep rock-cut ditches and draw-bridges, flanked by two towers – one of which was round. At either end of the ridge, D-shaped towers were placed to guard the northern and southern approaches. Such towers are typical of Welsh castles, and a fine example is to be seen at Ewloe in Clwyd. Here at Castell y Bere, the southern tower originally stood alone, cut off from the remainder of the castle by a rock-cut ditch. It probably contained private apartments, and could have held out as a last resort if the courtyard had fallen in time of siege. Finds of highly-decorated stone sculpture in the north tower reveal rooms of some quality, with

suggestions of a chapel on the first floor. The workmanship bespeaks of English inspiration, and bears eloquent testimony to Llywelyn's cultural ambitions and grandeur. The powerful rectangular tower on the summit of the ridge appears to have served as the central strongpoint or keep.

After a siege of ten days, Castell y Bere fell to the forces of King Edward I on 25 April 1283. Following the departure of the army five masons and five carpenters remained to carry out various works, though we cannot be sure what was done. If anything, it seems likely that the walls joining the keep to the southern tower were added at this time. The castle was subsequently besieged in the Welsh uprising of 1294, when it was quite possibly burnt. This was almost certainly the end of its military history, and in the late sixteenth century it was described as 'destroyed and cast to the ground'. It remains a tranquil and atmospheric site, with superb views in all directions.

Conwy Castle and Town Walls

Conwy Castle was raised in a frenzied period of building activity, over a few summer seasons between 1283 and 1287. It remains one of the most outstanding achievements of medieval military construction, and is universally regarded as one of the great fortresses of Europe. For many it is the most attractive of all King Edward I's castles in north Wales. Its eight handsome towers seem to spring from the very rock which dictated the castle's eventual layout. Seen from across the river estuary, first impressions are of enormous strength, an overwhelmingly dominant position, and a remarkable unity and compactness in design. As with Edward's other Welsh masterpieces, the planning and building operations were in the hands of the brilliant James of St George, Master of the King's Works in Wales. At Conwy, however, he somehow created a building which, perhaps more than any other, demonstrates his genius for understanding both the practical and the symbolic, or propagandist, roles of great military architecture.

It was in March 1283 that King Edward gained control of the Conwy valley, during his second and final campaign against the Welsh prince, Llywelyn ap Gruffudd. Work began almost immediately on a fortress to secure the estuary crossing. The natural advantages of the site were judged to be far superior to those of the older castle at Deganwy on the opposite side of the river. Such was the ruthlessness and the determination in the king's plan that, in order to accommodate his adjacent fortified town, he removed the Cistercian abbey of Aberconwy to a new site some miles higher up the river valley. Indeed, as the burial place of Llywelyn the Great, the removal of Aberconwy Abbey would also suit Edward's purpose in further eclipsing the native dynasty of princes. The abbey buildings were quickly pressed into service as stopgap accommodation for financial and administrative officials. In June, 20 men were busy clearing a site to put up the king's tents and pavilions 'beside the abbey'. When, towards the end of the month, the queen's temporary chamber was nearly ready, a lawn was made beside it. Turf was brought specially from up river, and the lawn was fenced with staves from an empty barrel. On a warm July evening, one of her squires was paid 3d. for attending to its first watering.

These tasks were, of course, far and away subordinate to the main priority of raising not only an entirely new castle, but also a complete walled town. Both castle and town walls were built at break-neck speed, and in just two years some £6,000 was spent on the works. During the summer of 1285 the construction was at its height, with the labour force comprising something like 1,500 craftsmen and general labourers. By the autumn of 1287 the magnificent fortress, together with the superb circuit of town walls and towers, stood substantially complete. The total cost cannot have been far short of a staggering £15,000.

Unlike most of King Edward's other new castles in Wales, Conwy was not built to a 'concentric' plan. The nature of the rock outcrop dictated a linear outline, with a lower barbican outwork at each end. The interior was sharply divided by a cross wall into two quite separate wards, so that either could hold out independently if the other should fall. When completed, the walls and towers would have been covered with a white plaster rendering, traces of which can still be seen clinging to the outer faces. Together with royal shields of arms, and the decoratively pinnacled battlements, the complete effect must have been quite awe-inspiring. Another feature to note in the masonry of the castle and town walls, particularly in the towers, is the lines of small holes set on a slant. These are 'putlog holes', used to support inclined or spiral scaffolds, a common feature in Edward's Welsh castles.

The original entrance to the outer ward was by way of a huge stepped ramp, leading up from the present roadway, to the west barbican, which was defended by a drawbridge and portcullis. Next, an attacker would have had to negotiate a right-angled turn to pass through the heavily barred main gate. All the while, defenders could release their missiles from the walls above. Inside the outer ward, visitors will soon be aware that during the Middle Ages it would have been cramped for space. On the northern side are the foundations of kitchens and stables. Opposite is the impressive Great Hall, built to

Conwy Castle – a masterpiece of medieval military architecture.

an unusual bowed plan to adapt to the rocky foundation, and stretching some 125 feet in length. Below part of the floor level there was a long narrow cellar, reached by steps leading down from the courtyard. With its fine windows and no doubt bright decoration, the hall must have appeared a glorious sight during great feasts. Originally, the roof was supported by wooden trusses, but a survey undertaken for Edward the Black Prince in 1343 shows that the entire roof was rotten for want of lead. The hall was repaired in 1346–47 when stone arches were installed. The four towers of the ward would have provided some accommodation for the garrison, and in the base of the Prison Tower there is a gloomy dungeon.

At the far end of the outer ward is the castle well, 91 feet deep, and beyond this another drawbridge protected a small gatehouse into the heart of the castle. At this point, too, even the wall-walks above could be shut off from the rest. For within the inner ward lay the private quarters of the king and queen. They included a hall and a sumptuous presence-chamber, though only the shells of the once lavish windows remain to give us some indication of their former splendour. As further evidence for the symbolic significance of the inner ward, the tops of the towers are crowned with turrets,

where the royals standards would have billowed when Edward and Queen Eleanor were in residence. It was in the presence-chamber that councils were held and distinguished visitors received an audience. The room has three windows looking out over the east barbican and the river. A beautiful little chapel royal gives one tower its name. It is situated on the first floor, with the main circle of the room forming the nave, the chancel being contrived within the thickness of the eastern wall. The first and second floors of the King's Tower were probably royal bedchambers. Each has a fine hooded fireplace and a large window.

The east barbican gave added security to the royal apartments, and it also had its own access to the river, via a small water gate in the gap beside the Chapel Tower. The stepped ramp which curved around the rock down to the water below has long since vanished. The barbican itself seems always to have been planted as a garden, probably at the request of Queen Eleanor, who was clearly keen to add such touches to a number of sites. She also had gardens at Caernarfon and Rhuddlan.

As well as establishing his great fortresses, King Edward I used the planted town as the prime instrument for introducing an English civilian presence in the newly-conquered pro-

The outer ward at Conwy.

vince. At Conwy, as at Caernarfon or Denbigh, the walls were integrated with those of the castle itself. The constable of the castle was also the mayor of the newly-born borough. The burgesses, or townsmen, were obliged to defend the walls of the town and to provide the castle garrison with supplies. Here at Conwy the surviving town walls represent one of the finest and most complete sets in Europe. It is still possible to walk much of their length, and they reveal a great deal of interest. The circuit extends for around 1,400 yards, with 21 towers and three double-towered gateways spaced at every 50 yards or so. The tops of the walls and towers were surmounted by battlements pierced

The chancel of the delightful chapel in the Chapel Tower at Conwy.

by arrowloops with perfect regularity. All in all, a rough calculation reveals there must have been something like 480 loopholes.

The most imposing stretch of wall is the uphill section between the quay and the tower at the highest point of the town. From this tower there are superb views back towards the castle. Nearby is the Upper Gate, which, as the only landward entry into medieval Conwy, was accordingly elaborately defended. These defences included a barbican, with a portcullis and heavy two-leaved wooden doors shutting off the gate-passage. The South, or Mill, Gate once led down to the Gyffin stream and the king's water mill. Adjacent to this gate, there is a neat row of 12 latrines projecting out from the wall face. Nowhere else, apart from the latrines at some of the great monastic houses, is there left to us such an extensive and remarkable example of a multiple medieval sanitary arrangement. The latrines were constructed in 1286 at a cost of £15, and probably served two groups of staff whose offices lay just inside the walls at this point: those of the Wardrobe department, and those under the master of the works.

During the revolt of Madog ap Llywelyn, King Edward was actually besieged at Conwy. Though food supplies ran low, the walls stood firm. In fact, the greatest battle the castle ever had to face was the one against decay. By 1627 the whole building was apparently in decline and dangerous to enter. During the Civil War, John Williams, archbishop of York, spent large sums on restoring and fortifying Conwy for the king. Having backed the losing side, and receiving no thanks, he threw in his lot

The castle and town walls at Conwy about 1770, by Paul Sandby (1725–1809).

with Parliament. The town was taken in August 1646, though the castle held out for a further three months. Following the war it was rendered untenable.

A handsome new visitors' centre has recently been opened at Conwy, and now forms the entrance to the castle, with a bridge across to the west barbican. It houses a comprehensive exhibition covering the castles of King Edward I. In the Chapel Tower there is a fascinating model of the castle and town at the end of the thirteenth century.

Criccieth Castle

Initially raised by Welsh princes, and modified by English kings, Criccieth is an intriguing castle which continues to be the subject of a lively debate. The surviving remains are fragmentary, but clearly demonstrate several main constructional phases. Since none of these is directly recorded, the controversy centres upon just who was responsible for what, and when. Visitors to this attractive seaside location, how-

ever, are bound to be struck first by the impressive siting of the fortress. It stands in a commanding position, high above the town, on a rocky promontory overlooking the waves of Tremadog Bay. From the castle itself, on a fine day, the views are superb: westwards out to the tip of the Lleyn peninsula, north-eastwards towards the rugged heart of Snowdonia, and across the bay lies the unmistakable profile of the mighty stronghold at Harlech.

The earliest mention of Criccieth Castle comes from the Welsh Chronicle of the Princes – the *Brut y Tywysogyon* – where it is recorded that in 1239 Dafydd ap Llywelyn imprisoned his unruly half-brother, Gruffudd, within its walls. It was their father, Prince Llywelyn the Great, who had begun the construction of the castle just a few years earlier. His contribution was almost certainly the small but powerful inner ward, where the substantial twin-towered gatehouse continues to dominate the site as a whole. In fact, the gate has been at the centre of much recent debate, largely since it has no true parallel among any of Llywelyn's other fortifications. It is undoubtedly one of the most sophisticated works to survive at any Welsh princely castle. None the less, we should not

145

An aerial view of Criccieth, a castle of the Welsh princes modified by Edward I.

underestimate Llywelyn's pre-eminent position in Wales during the 1230s, nor overlook his willingness to learn from advances in castle-building among his Anglo-Norman neighbours in the March. The gatehouse bears a distinct resemblance to one raised by the prince's ally Ralph de Blundeville, earl of Chester, at Beeston in Cheshire during the 1220s. It is also very similar to another built during the same period by his adversary, Hubert de Burgh, on behalf of the young King Henry III at Montgomery. Indeed, there is every reason to suppose that the Criccieth design was influenced by these up to date constructions on the fringes of Llywelyn's great north Wales principality.

Each of the large D-shaped towers of the gatehouse has three outward facing arrowloops, and the square holes below the battlements once held beams to support a timber fighting platform which extended out from the wallface. The entrance passage was protected by a portcullis and doors, and no doubt missiles could be dropped from the floor above. The ground-floor rooms served as guardchambers, with relatively comfortable accommodation on the upper floors. A fine thirteenth-century crucifix, found during excavations in the gatehouse, suggests that one of the upper rooms may have served as a chapel, at least in some phase of the castle's history.

146

It was probably Llywelyn's grandson, Llywelyn ap Gruffudd, who was responsible for the next major phase of building at Criccieth, sometime in the 1260s or early 1270s. He enclosed the remaining area of the hilltop, both to the north and south, with a curtain wall, adding new towers at the northern and south-western corners. In effect, he created an almost 'concentric' castle, surrounding the inner ward with a second outer ring of defences. A new gate, at the southern corner of this outer curtain, now became the principal entrance to the site. Although little remains of the south-western tower, when excavated it was found to contain various fragments of finely-dressed and decorated stone. The tower perhaps consisted of a basement with one of the chief apartments of Llywelyn's castle on the upper floor. It may well have resembled a similar tower built by Llywelyn the Great at Dolwyddelan.

Criccieth fell to the forces of King Edward I during his second war against the recalcitrant Prince Llywelyn, early in 1283. We have no record of the castle's actual capture, though it was certainly in English hands by 14 March. Between 1283 and 1292, the king spent considerable sums – in the region of £500 – refortifying and strengthening the castle to his own advantage. The most recent interpretation of this royal expenditure suggests that it comprised substantial repair and rebuilding, rather than any completely new constructions. The level of the inner gatehouse, for example, was raised, and new floors could have been added to the south-eastern and south-western towers. Moreover, the northern tower – also known as the 'Engine Tower' – was perhaps remodelled to mount either a catapult, or a larger stone-throwing machine, hence the name 'engine'.

Over the winter of 1294–95, during the Welsh rebellion under Madog ap Llywelyn, the coastal location and strengthening of Criccieth proved their worth. The garrison of some 29 men, under Sir William of Leyburn, held out against a siege lasting several months, with victuals coming in by ship from Ireland. The supplies taken in were certainly prodigious, with one shipment including 6,000 herrings, 550 large salt fish, 30 quarters of wheat, 27 quarters of beans, 20 pounds of twine for crossbows, 50 stockings and 45 pairs of shoes.

Money was again spent on the castle in the

Arrowloops in one of the D-shaped towers of the Criccieth gatehouse.

reign of Edward II, and some of this seems to have gone on raising the towers of the inner gate. The result of the work can still be seen in the surviving masonry, where the embrasures of Edward I's gatehouse have been clearly blocked up and the whole structure raised several feet. Later in its history, under Edward the Black Prince, Criccieth had a notable Welsh constable. Sir Hywel ap Gruffudd had distinguished himself on the field of Crécy (1346) with the prince, and was known as 'Sir Howel of the Battle-axe'. As a local man he returned with great honour, and remained constable until his death in 1381.

The castle's end came abruptly in 1404, during the Welsh uprising under Owain Glyndŵr. Deprived of seaborne provisions by a French fleet active in the Irish Sea in support of the rebels, the English garrison could do little but surrender. The castle was sacked and burnt, never again to be used as a fortress. Today, there is an interesting exhibition at the site, telling more of Criccieth within the wider context of castle-building by the native Welsh princes at large.

The Cistercian abbey of Cymer, founded in 1198.

Cymer Abbey

The Cistercian abbey of Cymer was founded under the patronage of Maredudd ap Cynan, lord of Meirionnydd, in 1198, and was colonized by monks from the mother house at Cwmhir, Powys. Its remote but serene and lovely setting, at the head of the Mawddach estuary, is typical of the locations sought by the austere Cistercians. Indeed, it was the position by the confluence ('cymer' in Welsh) of the rivers Mawddach and Wnion which gave rise to the abbey's name. Other initial benefactors included Maredudd's brother Gruffudd, and his nephew Hywel up Gruffudd, as well as Prince Llywelyn ab Iorwerth. None the less, it was destined to be something of a poor house, and certainly suffered during the Welsh wars of King Edward I.

There are few surviving details on the internal history of the abbey, though dairy farming may have been important in its economy, and access to the sea afforded some potential for shipping and fishing. The brothers also kept a stud and reared high-quality horses, rendering two of them yearly to Llywelyn the Great. Surprisingly for a small house, mining and metallurgy were also significant sources of wealth. Cymer was a distinctly Welsh monastery, a fact not least recorded in the few names of its monks which have survived. Moreover, in the decade or so before Edward I's conquest, Llywelyn the Last appears to have enjoyed a close relationship with the abbey. On several occasions he used their grange at Abereiddon as a headquarters, transacting business there.

The remains of the early thirteenth-century abbey buildings reveal that the monks were unable to complete the original scheme. Never more than the merest shadow of the great Cistercian houses upon which its plan was based, the church lacks the usual crossing, transepts and presbytery at the east end, and thus has a simple rectangular rather than a cruciform shape. The east wall, with its surviving lofty lancet windows, was probably meant to be temporary, but in fact no more was ever built beyond. The high altar would have stood below these windows, and there is a *piscina* – a basin for washing the sacred vessels – and a *sedilia* in the south wall close by. The monks worshipped in the nave, and their choir stalls extended back to the sturdy octagonal arcade pillars. The tower at the west end was added in the fourteenth century. It is unusual in Cistercian churches, but probably marks the abandonment of hopes for a central tower.

Little remains of the cloister to the south, though its layout has been preserved. The chapter house entrance can be identified to the east, and the monks' dining hall ran parallel to the church along the southern range. The west range may never have been built in stone. The adjacent farmhouse (the home of the present key keeper) almost certainly incorporates parts of the monastic guest house.

It may well have been the wars of Edward I which eventually curbed the ambitious building programme. The monks, for example, received £80 by way of compensation for war damages, but evidently this was not enough. There were just five monks here in 1388, and Cymer was finally dissolved in 1536/37 at which time its net income was assessed at a little over £51.

Dolbadarn Castle

Dolbadarn is without doubt one of the most magnificently sited castles in Wales. The powerful circular tower continues to preside over Llyn Padarn in a landscape of breath-taking grandeur. From its precipitous location above the lake, this castle of the Welsh princes commanded the entrance to the Llanberis Pass. Although there is no surviving documentary reference to the site before the conquest of Gwynedd by Edward I, it seems certain that the builder was Llywelyn the Great. Learning from his English adversaries, the prince was clearly concerned to control the ancient routeway from Caernarfon to the upper Conwy valley. Moreover, lying in the commote of Arfon, the castle must have eclipsed the older centre of the district as a place of government.

Apart from the round tower, the surviving curtain wall and associated structures are built of unmortared slabs of slate or gritstone. This work probably dates to the early thirteenth century, but it is very difficult to be certain of the precise phasing. At the northern end of the site, a large building with doorways at one end may have served as a hall, and there appear to

Llywelyn the Great's round tower at Dolbadarn, based on examples in the southern March.

Dolwyddelan, a castle of the Welsh princes taken by King Edward I in 1283.

Dolwyddelan Castle

have been towers guarding the western and southern approaches. It is, however, the circular tower which is the dominating feature. Standing almost 50 feet high, in contrast to the rest of the castle, this is a well built and fully developed round keep. Llywelyn had no doubt observed the strength of similar towers built by his rivals in the southern March, such as Hubert de Burgh's Skenfrith or William Marshall's Pembroke. Here at Dolbadarn, in the 1220s or 1230s, he raised a keep in every way a match for those of the Marcher lords. It was entered at first-floor level through a heavily barred doorway protected by a portcullis – an unusual feature in such towers. The basement could only be reached by a trap door, but a small stair in the thickness of the wall climbs up to the second floor. The projecting latrine block is also an unusual feature of the keep.

Dolbadarn is traditionally the place where Owain Goch was imprisoned by his brother Llywelyn the Last for more than twenty years. After Edward I's conquest, the castle lost its importance, and a record of 1284 records the removal of timber from here to the king's new fortress rising at Caernarfon.

Travellers driving through the scenic landlocked pass between Blaenau Ffestiniog and Betws y Coed cannot fail to notice Dolwyddelan; its solitary square tower rises impressively above the roadside, as it has done for more than 600 years. The castle overlooks the Lledr valley, and stands on a ridge which extends from the great mountainous mass of Moel Siabod. There is a tradition that Llywelyn the Great was born in this place in 1173. If this were the case, an earlier castle which stood on a rocky outcrop on the floor of the valley close by seems the more likely location. Here at the later site, the primary structure – the keep – dates to the early thirteenth century, and although no written record survives it seems certain that it was raised by Llywelyn himself.

This stern but functional building remains remarkably intact, though the upper levels and the battlements were restored in the nineteenth century. Originally, it would have consisted of two storeys, entered via a porch or forebuilding at the top of the steps, with a small drawbridge protecting the doorway. Llywelyn's keep would not, however, have stood alone. Various timber buildings were probably scattered in the courtyard below, and these were eventually enclosed by a stone curtain wall. Dolwyddelan remained a significant stronghold of the princes of Gwynedd and served as a centre of the royal court. It is alleged, for example, that Llywelyn the Last kept his treasure here. Without doubt it was a site of major strategic importance – a fact all too apparent to King Edward I.

In his second war with Llywelyn the Last, by 18 January 1283 the king was at Betws y Coed, and on the same day his troops entered Dolwyddelan – perhaps following a secretly negotiated surrender. As Edward's strategy developed, Dolwyddelan was to occupy a key point in controlling the north – south routeway between the castles soon to rise at Conwy and Harlech. Building works and repairs were begun on the very day the site was taken. Documents tell us that the principal addition was a new *camera* or lodging, presumably the now ruined tower on the west side of the courtyard. The defences were also reinforced by a siege engine made at Betws and carried down the pass to be installed at the castle. Another fascinating item within the king's expenditure

reveals that the garrison was hastily equipped with camouflage clothing of white tunics and stockings, suitable for winter warfare in the mountains.

With the wars long over, the castle was probably abandoned in the fourteenth century. It was to see a further lease of life when, in 1488, it was acquired by Maredudd ap Ieuan, a Welshman who had married into a reasonably wealthy family with connections at court. Maredudd seems to have undertaken a substantial remodelling of the keep, raising the height and giving it a third floor. Today, the position of this extra floor is still marked by an offset and windows halfway up the walls.

The keep houses a small exhibition on the castle and its history. A stairway in the thickness of the walls leads up to the roof, where there are superb views of the rugged surrounding landscape.

Dyffryn Ardudwy Burial Chamber

Situated on sloping ground at the southern end of the village of Dyffryn Ardudwy, the site of

The Neolithic chambered tomb at Dyffryn Ardudwy, with origins as early as 3500 BC.

this Neolithic tomb commands extensive views across the northern end of Cardigan Bay. At first, the two distinct megalithic chambers – some 30 feet apart – standing in a cairn of boulders, may seem confusing. In fact, excavations in 1961–62 revealed that the chambers were not of the same date, and that the Dyffryn long cairn is an example of a composite or multi-period monument, similar to Trefignath in Anglesey.

First, perhaps as early as 3500 BC, the smaller western chamber was raised in the form archaeologists now call a 'portal dolmen'. It is of classic proportions, with the front of the tomb defined by three uprights in an H-shaped formation. A capstone covers the chamber, and tips markedly down the slope. At this time, a small oval cairn surrounded the upright slabs. Later, perhaps in a generation or so, the larger eastern chamber was built a little higher up the slope. A wedge-shaped cairn, about 100 feet long, was thrown up to cover this, and extended westwards to envelop the earlier tomb. The contents of the chambers had been considerably disturbed before excavation, but Neolithic pottery was recovered, and it seems the original burials were inhumations.

The extension of the grave cannot simply reflect architectural embellishment, but must have been prompted by the need for additional burial space. Dyffryn Ardudwy is, therefore, a good example of the way these Neolithic tombs served to demonstrate the ties of a particular group of people to a piece of land. By building a vast monument, in a prominent position, generation after generation could trace a direct link with the past, and to the territorial rights over a specific area.

Gwydir Uchaf Chapel

This lovely little structure, sometimes confused with the Gwydir chapel attached to Llanrwst

Gwydir Uchaf Chapel, near Llanrwst, built by Sir Richard Wynn in 1673. It is particularly notable for its fine painted ceiling.

The interior fittings at Gwydir Uchaf are well preserved, and include a gallery for singers.

parish church, was built in 1673 by Sir Richard Wynn as the private place of worship for Gwydir Uchaf House. The warm yellow sandstone of the walls, and the original thick slate roof, give the exterior a distinctly Gothic appearance. Inside, however, the mood is far more Classical. Like the somewhat earlier building at Rûg, near Corwen, this is another charming example of a seventeenth-century chapel which still retains many of its original fittings.

The interior walls are plastered above a panelled dado. At the west end a massive beam supports a gallery, probably intended for a small band – with singers – which provided the music. The enclosed pews are again original, though they may have been rearranged. On the south wall there is a large painted panel bearing the arms of King Charles II.

The chapel is especially notable for its contemporary painted ceiling, a design inspired by high Anglican or Roman Catholic liturgical tradition. The colours are simple: a blue background, angels dressed in red or white, with gilt wings, and lettering in black or gilt. All of the figures are two-dimensional, with no attempt to introduce perspective. The principal theme appears to be the Holy Trinity. At the eastern end, Christ is represented by the sacred monogram IHS. In the next bay is the seated figure of God the Father, and beyond the Holy Ghost is portrayed as a dove. Above the gallery, two trumpeting angels announce the Day of Judgement. At the base of each roof truss, emphasizing the blend of Gothic and Renaissance styles, there is a flat cut-out angel. This is typically medieval, with each angel holding between outstretched hands a scroll bearing Latin invocations or prayers. Altogether, the ceiling at Gwydir Uchaf is undoubtedly one of the most remarkable examples of this class of seventeenth-century art in Britain.

Harlech Castle, seen from the well-trodden bluff of rock to the south of the town.

Harlech Castle

In the late spring of 1283 the Cistercian monks of Cymer, longtime supporters of the Welsh princes, suddenly found themselves obliged to provide hospitality for officials of the king's household. With developments in Edward I's second campaign in Wales reaching their peak, members of the Wardrobe had taken up lodging at the abbey as a base for their all-important financial administration. As the main spending department of the government, the role of the Wardrobe was crucial in the unprecedented levels of funding required in the early stages of the king's castle-building in Wales.

One day, amid their services in the abbey church, the monks may well have observed a mounted party gathering in the outer court. Two panniers containing £100 in hard cash – many thousands of pounds at today's values – were strapped to a horse, and the party with its guarded escort set off for a location some 20 miles away on the western coast. That location was Harlech, where for several weeks preparations had been in hand for yet another major new royal stronghold. Building works were just beginning on a carefully chosen rocky crag, a dramatic site towering precipitously some 200 feet above the coastal flats of the *morfa*. The arrival of the cash was no doubt greeted with enthusiasm; it would be adequate to sustain the labour force and essential supplies for construction over the next month. Harlech, it had been decided, was to form part of the 'iron ring' of castles surrounding the coastal fringes of Snowdonia, eventually stretching from Flint in the north-east around to Aberystwyth in the southwest. King Edward had announced that he was firmly resolved to 'put an end finally to the matter that he has now commenced of putting down the malice of the Welsh'. This immensely powerful chain of fortifications was intended to break the spirit of the people, to prevent this region from ever again becoming a focal point of insurrection or a bastion of resistance.

Although the early records of progress with the work are scanty, one or two fragments of information fill out the details of those initial months. We learn that in mid June, for example, 20 stonemasons and quarriers, together with a packhorse to carry their tools, were dispatched from Conwy on a two-day journey through the mountain passes to report for duty at Harlech. By 1286 the work was reaching its height, and the surviving details are much fuller. The labour force had built up from just 60 men in the slack winter months of January and February, to almost 950 by midsummer – including 227 masons, 115 quarriers, 30 smiths, 22 carpenters and 546 labourers and minor workmen. Ships were bringing in supplies of building stone from Anglesey and Caernarfon. They also brought iron and steel from Chester, used in large quantities for nails, cramps, locks, hinges, tools and so on. The records for the 1289 season are particularly full, and reveal that much of the work was carried out on a task-work basis. Thus, Master William of Drogheda was paid £111 7s. 6d. for his labours on the

The gatehouse at Harlech, a magnificent 'fortified domestic' residence.

'north tower towards the sea' – 49½ feet high, at a rate of £2. 5s. per foot. John of Maghull, a master carpenter, made 423 joists at 10d. each, a total of £17 12s. 6d. and William of Thornton was paid 8s. to make a fireplace in one of the upper rooms of the gatehouse.

By the end of this 1289 season, Harlech Castle stood substantially complete, another masterpiece of medieval military construction. The design had once more been in the hands of the king's brilliant architect, Master James of St George. Here, with tremendous skill, his sophisticated plan made maximum use of the opportunities offered by the rugged promontory. He adapted the great natural strength of the site to accommodate the most up-to-date defensive requirements, combining these in a structure with a glorious sense of majesty. More than 700 years later, the scene from the well-trodden bluff of rock to the south of the town remains breath taking – a superb testament to the creative genius of Master James. From this point, visitors cannot fail to appreciate the beauty in the line and form of the building. The green flatlands and silver sea to the west, with Snowdon's peak as the climax to the superb backcloth of mountains, combine to make this one of the most familiar strongholds in Britain.

From the outset, Master James had planned a 'concentric' castle, with the small and compact inner ward crowning the rocky site. The ground falls away steeply on all sides, leaving little

King Edward I, the builder of Harlech, seen with his senior churchmen, from a manuscript of about 1285.

The turrets of the outer gate, and the powerful main gatehouse at Harlech Castle, begun in 1283.

room for the outer ward. The only possible direction of attack was from the east, where the defences were further strengthened by a deep and wide rock-cut ditch. It was this east side, too, which formed the main approach to the castle. Here, the perfect symmetry and scale of the facade throw down an insolent display of power and a feeling of overwhelming might. At the end of the thirteenth century, the overall effect would have been further emphasized by shields of royal arms bedecking the battlements and walls.

From the centre of the eastern curtain rises the great gatehouse, the most dominant feature at Harlech, and upon which the entire defence system hinges. Eventually, a substantial bridge – its piers still visible – thrust across the ditch towards the outer gate. Beyond this, the main gate-passage was protected by a succession of up to seven obstacles, including stout wooden doors and three portcullises. On either side of the passage were guardchambers, whereas the upper floors of this imposing structure provided two lavish suites of accommodation. The gatehouse was indeed a 'fortified domestic' residence of considerable comfort. The uppermost floor may well have been intended for guests or visiting dignitaries, such as the justiciar or the

chamberlain of north Wales, or perhaps the king himself. The lower floor, with its direct access to the courtyard and a small private chapel, must have been the lodgings of the constable and his family. The constable served as the king's lieutenant, with direct control of the garrison. The composition of the Harlech garrison was established as early as 1284, and was to include '30 fencible men of whom 10 shall be crossbow men', a chaplain, an artiller, a smith, a carpenter and a mason. In 1290, the king appointed none other than Master James of St George to the position of constable of Harlech at the handsome salary of 100 marks (£66) a year, and he no doubt resided in the gatehouse he had designed.

The inner ward is surprisingly small and, as the foundations reveal, a great deal of room was originally taken up by the surrounding ranges of domestic buildings. To the west, overlooking the sea, lay the great hall and kitchen. Against the north wall there was a chapel and bake-house, and to the south a granary and second hall. The four corner towers provided further accommodation. Visitors may care to climb one of the accessible sets of steps up to the wall-walks, from which there are fine views in all directions.

Another notable feature at Harlech is the remarkable 'way from the sea', a gated and fortified stairway plunging the 200 feet or so down to the foot of the castle rock. Once, this gave access to supplies from the sea, when the tide level or at least a tidal channel lapped the edge of the cliff. The sea has long since receded, leaving Harlech somewhat isolated upon its rock. During the Welsh uprising of 1294–95, under Madog ap Llywelyn, this maritime lifeline proved the saviour of the garrison. As at nearby Criccieth, the castle was supplied and victualled by ship from Ireland.

Harlech also played a key role in the national uprising led by Owain Glyndŵr, when, after a long siege, it fell to his forces in the spring of 1404. Together with the castle at Aberystwyth, it was one of Glyndŵr's greatest prizes, and he held it with the utmost determination for four years. In possession of these major strongholds he was no longer merely the leader of an insurrection, he was a sovereign prince and effective ruler of large parts of western Wales. As his chief residence and headquarters, it was one of the two places to which he summoned parliaments of his supporters. It was only following a further long siege and persistent cannon bombardment at the end of 1408, or early in 1409, that Harlech was retaken by an English force led by Harry of Monmouth – the future King Henry V.

During the Wars of the Roses, some 60 years later, the castle was held for the Lancastrian party. It was again besieged by a large Yorkist army under the leadership of Lord William Herbert of Raglan, and surrendered on 14 August 1468. It was this siege which is traditionally supposed to have given rise to the well-known song, *Men of Harlech*. Harlech Castle saw final military action in the Civil War when it was garrisoned for King Charles. Following its capture by Parliamentary soldiers in 1647, it is said to have been rendered untenable.

Pennarth Fawr Medieval House

Somewhat hidden on a minor road a few miles west of Criccieth, this is a charming example of a late medieval hall-house. In north and east

The medieval hall-house at Pennarth Fawr.

A detail of the fifteenth-century timbers in the roof trusses at Pennarth Fawr.

Wales, such buildings served not only as the homes of the peasantry, but were also much favoured among the aristocracy. Pennarth Fawr was probably built around the middle of the fifteenth century by Madog ap Hywel ap Madog, a member of the local minor gentry classes. Chief interest in the house stems from its fine timber roof and the large 'aisle-truss' situated at one end of the hall.

Hall-houses were generally divided into three units, with the hall – open to the roof – at the centre, and separate suites of rooms at either end. In this, Pennarth Fawr is no exception. The visitor now enters into the original 'cross-passage'; the doorway at the opposite end is now blocked. The area to the right of the cross-passage, although much altered in the nineteenth century, was occupied by the service rooms – such as a buttery dairy or pantry. To the left, the passage is separated from the central hall by the impressive aisle-truss. In essence this was not a structural feature, but rather it served as a symbol of aristocratic pride. Almost 20 other houses with aisle-trusses are known in north Wales, and in each case the story is

similar. When, as at Pennarth Fawr, the truss forms an open division between the hall and the passage, it is known as a 'spere-truss'. It seems likely that a movable screen was positioned between the two elaborately-carved posts to keep out draughts.

In the hall itself, there was once a central hearth in the middle of the floor. This was replaced in 1615 by the large fireplace in the east wall. At the end furthest from the passage, there was probably a raised dais upon which the high table stood. The house originally extended a little further north, but all trace of this third unit with its private apartments has now disappeared.

Pont Minllyn

Immediately down stream from the modern crossing of the Dyfi at Dinas Mawddwy, this delightful little bridge is a rare survival of its period. It is particularly notable as one of three

Pont Minllyn, an early seventeenth-century bridge.

public bridges said to have been built by Dr John Davies (1567–1644), one of the most distinguished Welsh scholars of his time. 'Parson Davies' was rector of nearby Mallwyd from 1604 until his death, and he is buried in the churchyard there. As a clergyman and magistrate he was held in high esteem for the various charities he undertook about the parish. Pont Minllyn has two arches which span about 60 feet across the river. It has no parapets at the sides, and is only about nine feet wide. As such, it probably served pedestrians and packhorses, whilst larger carts may still have found it necessary to cross the stream at some adjoining ford.

St Cybi's Well

Cybi is one of a group of early Welsh saints whose 'Lives' are to be found in a manuscript, copied around 1200, quite probably at Gloucester. All of these 'Lives' are largely composed of wondrous tales, and the material is to be taken as a blend of myth, folklore and legend, telling us more about the attitudes and beliefs of the twelfth century than for the periods to which it supposedly relates. Nevertheless, from the 'Life', St Cybi is traditionally believed to have settled in this part of Wales in the sixth century. He was granted the deserted fort at Caer Gybi on Anglesey, in which he established a monastery. By the twelfth and thirteenth centuries – at the latest – various places in Wales had become associated with his cult.

We can only speculate on the origins of St Cybi's well as a place of pilgrimage, though it was almost certainly attracting people throughout the Middle Ages. Although its reputation was to become fairly localized, the well survived the Reformation and appears to have seen a revival of fortunes in the eighteenth century. Pilgrims at this time came in the hope of curing warts, lameness, blindness, scurvy and rheumatism. Patients took quantities of both well and sea water, and then had to bathe in one of the pools once or twice a day.

The remains are located in a particularly

The holy well dedicated to St Cybi on the Lleyn peninsula.

attractive setting, and consist of two well chambers, a 'custodian's cottage', and a small detached latrine building. Although difficult to date, the large southern chamber could belong to the twelfth or thirteenth centuries. Built of massive rough hewn boulders, it may have begun as a free-standing building. Inside, there are niches or seats around the walls. The smaller well chamber to the north was probably added at a later date. Both chambers contain a bath surrounded by a ledge, with steps leading into

the water. The cottage is attached to the east of the large well chamber, and was probably built about 1750. It was modified perhaps sometime during the nineteenth century, and was occupied until at least 1870.

Segontium Roman Fort

Overlooking the modern town of Caernarfon, with Edward I's great castle beyond, the Roman fort of *Segontium* stands as one of the most famous in the kingdom. Long after the departure of the legions, its upstanding ruins assured it a place in legend as the *Caer aber Seint* – 'the fort at the mouth of the Saint river' – mentioned in *The Dream of Macsen Wledig*, one of the early Welsh tales of the *Mabinogion*. Today, it is the only site in Wales where it is possible to see something of the internal layout of a Roman auxiliary fort.

Segontium was almost certainly established in the late 70s AD, probably during the governor Julius Agricola's crushing offensive against the native tribe of north Wales, the *Ordovices*. The new fort was intended to guard the Menai Strait, and occupied a pivotal position in the Roman road system. It was part of an overall

The main well chamber at St Cybi's.

network of fortifications situated throughout Wales, a network designed as a rigid straight-jacket for the effective policing of the newly-conquered territory. Although effective, such a garrison could not be maintained indefinitely, and many of the forts were accordingly phased out wherever possible. *Segontium*, however, was held more or less continuously until around AD 395, if not slightly later. During the three centuries of occupation, the nature and arrangement of the fort buildings changed considerably, no doubt reflecting the varying role and composition of the garrison stationed here.

The outline of the fort was the usual playing-card shape, covering between five and six acres, and may have been originally designed for a unit of up to 1,000 auxiliary troops. The late first-century defences comprised a single earthen bank, possibly with inner and outer ditches, and probably four timber gates. Inside, all the buildings were of wood at this stage. Recent excavations in the south-east corner of the fort have revealed a complicated sequence of building, including several phases of timber barrack blocks dating to the late first and early second centuries. But we must await the full publication of this work before drawing too many conclusions. Reconstruction of parts of the fort in stone began in a piecemeal fashion after about AD 140. From an inscription, it is known that a new garrison arrived at *Segontium* about AD 198. The *First Cohort of Sunici*, a unit of about 500 men, was initially raised in the Cologne-Aachen region, though it was long resident in Britain before arriving in north Wales.

The defences were finally completed in stone in the early third century, when the water supply and headquarters building were also renovated. Once again, the recent excavations have uncovered fascinating evidence of a large residence arranged around a central courtyard, built in the south-eastern corner of the fort around this time. It was associated with a bath-house, and was possibly used by an official connected with the civil government of the region. The fourth century saw much further renewal, especially after 369, and a good deal that is currently visible dates from these later periods.

At the centre of the fort lay the headquarters building, the *principia*. This had a courtyard, an assembly hall, with the regimental 'chapel' or

The Roman fort of Segontium, on the outskirts of Caernarfon.

shrine to the rear where the standards of the unit were kept. In the third century an underground strongroom was constructed beneath the shrine. To the west was the commandant's house, which had four ranges of rooms opening on to a small central court or garden. The freestanding platform in one of the rear rooms is almost certainly the base of a domestic shrine. Barrack blocks lay to the north and south, and part of a granary can be seen near the north-east corner. South of the modern road, a footpath leads to the line of the southern fort wall with its central gate. The gate had a pair of passages, flanked by towers, and guardrooms can be seen in that to the right. The wall originally stood up to 17 feet high.

Traditionally, the garrison was finally removed by the rebel general Magnus Maximus, the Macsen Wledig of legend, in 383. The recent archaeological investigations have shown this was not the case, and occupation at some level continued through to the end of the century. There is a well laid out museum at the site run by the National Museum of Wales. Visitors will find more on the history of *Segontium* and its buildings, together with many of the finds discovered during excavations.

POWYS
The Central Marches and Mid Wales Hills

Powys is a large rambling county covering up to a quarter of Wales, yet it has a population of less than 120,000. Straggling along the English border, it stretches from the Brecon Beacons in the south to the fringes of Snowdonia in the north. Although the county is crossed by three beautiful east-flowing rivers – the Severn, Usk and Wye – it is entirely landlocked. The nearest it comes to the coast is the head of the Dyfi estuary near Machynlleth. Everywhere it is a region of hills, with much of the rich green landscape and many of the settlements lying over 1,000 feet.

Powys was created by the local government changes of 1974, when the counties of Breconshire, Montgomeryshire and Radnorshire were merged in a single jumbo administrative area. These earlier counties had themselves been established under the Act of Union in 1536, during the reign of King Henry VIII. They in turn had been carved from medieval Marcher lordships, and the native principality of Powys whose origins lay in pre-Conquest times.

The number of historic sites and monuments cared for by Cadw in the county is not great, though each offers something of unique interest. The strongholds at Bronllys, Tretower and Montgomery were essentially built by Marcher lords. Dolforwyn, however, represents the only castle raised entirely by Prince Llywelyn ap Gruffudd of Gwynedd. At the time Llywelyn was busy extending the borders of his principality, despite the wishes of his English neighbours. In this instance Llywelyn's policy for expansion was also at the expense of Gruffudd ap Gwenwynwyn (d. 1286), prince of southern Powys. In contrast, Tretower Court is far more domestic in character, and is a rare survival from the later Middle Ages.

The partial remains of other castles can be seen, for example, at Brecon, Crickhowell and at Hay on Wye. Further north, near Welshpool, the National Trust looks after elegant Powis Castle. This began as a fortress of the Welsh princes of Powys. It may have been Owain 'de la Pole' (d. 1293), the last of the native rulers of the region, who built the twin-towered gatehouse shortly before 1300. Almost three centuries later, Powis was bought in 1587 by Sir Edward Herbert who began the long process of transforming it into one of the grandest stately homes in Wales. The magnificent formal gardens were laid out in the late eighteenth century. Another site of considerable importance in the county is that of the Cistercian abbey of Cwmhir, near Llandrindod Wells. Although the remains are scanty they should not be overlooked. Had it been completed as planned, this would have been Wales's largest church, and it is generally held that Llywelyn ap Gruffudd was buried here in 1282.

Powys also has some of the more attractive and charming market towns of Wales. Brecon's fine cathedral began as a Benedictine priory founded about 1110 by the Norman lord Bernard de Neufmarché. Builth Wells is the home of the annual Royal Welsh Show, and also has the earthen remains of a huge Norman motte modified by King Edward I at the end of the thirteenth century. The market hall at Llanidloes, dating to about 1600, is the only timber-framed building of its type to survive in the country, and the superb early thirteenth-century arcade in the church of St Idloes almost certainly came from Cwmhir Abbey following the Dissolution of the Monasteries.

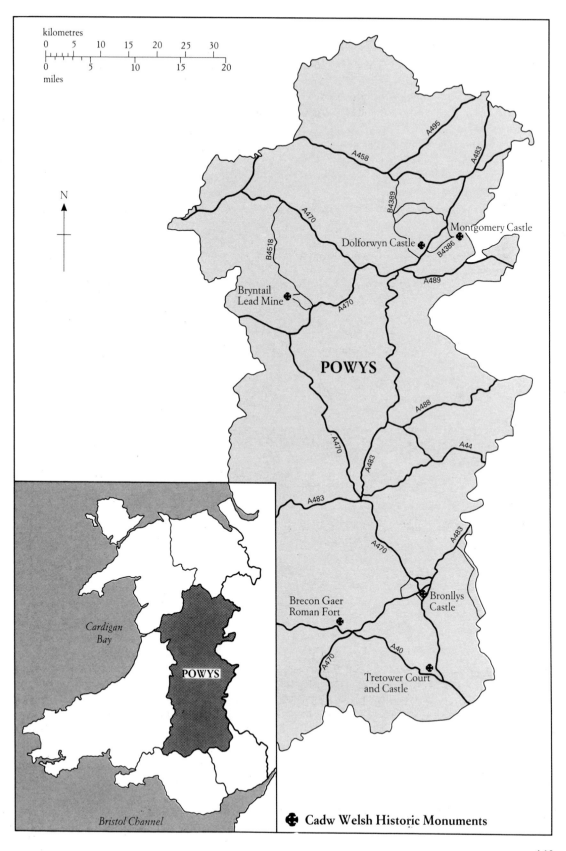

kilometres

miles

N

POWYS

A495

A483

A458

B4389

Montgomery Castle

Dolforwyn Castle

B4386

A470

B4518

A489

Bryntail
Lead Mine

A470

POWYS

A488

A470

A483

A44

A483

A483

A470

A483

Brecon Gaer
Roman Fort

Bronllys
Castle

A40

A470

Tretower Court
and Castle

Cardigan
Bay

POWYS

Bristol Channel

✤ Cadw Welsh Historic Monuments

Brecon Gaer Roman Fort

On the eve of the Roman conquest, the Usk valley was occupied by northern groups of *Silurian* tribesmen, who united to put up fierce resistance to the legions throughout south-east Wales from about AD 50 to AD 75. The subjugation of the *Silures* was only finally achieved in a series of concerted campaigns between AD 74 and AD 78. With a new legionary fortress at Caerleon, the governor Julius Frontinus laid plans for a tight network of forts throughout the hostile territory. Brecon Gaer must have been established no later than AD 80, and occupied an important pivotal position in the overall strategy. The site has sometimes been identified as the Roman *Cicucium*, but this is not universally accepted. However, we know from an inscription found nearby, that the first garrison was probably the Vettonian Spanish cavalry regiment, a unit of some 500 men.

The fort was first excavated in 1924–25 by Sir Mortimer Wheeler, at which time the general outline and details of several internal buildings were recovered. It was quite large for an auxiliary unit, occupying up to eight acres. The initial defences comprised an earthen bank, with two external V-shaped ditches. Unlike many forts in *Silurian* territory, Brecon Gaer continued in use well into the second century, and about AD 140 the earth and timber defences were replaced by stone walls and gates. The precise history of occupation and the arrangement of internal buildings is somewhat complex and requires further excavation. None the less, a small bath-building inserted in the north-east corner is now believed to date to about AD 100, and it may be that by this time the cavalry regiment had been replaced by a smaller unit. The headquarters block and commandant's house were also excavated in 1924–25, and their rebuilding in stone could date to the mid second century. Finds from the site suggest that occupation continued into the fourth century, but the extent and nature of activity cannot be defined without additional work. Wheeler

The remains of the west gate at the Roman fort of Brecon Gaer.

The Norman motte and early thirteenth-century round tower at Bronllys Castle.

further found evidence for timber buildings running northwards from the north gate, and these probably formed part of a civilian settlement. Finally, he excavated a large stone construction just to the north-west; probably an official rest-house or *mansio*.

Today, although none of the internal buildings are displayed, it is possible to see the remains of the west and south gateways. The west is the more elaborate, with its two carriageways and flanking guard chambers. The south gate was of different design, but still stands in places up to eight feet high. In both gateways, the visitor will notice pivot holes on which the actual gates were hung. The fort wall is well preserved along parts of the north rampart, standing to a maximum height of 11 feet. The north-east corner turret can also be seen.

Bronllys Castle

Bronllys is situated in lush and attractive countryside, near the junction of the Llynfi and Dulais rivers, and is one of a dozen or more castles in this area of the southern March distinguished by their prominent thirteenth-century round keeps. It began as a motte and bailey, probably raised by Richard fitz Pons soon after 1086. Richard had been among the Norman knights who had followed Bernard de Neufmarché into the Welsh kingdom of Brycheiniog, and in return was granted a mountainous strip of territory known as Cantref Selyf. He chose Bronllys as the centre from which to protect and administer this new lordship, a role which the castle maintained for much of the Middle Ages.

In 1188, Gerald of Wales recorded how a ruthless knight named Mahel met his end at Bronllys. He had been guilty of persecuting the bishop of St Davids, and as a divine punishment he received a mortal blow from a stone which fell from a tower during a fire. Believing the stone to have been hurled by St David himself, he died in misery, begging the bishop's forgiveness.

From the path which leads to the castle, visitors can readily appreciate the strength of Richard's motte, but this in turn is dominated by the circular stone keep. Towering upwards, such keeps were used as a simple and effective way of bringing outmoded earth and timber castles up to date in the early thirteenth century. The mound at Bronllys would have provided protection against siege engines, and a now vanished wooden gallery running around the top of the tower enabled archers to release their lethal fire in all directions. It was almost certainly built by fitz Pons's great-grandson, Walter de Clifford III, lord of Bronllys from 1221 to 1263. Indeed, Walter was a military colleague of the influential Hubert de Burgh, who had built a remarkably similar tower at Skenfrith.

The tower is entered by a wooden stair, similar no doubt to the medieval original. The private house and gardens beyond mark the site of the bailey, and a print of 1741 reveals a substantial medieval hall block where the stable now stands – perhaps the site where the hapless Mahel met his end. Inside the keep there is clear evidence of residential apartments, with fireplaces and comfortable window seats. The first floor, above a vaulted basement, retains its thirteenth-century windows. But on the second floor the windows were altered in the early fourteenth century when new openings with fashionable 'cinquefoil' heads were inserted. Moreover, the third floor may have been a completely new addition at this time. These changes represent a complete remodelling of the tower, probably the work of Master Rhys ap Hywel – a Welshman loyal to Edward I – who acquired the lordship about 1311. Bronllys, however, gradually fell into decay in the fifteenth century, and by 1521 it was described by a king's surveyor as 'beyond repair'.

Bryntail Lead Mine

The remains of the Bryntail lead mine are almost completely overshadowed by the soaring buttresses of the Clywedog dam. Built between

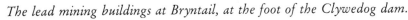

The lead mining buildings at Bryntail, at the foot of the Clywedog dam.

1964 and 1967, the dam towers 237 feet above the river bed and is claimed to be the tallest mass of concrete in Britain. From a viewing point above the dam there are superb vistas of the Llyn Clywedog reservoir, the gorge below, and virtually an aerial view of the mine buildings.

Lead ore occurs fairly widely in mid Wales, the Bryntail mine lying on the eastern edge of the so-called Van lode. The workings here are very old, and the best supplies were probably already taken before the mine's revival in the mid nineteenth century. A lease for the mine is recorded as early as 1770, but the really productive period was between 1845 and 1867 when nearly 2,000 tons of ore were mined. The highest recorded output for any year was 384 tons in 1851, with the level of production dropping off rapidly in the 1860s. In 1869 Bryntail became the Van Consols Mining Company, and soon afterwards production switched to the processing of barytes ('white lead'), which was used in the manufacture of paint. After struggling on financially through the 1870s, the mine venture eventually collapsed in 1884.

Visitors may care to follow the Clywedog gorge trail which has been developed by the Severn-Trent Water Authority. A footbridge below the dam crosses the river to the western mine workings. The ore itself was worked on the hillside and was carried down to the mills on an inclined railway. The surviving structures include two dressing buildings, each of which had a waterwheel providing the power to drive crushing rollers and other machinery. The wheel in the lower building was also harnessed to drive equipment to pump water out of the mine levels. There are also the remains of cottages or offices, and bins (hoppers) used for storing uncrushed ore. In the later history of the mine, the upper dressing building was converted to a barytes mill. The ore was brought in to the upper storey on trucks and was then crushed to powder. It was next left to bleach in great stone settling tanks inside the building. Finally it was dried out in earthenware pots placed in coal-fired ovens, the remains of which can also be seen.

The trail continues a short distance through Gelli Wood to the eastern mine workings. Here there are further remains including another stone-lined waterwheel pit and storage bins.

Dolforwyn Castle

Dolforwyn stands on a wooded hill, high above the fertile Severn valley – a scene so peaceful today that it is hard to picture it as one of military action or political animosity. It is a steep climb to the castle, but the visitor is rewarded with a glimpse of the only stronghold built entirely by Llywelyn the Last as a totally new foundation. Much of the site is still greensward, but excavations have been underway summer by summer since 1981, and gradually the buildings mentioned in a survey of 1321–22 are being uncovered: a square tower, round tower, chapel, hall, lady's chamber, pantry, buttery, kitchen, brewery, bakehouse, larder, granaries and cellar.

Building work probably began in the spring of 1273, and Llywelyn no doubt intended that the new castle would secure the south-eastern border of his territory against royal or baronial intrusion along the Severn valley from the direction of Montgomery. Moreover, it was a deliberate exhibition of his authority over Gruffudd ap Gwenwynwyn, prince of southern Powys. In June of that year, however, the English government wrote to Prince Llywelyn forbidding the construction of the castle and the creation of an associated borough and market. Llywelyn's response to the king was firm, and a masterpiece of ironic politeness: 'We have received a letter written in the king's name... forbidding us to construct a castle on our own land near Aber Miwl... We are certain that the said letter did not come forth with the king's knowledge, and that if the king were present in his kingdom [Edward was in Gascony at the time]... such a mandate would not be issued... For the king knows well that the rights of our principality are entirely separate from the rights of the king's realm... And the king has heard and in part seen that we and our ancestors had the power within our boundaries to build and construct castles and fortresses... without prohibition by any one'.

Llywelyn continued work on the castle, and by April 1274 he had invested £174 6s. 8d. in its construction. When, nevertheless, Edward I finally moved against the prince in 1277, Dolforwyn quickly fell to the English forces. Ironically, the garrison put up little fight and the

The 'square tower', recently excavated at Llywelyn the Last's castle of Dolforwyn.

castle was handed over to Roger Mortimer on 8 April after a short siege. The site was repaired by Mortimer and was garrisoned for a time, but gradually fell into decay and disuse; in 1398 it was described as 'ruinous and worth nothing'.

The excavations have so far recovered details, for example, of the 'square tower' of the 1321–22 survey – a very substantial keep-like structure on the south-western side of the ridge. The 'round tower' has also been exposed, and gradually the programme of work will progress to the buildings of the courtyard. A few banks and platforms, to the west of the castle, mark the position of Llywelyn's infant borough.

Montgomery Castle

On the eve of his sixteenth birthday, the young King Henry III was at the head of the royal army on a brief military campaign in the Marches. Llywelyn ab Iorwerth had been flexing the muscles of his power, and there was a need to tilt the balance of strength back in favour of the Crown. Having relieved Builth Castle, the army advanced through Hereford and Shrewsbury to Montgomery. Roger of Montgomery, from Ste Foi de Montgommeri in Calvados, had established an earth and timber castle to guard this important ford on the River Severn just a few years after the battle of Hastings. In the political climate of the 1220s, however, with Prince Llywelyn near the height of his success, it was clear that such a key border point could no longer be defended by an outmoded wooden fortification. So it was, in the words of a contemporary chronicler, that the king's advisers pointed out 'a suitable spot for the erection of an impregnable castle'. The site was about a mile from Earl Roger's motte and bailey, which in time became known as Hen Domen – the 'Old Mound' – itself under thorough excavation since 1960.

The principal adviser to the king was without doubt the justiciar, Hubert de Burgh, and the 'impregnable spot' was a high narrow ridge of rock, where the ruins of the castle continue to look down on this attractive border town.

Work on New Montgomery began immediately, and the site was divided into two wards with deep rock-cut ditches across the ridge. That autumn, carpenters set to work on raising temporary timber accommodation which would be replaced in stone over the coming years. King Henry spent substantial sums here and in 1228 he granted the castle to de Burgh. By 1233 work on the initial phase was complete.

Beyond the inner ditch, this ward was entered by a large twin-towered gatehouse – one of the earliest of its type in the country. Indeed, the Montgomery gate may have so impressed Prince Llywelyn that he adopted a similar design for his own castle at Criccieth. Projecting out from the west side of the ward, the well tower protected the castle's all important water supply. The rock-cut shaft of the well itself extends to a depth of about 220 feet.

Further sources reveal that it was probably in 1251–53 that the timber defences of the middle ward were replaced in stone. Even so, following the final conquest of independent Wales by Edward I, Montgomery lost much of its role as a front-line military spearhead. In the fourteenth century the castle was held by the Mortimers, earls of March. Their additions to the inner ward, such as the bakehouse, brewhouse and kitchen were domestic and manorial rather than military or defensive.

In the sixteenth century, the castle passed to one of the branches of the Herbert family, and in the 1620s Sir Edward Herbert – later Lord Herbert of Chirbury – raised one of the first brick houses in Wales in the middle ward. Some 600,000 bricks were used in the construction of what must have been an extremely elegant structure. Herbert himself was a lukewarm Royalist and in 1644 he surrendered Montgomery to Parliamentary forces who had placed a bomb under the outer gatehouse. A Royalist siege was led by Lord Byron in an attempt to recover the castle. When in turn the Parliamentary relief column arrived, it resulted in the battle of Montgomery, a crushing defeat for the Royalist cause. Following the Civil War, both the castle and Lord Chirbury's house were demolished by order of Parliament.

The 'new' castle of Montgomery, begun in the 1220s for the young King Henry III.

169

The early medieval castle at Tretower, with the later court in the distance.

Tretower Court and Castle

To those familiar with the warm glow of the red sandstone on a summer evening, or with the distinct smell of the ancient and precious seasoned timbers, Tretower is something of a well kept secret. Lying on the lush northern bank of the River Usk, the site announces itself from afar by the great thirteenth-century round keep which rises from the valley floor. The place name is derived from this tower, but its attraction lies as much in a glorious late medieval house, as in the earlier castle stronghold it replaced. Quite simply, Tretower offers the visitor a group of medieval buildings difficult to parallel anywhere in Wales.

An earth and timber motte and bailey castle was built here by the Norman knight Picard, a follower of Bernard de Neufmarché in his conquest of the Welsh kingdom of Brycheiniog. About 1150, Picard's son or grandson raised a stone shell keep on the summit of the motte, and much of this still survives despite later alterations. It was entered by a small gatehouse, and inside a hall and a private chamber stood at first-floor level. Delicate traces of Romanesque carving can be seen around the edges of the blocked up windows of this period. Around 1220–40, however, the castle was completely remodelled and brought right up to date in terms of military development. The interior of the shell keep was gutted to make way for a massive circular tower, characteristic of this area of the southern March. The tower resembles that built by the powerful Marcher lord Hubert de Burgh at Skenfrith, or even the work of William Marshall at Pembroke. The Picards were of course adopting the idea from their influential neighbours, just as surely as Walter de Clifford was doing at nearby Bronllys.

At Tretower, as elsewhere, the keep was entered at first-floor level. Inside, above a basement, there is evidence of three floors. The first two were particularly comfortable apartments with elaborate hooded fireplaces and spacious window seats. The top of the tower is likely to have carried a projecting wooden gallery, or fighting platform, from which archers could cover the ground on all sides. Outside the tower, the outer face of the earlier shell keep now served as a curtain wall, and was heightened to carry a wall-walk. It was at this time, too, that the castle bailey was surrounded by a stone wall with rounded towers at the angles. The bailey is now a working farm, and is not accessible to visitors, but traces of the walls can be seen from the meadow between the castle and the court.

The cramped conditions of this defensive stronghold could never have proved ideal, and there is evidence that by the early fourteenth century the family had largely abandoned the castle in favour of the more spacious Tretower Court. The earliest part of the house is the north range, where various features indicate it was first built in the early 1300s. At the time, it would have been a single-storey building with a large central hall open to the roof. Eventually, this was to be transformed out of all recognition into the building we see today. One man, more than any other, was responsible for this transformation: Sir Roger Vaughan, allegedly the richest commoner in Wales at the height of his power.

Vaughan received Tretower as a gift from his half-brother, Sir William Herbert of Raglan Castle. Both men were prominent Yorkists, and rose to power by their timely support for Edward IV in the Wars of the Roses. Herbert's own success is reflected in his sumptuous building at Raglan, but he also used his position of influence to secure Vaughan a series of grants in Brecon and Glamorgan. With these resources, though much less than those of his kinsman, Sir Roger began reconstructing Tretower on a scale befitting his position as one of the leading royal retainers in Wales.

The existing north range was completely refashioned by dividing it into two storeys, and by the addition of a noteworthy timber gallery. Moreover, Vaughan went on to more than double the extent of his accommodation by adding the extensive west range. It comprised a new ground-floor hall, open to the roof, buttery and pantry areas, and various private chambers. There was also a retainers' hall, since the employment of retainers – men at arms –

The interior of Tretower Court.

was a practical necessity for any gentleman of position at this date. Many of the details of this late fifteenth-century arrangement can still be seen. The magnificent roof and timber panelling in the hall, for example, is particularly memorable. No less impressive are the beams in the older north range, where the sliding wooden shutters have also been restored along the gallery.

Sir Roger Vaughan was beheaded following the battle of Tewkesbury in 1471, but his son Sir Thomas added the gatehouse to Tretower and enclosed the courtyard with a battlemented wall-walk. Generations of the family continued to live here until the last major alterations were undertaken in the 1630s by Sir Charles Vaughan. It was Sir Charles who introduced the classical style windows which give the court much of its present aspect, though his scheme meant the removal of the gallery along the western range. The ingenious design also involved roofing the wall-walk and adding windows on the south side, giving the appearance of a much larger house with an additional range of rooms.

In the eighteenth century the family took up residence at Scethrog, in a property acquired by marriage. Tretower was eventually sold off and became a farm, gradually falling into a state of neglect and decay until restoration works began in the 1930s.

SUMMARY
OF DATES

This table is offered as an approximate chronological guide to the monuments in the care of Cadw: Welsh Historic Monuments. In all, the sites span some 6,000 years, stretching from the so-called Neolithic era, right through to the end of the nineteenth century. The left-hand column represents no more than an alphabetical listing of the monuments divided into broad period groups. The right-hand column, on the other hand, is presented as a more detailed chronology of events.

With regard to the prehistoric period, the compilation of a basic table of dates might seem a straightforward task, but it is far from it. The traditional 'Three Age' system – Stone, Bronze and Iron – has been under strong attack for some years. Archaeologists no longer see a distinct division between the phases, and the idea of successive waves of invasion to explain the differences is no longer accepted. The advent of radiocarbon dating has had a profound effect on our understanding of prehistory. However, there is still a great deal of dispute over the extent to which radiocarbon dates can be 'recalibrated' as absolute calendar years. Thus, the prehistoric dates given in this table are, of necessity, a general approximation, liable to change or refinement as more investigation is undertaken.

For the historic periods, the information is, of course, based on much firmer ground. In the left-hand column, in order to create some subdivision, the medieval monuments have been divided into two groups. Although the life of a castle or an abbey might span the entire Middle Ages, sites have been allocated to the period during which the principal surviving remains were first constructed; that is before or after 1216. A question mark denotes some doubt as to the precise date of origin.

Finally, the chronology of events concentrates on the historic periods, and in the main it focuses upon those centuries of greatest relevance to the monuments covered in this volume. Events and dates relating more specifically to Wales are printed in *italic* script.

Earlier Neolithic (*c.* 4500–3000 BC)

Bodowyr Burial Chamber	*c.* 4500	Beginning of the so-called Neolithic (New Stone Age).
Capel Garmon Burial Chamber		
Carreg Coetan Arthur Burial Chamber	*c.* 4000–3500	Arrival of the 'first farmers',
Din Dryfol Burial Chamber		and the beginnings of settled
Dyffryn Ardudwy Burial Chamber		agriculture; gradual
Lligwy Burial Chamber		appearance of earth covered
Parc le Breos Burial Chamber		'long barrows' in southern England, and chambered

Presaddfed Burial Chamber
Pentre Ifan Burial Chamber
St Lythans Burial Chamber
Tinkinswood Burial Chamber
Trefignath Burial Chamber
Tŷ Newydd Burial Chamber

(megalithic) tombs in the north and west; introduction of earliest pottery.

Later Neolithic – Bronze Age (*c.* 3000–800 BC)

Sites	Date	Description
Barclodiad y Gawres Burial Chamber	*c.* 3000–2500	Appearance of 'henge' monuments; earliest phase at Stonehenge near beginning of this period.
Bryn Celli Ddu Henge/Burial Chamber		
Castell Bryn Gwyn		
Holyhead Mountain Hut Circles		
Penrhos Feilw Standing Stones	*c.* 2700–2500	*Passage graves in north Wales.*
Tregwehelydd Standing Stone		
Tŷ Mawr Standing Stone	*c.* 2500	The earliest appearance of 'Beaker' pottery; first metalwork, marking the beginning of the so-called Bronze Age.
	c. 2500–1500	Stone circles and standing stones raised across landscape.
	c. 1000–800	Early defended hilltop enclosures – hillforts.

Iron Age (*c.* 800 BC–AD 50)

Sites	Date	Description
Caer y Tŵr Hillfort	*c.* 800–600	Renewed phase of hillfort building; gradual appearance of iron tools and weapons, marking the beginnings of the so-called Iron Age.
Chepstow Bulwarks Camp		
Llanmelin Wood Hillfort		
	c. 600 BC– AD 50	*Spread of hillforts and smaller lowland defended enclosures across Wales; regional differences eventually consolidated in the form of tribal areas: Cornovii and Deceangli in north-east, Ordovices in north-west, Demetae in south-west, and Silures in south-east.*
	AD 43	Roman invasion of Britain.

Roman (*c.* AD 50–400)

Brecon Gaer Fort	*c.* 55–60	*Roman frontier advanced into south Wales; legionary fortress established at Usk.*
Caer Gybi Fortlet		
Caer Lêb (?)		
Caerleon Fortress	*c.* 75	*Legionary fortress established at Caerleon.*
Caerwent Town		
Din Lligwy Hut Group	*c.* 75–80	*Final Roman conquest of Wales; auxiliary forts established throughout the country, including Brecon Gaer and Segontium.*
Segontium Fort		

Fragment of Roman mosaic found at Caerleon.

	c. 122–28	Construction of Hadrian's Wall.
	c. 383–88	Usurper emperor Magnus Maximus withdraws troops from Britain to invade Continent.
	c. 410	Towns of Britain told to look to their own defences by central administration; official Roman presence in Britain ceased.

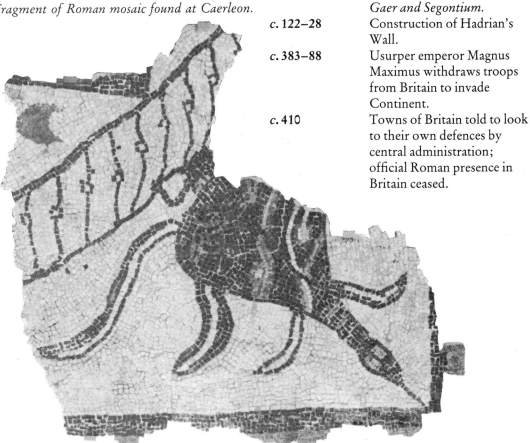

Early Medieval (*c.* AD 400–1066)

Carew Cross	*c.* 450–600	*Emergence of early kingdoms in Wales, including Dyfed in south-west, Glywysing in south-east, Gwynedd in north-west, and Powys in north-east; traditional 'Age of Saints', with spread of Christianity.*
Eliseg's Pillar		
Maen Achwyfan Cross		
Margam Stones		
Penmon Cross		
Penmon, St Seirol's Well (?)		

c. 784–96	Construction of Offa's Dyke, marking first effective frontier between England and Wales.
852–78	*Earliest Viking raids on Wales.*
921	*Edward the Elder, Saxon king of Wessex, establishes a fortified 'town' at Rhuddlan.*
c. 940–50	*Laws of Wales assembled and revised by Hywel Dda – Hywel the Good (d. ?950).*
c. 950–1000	*Renewed phase of Viking attacks on Wales.*
1039–63	*Gruffudd ap Llywelyn seizes power in Gwynedd, and succeeds in bringing unity to much of Wales.*
1066	Battle of Hastings: Norman victory over English.

The celebrated sixth-century Bodvoc (Bodvocus) stone at Margam Stones Museum. It is one of three stones at Margam which provide some of the earliest evidence for Christianity in post-Roman Wales.

Medieval (*c.* 1066–1216)

Basingwerk Abbey
Bronllys Castle
Capel Lligwy
Chepstow Castle
Coity Castle
Cymer Abbey
Dinefwr Castle (?)
Ewenny Priory
Grosmont Castle
Haverfordwest Priory (?)
Kidwelly Castle
Laugharne Castle
Llansteffan Castle
Llanthony Priory
Llawhaden Castle
Loughor Castle
Monmouth Castle
Neath Abbey
Newcastle Castle

1066–87	William I (the Conqueror), king of England.
c. 1067–71	*Norman lord, William fitz Osbern, overruns much of Gwent, and builds first stone castle in Wales at Chepstow.*
c. 1071–93	*Initial Norman advance and conquest of north Wales.*
1087–1100	William II, king of England.
1100–35	Henry I, king of England.
1131	*First Cistercian abbey founded in Wales at Tintern.*
1135–55	Stephen, king of England.
1137–70	*Owain Gwynedd reasserts the authority of Gwynedd.*
c. 1147–97	*Rhys ap Gruffudd rebuilds the strength and authority of the kingdom of Deheubarth in south-west Wales.*

Ogmore Castle	**1154–89**	Henry II, king of England.
Penmon Priory	**1157**	*Henry II on campaign in*
Rhuddlan, Twthill		*Wales in an attempt to curb*
Runston Chapel		*the power of Owain*
St Cybi's Well (?)		*Gwynedd.*
St Davids Bishop's Palace	**1176**	*Rhys ap Gruffudd holds the*
St Dogmaels Abbey		*first 'national eisteddfod' at*
St Non's Chapel (?)		*Cardigan.*
Strata Florida Abbey	**1188**	*Gerald of Wales accompanies*
Talley Abbey		*the archbishop of Canterbury*
Tintern Abbey		*on a major journey around*
Tretower Castle		*Wales, gathering recruits for*
Valle Crucis Abbey		*the Third Crusade.*
White Castle	***c.* 1194–1201**	*Llywelyn ab Iorwerth takes*
		control of Gwynedd, and
		becomes effective ruler of
		north Wales.
	1197	*Death of Rhys ap Gruffudd.*
	1189–99	Richard I (the Lionheart),
		king of England.
	1199–1216	John, king of England.
	1205	*Llywelyn ab Iorwerth*
		marries King John's
		illegitimate daughter, Joan.
	1211	*King John leads two*
		campaigns into the heart of
		Gwynedd to curb the power
		of Llywelyh an Iorwerth.
	1215	Magna Carta first issued.

Ogmore Castle. The fine twelfth-century keep stands up to 40 feet high.

Llansteffan Castle, on an ancient site overlooking the Tywi Estuary.

Medieval (*c.* 1216–1500)

Beaumaris Castle	**1216–72**	*Henry III, king of England.*
Beaupre Castle	**1218–40**	*Llywelyn ab Iorwerth at the*
Caernarfon Castle		*height of his power, with*
Caerphilly Castle		*superiority over all of native*
Carreg Cennen Castle		*Wales.*
Carswell Medieval House	**1238**	*Llywelyn ab Iorwerth*
Castell y Bere		*summons all the native lords*
Cilgerran Castle		*of Wales to Strata Florida*
Conwy Castle		*Abbey, to give allegiance to*
Criccieth Castle		*his son and heir.*
Denbigh Castle	**1240**	*Death of Llywelyn ab*
Denbigh Friary		*Iorwerth; decline in the*
Denbigh, St Hilary's Chapel		*power of Gwynedd follows.*
Derwen Churchyard Cross	**1255**	*Llywelyn ap Gruffudd,*
Dolbadarn Castle		*grandson of Llywelyn ab*
Dolforwyn Castle		*Iorwerth, emerges as sole*
Dolwyddelan Castle		*master of Gwynedd.*

Dryslwyn Castle	**1267**	*Treaty of Montgomery;*
Ewloe Castle		*Llywelyn ap Gruffudd near*
Flint Castle		*the height of his power;*
Harlech Castle		*recognized as Prince of Wales*
Hen Gwrt Moated Site		*by Henry III.*
Lamphey Bishop's Palace	**1272–1307**	Edward I, king of England.
Llangar Old Parish Church (?)	**1276–77**	*Edward I's first Welsh War;*
Montgomery Castle		*castles begun at Flint and*
Newport Castle		*Rhuddlan.*
Pennarth Fawr Medieval House	**1282–83**	*Edward I's second Welsh*
Raglan Castle		*War; death of Llywelyn ap*
Rhuddlan Castle		*Gruffudd; castles begun at*
Skenfrith Castle		*Caernarfon, Conwy and*
Swansea Castle		*Harlech.*
Tretower Court	**1284**	*Statute of Wales issued at*
Weobley Castle		*Rhuddlan; former*
		principality of Gwynedd
		carved into the shire counties
		of Anglesey, Caernarfon and
		Merioneth; new county of
		Flintshire.
	1294–95	*Revolt of Madog ap*
		Llywelyn; Beaumaris Castle
		begun.
	1301	*King Edward I creates his*
		son, Edward of Caernarfon,
		Prince of Wales.
	1307–27	Edward II, king of England.
	1316	*Llywelyn Bren leads furious*
		rebellion in Glamorgan.
	1326	*King Edward II 'in hiding' in*
		south Wales.
	1327–77	Edward III, king of England.
	1337–1453	Hundred Years War with France.
	1377–99	Richard II, king of England.
	1381	Peasants' Revolt.
	1399–1413	Henry IV, king of England.
	1400–10	*Owain Glyndŵr proclaimed*
		prince of Wales; Welsh rise in
		general rebellion.
	1404	*Owain Glyndŵr at the*
		height of his power; English
		control in Wales reduced to a
		few coastal areas.
	c. 1415	*Death of Owain Glyndŵr.*
	1413–22	Henry V, king of England.
	1422–61	Henry VI, king of England.
	1455–87	Wars of the Roses.
	1461–83	Edward IV, king of England.
	1483–85	Richard III, king of England.

Conwy in about 1600, from a contemporary drawing.

	1485	Henry Tudor's march through Wales, and defeat of Richard III at the battle of Bosworth.
The west view of Dolbadarn Castle, by Samuel and Nathaniel Buck, 1742.	1485–1509	Henry VII, king of England.

Post Medieval (*c.* 1500–1750)

Denbigh, Leicester's Church	1509–47	Henry VIII, king of England.
Gwydir Uchaf Chapel		
Monmouth, Great Castle House	1536–40	Dissolution of the Monasteries in England and Wales under Henry VIII.
Oxwich Castle		
Penmon Dovecot		
Pont Minllyn	1536–43	*Act of Union; Wales merged wholly with England, and Welsh shires henceforward represented in English Parliament.*
Rûg Chapel		
St Winifred's Chapel and Holy Well		
	1553–58	Mary I, queen of England.
	1558–1603	Elizabeth I, queen of England.
	1588	*Bishop William Morgan produces the first Welsh translation of the Bible.*
	1625–49	Charles I, king of England.
	1642–48	Civil War between Royalist and Parliamentarian brings many medieval castles back into use.
	1660–85	Charles II, king of England.

Dyfi Furnace, as depicted in 1804 by P.J. De Loutherbourg.

Industrial and Recent (*c.* 1750–1900)

Blaenavon Ironworks	**1760–1820**	George III, king of England.
Bryntail Lead Mine	**1789**	*Earliest production of iron at Blaenavon.*
Castell Coch		
Dyfi Furnace	**1837–1901**	Victoria, queen of England.
	1875	*The third marquess of Bute and William Burges begin work on Castell Coch.*

BIOGRAPHICAL NOTES
Key Historical Figures

These notes will provide readers with a few brief details on some of the key historical personalities featuring in the main text.

King Edward I (1239–1307)

From a later inscription on his tomb, King Edward I is generally remembered as the 'hammer of the Scots', yet it is through his awesome determination to finally conquer independent Wales that he so forcibly left his imprint. Edward's north Wales castles represent some of the most magnificent strongholds built anywhere in medieval western Europe.

The son of King Henry III, he was born at Westminster on 17 June 1239. The choice of Edward as a name undoubtedly reflects his father's devotion to the cult of Edward the Confessor, who had been canonized in 1161. The young Lord Edward entered public life at the age of 13, and two years later he was married to Eleanor of Castile. From the chronicles of Nicholas Trivet, he appears to have been an impressive man in physical terms (there is a manuscript illustration of the king on page 155).

Statues of King Edward I and Queen Eleanor at Lincoln Cathedral.

In his youth he devoted himself to the practice of arms: long arms gave him an advantage as a swordsman, long thighs one as a horseman. His otherwise handsome features were marred by a drooping left eyelid, and he apparently had a lisp. Even so, Edward stood quite literally head and shoulders above ordinary men. When his tomb was opened in 1774, the body measured 6 feet 2 inches. His chief leisure pursuits seem to have been chess-playing and hunting, particularly falconry.

In 1254 Edward was granted all the lands then held by the king in Wales. He was to gain valuable military experience in the baronial wars against his father in 1263–65, and during his own crusade to the Holy Land in 1270–72. It was on his return from this crusade that he learned of the death of his father in November 1272. Edward thus became king at the age of 33, and soon became a formidable ruler and a particularly able administrator and legislator. King Edward was insistent upon the rights of the English crown, and this in a large part accounted for his wars in Wales, France and Scotland. He remained devoted to his beloved queen, Eleanor, who died near Lincoln in 1290. Edward erected the famous Eleanor crosses, 12 in all, at the resting places of her funeral procession from Lincoln to Westminster.

The 1290s marked a turning point in his reign, with crippling financial problems associated with his wars against the French and the Scots. It was on his way to yet another campaign in Scotland that Edward died at Burgh-on-Sands, near Carlisle, on 7 July 1307.

Hubert de Burgh (d. 1243)

Hubert de Burgh was born of a modest Norfolk family, probably around the year 1175. His military and political career was a remarkable one. He rose to high office as justiciar of England, and entered the ranks of the aristocracy when he was created earl of Kent in 1227. At various stages in his life he held lands in 27 counties of England, and also controlled an important series of castles and estates in Wales.

Hubert appears to have entered the household of Prince John through the influence of his family's neighbours – the powerful de Warenne family, earls of Surrey, who held the Norfolk stronghold at Castle Acre. When John became king, Hubert served him as chamberlain and at first he was well rewarded. In 1201 the king granted him the three castles of Grosmont, Skenfrith and White Castle 'to sustain him in our service'. Eventually, they became known as 'the three castles of the justiciar'. By the end of 1203, de Burgh was posted in France as the constable of Chinon Castle, which he held during a year-long siege by the forces of King Philip Augustus until its fall in June 1205. The seemingly luckless Hubert was held as a prisoner of war for two years, during which time he lost the three castles. On his return to England in 1207, however, he soon regained his prosperity, acquiring great influence at the court, and eventually receiving the office of justiciar from King John in 1216.

John's reign ended in a national crisis, culminating in an attempt by Prince Louis of France to take the English throne. In July 1216 the prince's forces laid siege to Dover Castle, 'the key to England', and once more it was the heroic defence by Hubert de Burgh that saved the day. Following the siege, the justiciar was responsible for the complete redesign of the approaches to this enormous stronghold. Indeed, it was his early military experience in France, together with the lessons learnt at Dover, that were put to such good effect at Grosmont, Skenfrith and Montgomery.

In fact, it was in 1219 that the justiciar regained the so-called 'Three Castles', and gradually rose to the height of his power under the young King Henry III. He had already made two good marriages, and in 1221 he capped these through his wedding to Margaret, daughter of the king of Scotland. In 1227 he became a belted earl, and two years later he was granted the important castles at Cardigan and Carmarthen. By 1231 he had become master of the southern March.

Earl Hubert's success was short lived. In 1232 he fell from the king's favour, and was forced to seek sanctuary at Merton Priory (illustration, page 127). His last ten years were difficult ones, and he never fully recovered the trust of the king. In May 1243, 'after the many gratuitous attacks and persecutions of the king and after so many fluctuations of fortune', Hubert de Burgh died peacefully at his Surrey manor of Barnstead.

Master James of St George

James of St George was the brilliant master mason whose genius inspired King Edward I's castle-building in Wales for nearly three decades; the man who wrote in 1296: 'But as you know, Welshmen are Welshmen, and you need to understand them properly'.

Master James was probably born around 1230, though he is first mentioned in 1261. At the time he was working with his father in Savoy (on the present French-Swiss-Italian border), at the castle of Yverdon. Later, James worked on another great Savoy castle, St Georges d'Esperanche – from which he took his name – and it was here, on return from crusade in 1273, that Edward I must have first encountered him. The king was clearly impressed with his skills, and by early 1278 – at the beginning of the Welsh wars – James had been recruited to work in Wales, 'to ordain the works of the castles there'.

James was responsible for significant aspects in the planning and design of up to 12 castles in Wales, including the masterpieces at Beaumaris, Caernarfon, Conwy, Flint, Harlech and Rhuddlan. He was to all intents and purposes a true architect, in something like the modern sense of the word. James was not, however, the only Savoyard to work on the new royal strongholds. Certain distinct architectural details in the castles can be paralleled only in Savoy, and serve to underline not only the formative role of Master James, but also the influence of various other craftsmen who travelled from the Continent to work for King Edward.

As 'master of the king's works in Wales', from 1284 James was paid the handsome daily wage of three shillings (more than many craftsmen earned in a week), and in 1290 he was appointed constable of Harlech Castle for three years. This was indeed a high reward for a craftsman, unequalled throughout the Middle Ages. From 1295 he held a life tenancy of the Flintshire manor of Mostyn. Between 1298 and 1305 Master James went on to work for the king in Scotland. He died about 1309.

Llywelyn ab Iorwerth ('Llywelyn the Great') (1173–1240)

Llywelyn ab Iorwerth was born in 1173, probably at Dolwyddelan. He was the son of Iorwerth Drwyndwn (flat-nose), and grandson of Owain Gwynedd. In his youth, a series of family feuds had broken the strength of Gwynedd, but from 1194 Llywelyn began to exert his authority. His rise to power was meteoric. Llywelyn expelled his uncle, Dafydd, and brought other members of the dynasty under his firm control. By 1202 he had become the effective master of Gwynedd, a position he held until his death in 1240. Moreover, from this secure base, Llywelyn was able to utilize his power and resources to further his wider ambitions in Wales.

In 1205 he demonstrated his determination to play more than a parochial part in the politics of the day, when he married Joan, the daughter of King John. As Llywelyn's power in Wales grew, his relations with the king deteriorated, and in 1211 John invaded Gwynedd. In the event, it proved merely a temporary setback, since the king was soon embroiled in his own political difficulties, with the growing storm of baronial discontent culminating in *Magna Carta*. Llywelyn exploited this situation to the full, making devastating advances into the southern March in 1215. In 1218, he capitalized upon this military success by a political settlement with the councillors of the young King Henry III – the Treaty of Worcester.

From this point on his authority went unchallenged. Llywelyn enjoyed territorial superiority over a greater area than any other Welsh prince since the coming of the Normans. He exercised an overlordship based on strong military might and leadership. Llywelyn was a man of great passion; his wrath could be terrible – as William de Braose found to his cost in 1230, when he was publicly executed for allegedly having an affair with Llywelyn's wife.

From 1230 Llywelyn began to style himself prince of Aberffraw and lord of Snowdon, but he had become effectively prince of Wales. His main object from then on was to secure the succession for his son, Dafydd. There was a flaw in this ambition. Everything he had achieved was based on his own personality; there was no institutional framework to sustain the strength of the Gwynedd principality. Following Llywelyn's death in 1240, Dafydd was soon forced to relinquish his father's conquests to Henry III. But this should not belittle Llywelyn's achievements. He had dominated the history of Wales for 40 years. Small wonder that within a few decades the title 'the Great' had been bestowed upon him.

Llywelyn ap Gruffudd ('Llywelyn the Last') (d. 1282)

Following Llywelyn ab Iorwerth's death in 1240, his sons – Dafydd and Gruffudd – were soon engaged in power struggles in Gwynedd. Dafydd was forced to submit to Henry III, and in 1244 Gruffudd was killed whilst trying to escape from the Tower of London. It was not until Llywelyn's grandson, Llywelyn ap Gruffudd, emerged as the sole ruler of Gwynedd in 1255 that native Wales had once more found a

A stone head possibly of Llywelyn ab Iorwerth, the effective master of Gwynedd from 1202 to 1240.

Memorial stone at Cilmeri, near Builth Wells, commemorating Llywelyn ap Gruffudd.

leader. In this role, Llywelyn the Last quickly showed his true metal, and by 1258 he had received oaths of homage and allegiance from virtually all the Welsh princes. He went on to exploit the difficulties encountered by Henry III during the civil war with his barons (1264–65), led by Simon de Montfort. Exhausted by this continuing political dissension in both England and Wales, the king was forced to accept Llywelyn's territorial gains, and to acknowledge his proud title as prince of Wales by the Treaty of Montgomery (1267).

This was to prove but a temporary taste of power, lasting just ten years. Llywelyn was to totally misjudge the strength of Edward I, England's new ruler. Edward came to the throne in 1272, and from the outset the prince seemed almost to go out of his way to court the king's anger. In particular, he refused to yield the homage and money payments owing to the king under the terms of the Treaty of Montgomery. Llywelyn tempted fate yet further by arranging to marry Eleanor, daughter of the rebel baron Simon de Montfort, an act destined to strain Edward's patience to the limit.

Enough was enough, and by 1276–77 Edward had decided to settle accounts with the recalcitrant Welsh prince. Following his defeat, Llywelyn's power was restricted under the Treaty of Aberconwy (1277). An uneasy peace ensued for a few years, until Llywelyn's brother, Dafydd, broke into open revolt in the March of 1282. The king was outraged and moved with all speed to prevent disaster. He was determined that the solution would be permanent and annonced that he would 'put an end finally to the matter that he has now commenced of putting down the malice of the Welsh'.

Llywelyn was keen to avoid a repeat of 1277 and broke out from his Gwynedd stronghold to the south, possibly in an attempt to take Builth Castle. Athough the details are not clear, in December 1282 he was killed a few miles from Builth, in or after a major skirmish with a larger Marcher force. With him died all hopes of an independent Wales. 'It is the end of the world' mused one of the poets; another cried 'Oh God! That the sea might engulf the land . . . Why are we left to our long drawn weariness?'.

Owain Glyndŵr

Owain Glyndŵr is probably the best known hero of medieval Wales, and like all medieval heroes there is much about him that is shrouded in an air of mystery – he remains a shadowy and elusive figure. At least one contemporary chronicler believed he dabbled in the arts of magic, and in Shakespeare's *Henry IV* he is 'that great magician, damned Glendower'.

Owain belonged to a well-to-do native Welsh family, though we cannot be sure when he was born. In his youth he probably served a period of legal training at the Inns of Court, before turning to the profession of arms: he served as a squire in a number of Richard II's campaigns. He was in due course able to provide himself with a comfortable moated homestead at the family seat at Sycharth, near Llangollen. There is, however, little in his career before 1400 that suggests a budding national leader.

None the less, the final Edwardian conquest had left the Welsh an aggrieved people, and in the fourteenth century there were various hints that the smouldering flames of resentment could fire the nation to revolt at any point. Owain may have been stung into action by a territorial dispute with his English neighbour Reginald Grey of Ruthin. Whatever the case, the storm of revolt broke in September 1400, when Glyndŵr was proclaimed prince of Wales by some of his supporters at Glyndyfrdwy (Clwyd) and immediately set out on a raid of the English boroughs in north-east Wales. It quickly turned into a national uprising under Glyndŵr's charismatic leadership.

Central to Owain's role at the head of his people was his distinguished descent. Through his father he descended from the princely dynasty of northern Powys, and through his mother from the yet more distinguished stock of the Lord Rhys of Deheubarth. Owain saw the revolt as a way to free the Welsh people from the captivity of the English. Indeed, in 1403, he told the king of France how 'my nation has ... been trodden underfoot by the fury of the barbarous Saxons'.

By the autumn of 1403 the revolt was nearing its height, with the French lending practical help to the rebels at the sieges of Caernarfon and Kidwelly castles. The following year Owain achieved his greatest success, taking the castles of Aberystwyth and Harlech, and assembling his own parliament at Machynlleth. He had become a sovereign prince and effective ruler of large parts of western Wales. English control had been reduced to a few coastal and lowland areas, to isolated castles and boroughs.

Almost as quickly, the revolt seemed to die. The support of the French waned, and in 1408

The seal of Owain Glyndŵr, who was proclaimed prince of Wales in 1400.

Aberystwyth and Harlech were at last recaptured after long sieges. Owain himself was never taken, and English garrisons remained nervous for some time. Enigmatic to the end, Glyndŵr simply disappears from the records in 1415.

Rhys ap Gruffudd ('The Lord Rhys') (d. 1197)

The first appearance of Rhys ap Gruffudd in the records is in 1146, when as a young prince in his early teens he was present at the Welsh capture of Llansteffan Castle. From virtually that point, through until his death in 1197, he was to occupy centre stage in the world of Welsh politics; the Lord Rhys as he is generally known was without doubt the most powerful and influential native ruler of his day.

The course of his early career was not entirely smooth. In 1158, for example, King Henry II led a punitive campaign into south-west Wales, and Rhys was compelled to make formal submission, to give hostages, and to hand back various lands and castles to Anglo-Norman lords. Rhys was not, however, a man who would totally yield to such a crushing defeat, and gradually through calculated military actions and great statecraft he rebuilt the authority of the kingdom of Deheubarth. He eventually reached an accord with the king, sealed in negotiations at Pembroke and Laugharne in 1171–72. Henry eventually recognized the status of Deheubarth, and in effect appointed Rhys his 'justiciar'.

Rhys ruled from his two major strongholds at Dinefwr and Cardigan, and assumed for himself the title rightful prince of south Wales. He was, too, a pious man, and was an early benefactor to the Cistercians at Whitland Abbey. Strata Florida was virtually his foundation, and at Talley he established the only colony of Premonstratensian canons in Wales. The Lord Rhys was also determined upon a display of the cultural eminence of his court, and in 1176 he held a great assembly of poets and musicians from all over Wales at Cardigan – hailed as the first 'national eisteddfod'. In due course, the poets justifiably praised him as Rhys the Great, Rhys the Good – 'the unconquered head of all Wales'.

Rhys died in 1197 and was buried at St Davids (illustration, page 76), at the shrine of his and the nation's premier saint. His success had been based largely on his own remarkable stamina and skill, but also upon the good will of the Crown. Ironically, the strength of Deheubarth was not to outlive his death, and in the following century its power was eclipsed as that of Gwynedd in the north rose to new heights.

GLOSSARY

The following is a glossary of the various terms used in the body of the text which may be somewhat familiar to general readers. Many of them should, hopefully, be relatively clear from their general context, but this list will provide a source of easy reference. The glossary may also be of use to those readers who visit the monuments themselves. The terms will be found in wide use in Cadw's guidebooks, exhibitions and other site interpretation.

Aisle The part of a church on either side of the nave or presbytery, usually separated off behind columns.

Antiphoner A book of psalms or hymns, with music, for use in the divine office.

Apse The semicircular termination of a chancel or chapel in a church.

Apsidal Apse shaped; as in the D-shaped towers of native Welsh castles.

Arcade A row of columns supporting open arches, as in 'nave arcade'.

Ashlar Squared dressed stone laid in regular courses, with fine joints.

Augustinian Communities of clerics (also known as Austin or Regular Canons), who adopted the Rule of St Augustine. First officially recognized in the later eleventh century.

Bailey The defended outer court of a castle (see Ward).

Ballflower A small carved ornament of flower petals around a ball, common in the early fourteenth century.

Barbican An outer defence work, usually an enclosure, but often also a gated bridge or ramp, before a main gate of a castle.

Bastide Medieval fortified township, particularly those established by the kings of England and France in Gascony. The term is often used for King Edward I's new towns in Wales.

Bay A vertical division of a building, marked on the outside by windows or buttresses, and inside by columns or units in the roof vaulting.

Beaker A form of distinct pottery vessel, making its first appearance as early as 2500 BC and frequently deposited with burials.

Bellcot A small structure to hang a bell or bells, usually on the gable end of a church.

Benedictine The oldest of monastic orders (also known as 'black monks' from the colour of their habits). The monks observed the

188

St Benedict, upon whose Rule the Bendictine and Cistercian orders based their monastic lives.

Detail of a corbel in the chapel at Raglan castle.

	Rule of St Benedict.
Boss	A carved decorative knob at the intersection of vaulting ribs.
Burgage Plot	A plot of land, usually long and narrow, forming the unit of property in a medieval borough.
Burh	An Anglo-Saxon fortified town or other major defended place.
Buttress	A vertical mass of masonry projecting from a wall to give it extra strength.
Cairn	A heap or mound of stones covering a prehistoric burial or a chambered tomb. Some, however, served ceremonial and ritual purposes.
Cantref	The main Welsh administrative unit, occuring as a territorial division in pre-Norman times. By the late eleventh century most cantrefi had been subdivided into two or more commotes.
Capital	The head of a column, usually carved with decoration.
Carmelite	An order with obscure origins, taking its name from Mount Carmel in Palestine. Reorganized as friars (the 'white friars') in the thirteenth century.
Chancel	The eastern part of a church, usually with the high altar, and reserved for the clergy (see Presbytery).
Choir	The part of a church, fitted with choir stalls, where the monks or clergy met to sing and pray.
Cinquefoil	Five leaf, or foil shape, often found in the head of a window opening in Gothic architecture.

Cist A stone-lined or slab-built grave. The term long cist is sometimes used to describe the form of chambers in a Neolithic tomb.

Cistercian Reformed Benedictine monks, established at Cîteaux in 1098, and later greatly expanded under the leadership of St Bernard (d. 1153); also known as the 'white monks'.

Civitas The name given to a tribal area by the Romans; a unit of local self government.

Clas A Welsh term; a pre-Conquest community of canons at a 'mother church', exercising ecclesiastical independence and authority in a respective district.

Clerestory The upper storey of the main walls of a church, usually pierced by windows.

Commote A Welsh administrative unit; a sub-division of an ancient cantref. The commote was often converted to a Norman lordship.

Constable The governor of a castle.

Corbel A stone projection from the face of a wall intended to support a floor or roof beam.

A roof boss from the Presbytery, Tintern Abbey.

Clerestory windows on the south side of the nave at Tintern Abbey.

Crossing The intersection in a church of the nave, transepts, and presbytery or chancel; often there is a tower above.

Curtain The wall, often with angle towers, which encloses the courtyard of a castle.

Dais A low platform at the upper end of a hall, reserved for the high table of the lord or head of the family.

Decorated The phase of English Gothic architecture lasting from about 1250 to 1360.

Donjon The great tower of a castle (see Keep).

Drum Tower A circular tower – drum shaped.

Early English The phase of English Gothic architecture lasting from about 1190 to 1250.

Embrasure A splayed opening in a wall or parapet, to take a window, or to accommodate bowmen.

Henge Circular ceremonial earthwork surrounded by a ditch, with an inner or outer bank; one or more breaks in the ditch and bank forming entrances. Frequently there are additional internal features such as circles of timber or stone, pits or sometimes burials. The name derives from the most famous example, Stonehenge.

Hipped Roof A pitched roof with sloping ends, as opposed to vertical gables.

Hoarding (Hourd) A timber gallery projecting from a castle tower or wall and supported on joists. Usually with openings in the floor through which to drop missiles.

Jamb The straight side of a door, window, or archway.

Justiciar The king's chief minister in the early Middle Ages. Edward I made similar appointments in Wales, where the justiciars in the north and south acted as governor-generals.

Keep The principal tower of a castle, generally containing the residential quarters of the lord.

The keep at Skenfrith Castle.

Lancet A narrow pointed window without tracery, and characteristic of the Early English period.

Loop An arrowslit or loophole.

Machicolation Opening in the floor of a projecting parapet or fighting gallery, through which missiles could be directed at attackers. Frequently the term is also applied to the entire projecting structure.

March From the French word 'marche' meaning frontier; generally applied to the south coast and eastern borders of Wales under Anglo-Norman control.

Marcher Lordship A lordship in the March of Wales, whose baron exercised virtually independent powers under the king. The Marcher lordships eventually swung in a great arc from Chester in the north to Chepstow in the south, and then west to Pembroke and Haverfordwest.

Megalith(ic) Large stone; a term widely applied to the construction of Neolithic chambered tombs.

Motte A castle mound, introduced by Normans, characteristically shaped like an upturned basin.

Mullion Vertical bar between the openings of a window.

Murder Hole A hole contrived in the vault or roof of a gatehouse passage, through which missiles could be dropped on attackers.

Neolithic New Stonge Age; the period of the earliest agriculturalists, beginning in Britain at least 4000 BC and lasting to around 2500 BC.

Newel Stair A circular stair winding around the newel, or central pillar.

Norman The architectural style described on the Continent as Romanesque, and characterized by round-headed arches.

Oriel Window An angular or curved projecting window. Sometimes the term is reserved for upper floors.

Perpendicular The phase of English Gothic architecture lasting from about 1330 to 1550.

Pier A pillar of masonry.

Piscina Latin for basin; a niche close to an altar for washing the priest's hands and the sacred vessels during mass.

Plinth The projecting base of a wall or column.

Portal Stone The stone at the entrance to a chambered tomb.

Portcullis A heavy grating designed to close off an entrance passage, sliding vertically in grooves cut on either side to receive it.

Premonstratensian An order of canons (the 'white canons'), founded by St Norbet at Prémontré, and observing the Rule of St Augustine.

Principia The headquarters building in a Roman fortress or fort.

Presbytery The eastern arm of a large church, east of the choir and containing the high altar (see Chancel).

Pulpitum A screen wall dividing the nave from the choir in large churches; generally forming a backing for the return choir stalls.

Putlog Hole One of a series of holes in a masonry wall, that originally carried the horizontal timbers of the scaffolding used during construction.

Revetment A retaining wall or facing supporting the core of a defensive bank or curtain.

Rib An arch carrying the vault, or placed across the sections of a vault (see Vault).

Ringwork An early earthwork castle, making its first appearance at the same time as mottes. Usually circular or oval in plan, the defences consist of a steep bank and external ditch.

Rule The code of religious life followed by a monastic order. Two major Rules governed in the medieval western world: those of St Benedict of Monte Cassino (d. about AD 547), and St Augustine of Hippo (d. AD 430).

Savigniac An order of monks founded at Savigny in 1105, originally as a colony of hermits. The order merged with the Cistercians in 1147.

Screens Passage The space at the service end of a medieval hall, between the screen and the entrance to the kitchen, buttery or pantry.

Sedilia Latin for seats. Seats for the clergy officiating at services, situated on the south of the chancel or presbytery, and often three in number.

Shell Keep A tower contrived by circling the summit of a castle mound with a stone curtain wall.

Solar A private chamber, generally of a lord, often placed at the dais end of a hall.

Springer The lowest stones in the arches of a vault; the point at which an arch meets its supporting member.

String Course A projecting horizontal band or strip of masonry, intended for decorative effect, across a wall face.

Tironensian Monastic order founded by Bernard (d. 1117) at Tiron, and much influenced by the Cistercians.

Tithes A tax payable to the church of one tenth of all agrarian produce.

Tracery Geometrical patterns of cut stone, found in windows or as blank patterns on walls.

Transept The transverse (short) arms of a cross-shaped church, linking the nave and presbytery at the crossing.

Truss A timber frame in which the wood is jointed and braced to retain its shape under a load. A roof truss is composed of a series of timbers framed together and placed at bay intervals along a building to support the various rafters.

Undercroft A ground-floor chamber or basement, often vaulted.

Vault An arched stone roof, with many variants: barrel vault, fan vault, groined vault, rib vault.

Wall-Walk A passage, path or fighting platform behind the parapet of a curtain wall.

Ward A court or bailey of a castle.

A view of the upper ward of Caernarfon Castle.

GAZETTEER
The Location of Properties and Details of Access

Admission

The following list includes all those monuments cared for by Cadw: Welsh Historic Monuments on behalf of the Secretary of State for Wales. Those sites where a charge is made for admission are marked with an asterisk (*). Elsewhere entry is free at all reasonable hours. At several monuments, current programmes of archaeological excavation and conservation works mean that access is of necessity limited, and these are noted accordingly in the gazetteer entries. The standard hours of admission do vary seasonally, and there are also slight differences from site to site. All monuments are closed Christmas Eve, Christmas Day, Boxing Day and New Year's Day. Full details of hours are available from the Cadw main office (address below).

Heritage in Wales Membership Scheme

Visitors may care to take advantage of the 'Heritage in Wales' membership scheme, which provides free access to all sites, together with a series of other benefits. Details are available at many monuments, or once again from the Cadw main office.

Location

This gazetteer provides basic information on the location of sites, together with the Ordnance Survey (OS) 1:50,000 Landranger map number. The National Grid References (NGR) will assist the reader to identify those smaller sites which may be particularly difficult to locate.

Further Information

Telephone numbers are provided for those sites in custodial care, or where a key keeper is on hand. As all information is subject to change, in order to avoid disappointment, enquiries for further details may be directed to the monument, or to:

Cadw: Welsh Historic Monuments,
Brunel House,
2 Fitzalan Road,
CARDIFF, CF2 1UY.

Tel: (0222) 465511

BARCLODIAD Y GAWRES BURIAL CHAMBER
Just off A4080, 2m NW of Aberffraw, Isle of Anglesey, Gwynedd
A key can be collected at the 'Wayside Shop', Llanfaelog
Tel: (0407) 810153 – Key keeper
OS Map 114: NGR SH 329707

BASINGWERK ABBEY
Just S of A548, near Greenfield, 1m NE of Holywell, Clwyd
OS Map 116: NGR SJ 196774

BEAUMARIS CASTLE*
Beaumaris, Isle of Anglesey, Gwynedd
Tel: (0248) 810361
OS Map 114: NGR SH 607762

BEAUPRE CASTLE
1m SW of St Hilary, off A48, near Cowbridge, South Glamorgan
Tel: (044 63) 3034 – Key keeper
OS Map 170: NGR ST 009720

BLAENAVON IRONWORKS*
Blaenavon, Gwent
OS Map 161: NGR SO 249092

BODOWYR BURIAL CHAMBER
Near Bodowyr farm, 1¼m E of Llangaffo, off
B4419, Isle of Anglesey, Gwynedd
OS Map 114: NGR SH 462681

BRECON GAER ROMAN FORT
2¾m WNW of Brecon, off A40, near
Aberyscir, Powys
OS Map 160: NGR SO 004296

BRONLLYS CASTLE
¾m NW of Talgarth, on A479, 9m NE of
Brecon, Powys
OS Map 161: NGR SO 149347

BRYN CELLI DDU BURIAL CHAMBER
N of A4080, 1m ESE Llanddaniel Fab, Isle of
Anglesey, Gwynedd
OS Map 114: NGR SH 506701

BRYNTAIL LEAD MINE
At foot of Clywedog dam, off B4518, 3m NW
of Llanidloes, Powys
OS Map 136: NGR SN 917864

CAER GYBI ROMAN FORTLET
Overlooking harbour, Holyhead, Isle of
Anglesey, Gwynedd
OS Map 114: NGR SH 247826

CAER LÊB
¾m WNW of Brynsiencyn, off A4080, Isle of
Anglesey, Gwynedd
OS Map 114: NGR SH 473674

CAERLEON ROMAN FORTRESS*
Amphitheatre, Fortress Baths, Fortress
Defences, Prysg Field Barracks, situated around
small town of Caerleon, off M4, 2m NE of
Newport, Gwent
Tel: (0633) 422518
OS Map 171: NGR ST 337906

CAERNARFON CASTLE*
Caernarfon, Gwynedd
Tel: (0286) 77617
OS Map 115: NGR SH 477626

CAERNARFON TOWN WALLS
N of castle, Caernarfon, Gwynedd
OS Map 115: NGR SH 477628

CAERPHILLY CASTLE*
Caerphilly, Mid Glamorgan
Tel: (0222) 883143
OS Map 171: NGR ST 155870

CAERWENT ROMAN TOWN
Caerwent, just off A48, 5m SW of Chepstow,
Gwent
OS Map 171: NGR ST 469905

CAER Y TŴR HILLFORT
On summit of Holyhead Mountain, 1¾m W of
Holyhead, Isle of Anglesey, Gwynedd
OS Map 114: NGR SH 218830

CAPEL GARMON BURIAL CHAMBER
¾m S of Capel Garmon, 5m S of Llanrwst, off
A5, Gwynedd
OS Map 116: NGR SH 818543

CAPEL LLIGWY
¾m N of Llanallgo, off A5025, Isle of
Anglesey, Gwynedd
OS Map 114: NGR SH 499863

CAREW CROSS
Carew, off A477, near castle, 4m NE of
Pembroke, Dyfed
OS Map 157: NGR SN 047038

CARREG CENNEN CASTLE*
Near Trapp, off A483, 4m SE of Llandeilo,
Dyfed
Tel: (0558) 822291
OS Map 159: NGR SN 668191

**CARREG COETAN ARTHUR BURIAL
CHAMBER**
Near Newport, off A487, 6m E of Fishguard,
Dyfed
OS Map 145: NGR SN 060394

CARSWELL MEDIEVAL HOUSE
1m E of St Florence, off B4318, about 3m W of
Tenby, Dyfed
Limited access
OS Map 158: NGR SN 098010

CASTELL BRYN GWYN
1¼m W of Brynsiencyn, off A4080, Isle of
Anglesey, Gwynedd
OS Map 114: NGR SH 465670

CASTELL COCH*
Near Tongwynlais, off A470, 5m NW of
Cardiff, South Glamorgan
Tel: (0222) 810101
OS Map 171: NGR ST 131826

CASTELL Y BERE
Near Llanfihangel y Pennant, off B4405, 6½m
NE of Tywyn, Gwynedd
OS Map 124: NGR SH 667085

CHEPSTOW BULWARKS CAMP
1m S of Chepstow, Gwent
OS Map 162: NGR ST 538927

CHEPSTOW CASTLE*
Chepstow, Gwent
Tel: (029 12) 4065
OS Map 162: NGR ST 533941

CHEPSTOW TOWN WALL
From castle, across town, to River Wye,
Chepstow, Gwent
OS Map 162: NGR ST 533937

CILGERRAN CASTLE*
Cilgerran, 3m S of Cardigan, off A478, Dyfed
Tel: (0239) 615136
OS Map 145: NGR SN 195431

COITY CASTLE*
Coity, 2m NE of Bridgend, off A4061, Mid
Glamorgan
A key can be collected at 94 Heol West Plas,
Coity
Tel: (0656) 652021 – Key keeper
OS Map 170: NGR SS 923815

CONWY CASTLE*
Conwy, Gwynedd
Tel: (0492) 592358
OS Map 115: NGR SH 783774

CONWY TOWN WALLS
N and W of castle, enclosing much of town,
Conwy, Gwynedd
OS Map 115: NGR SH 781776

CRICCIETH CASTLE*
Criccieth, Gwynedd
Tel: (0766) 522227
OS Map 123/124: NGR SH 500377

CYMER ABBEY*
Near Llanelltyd, off A470, 1½m N of
Dolgellau, Gwynedd
Tel: (0341) 422854 – Key keeper
OS Map 124: NGR SH 721195

DENBIGH CASTLE*
Denbigh, Clwyd
Tel: (0745) 713979
OS Map 116: NGR SJ 052658

DENBIGH FRIARY
E outskirts of Denbigh, Clwyd
OS Map 116: NGR SJ 059666

DENBIGH, LEICESTER'S CHURCH
Near castle, Denbigh, Clwyd
OS Map 116: NGR SJ 053659

DENBIGH, ST HILARY'S CHAPEL
Near castle, Denbigh, Clwyd
OS Map 116: NGR SJ 052659

DENBIGH TOWN WALLS
Denbigh, Clwyd
A key to the walls is available from the castle
custodian
OS Map 116: NGR SJ 051657

DERWEN CHURCHYARD CROSS
Derwen, off A464, 5m N of Corwen, Clwyd
OS Map 116: NGR SJ 070507

DIN DRYFOL BURIAL CHAMBER
2m N of Bethel, off B4422, near Fferam Dryfol,
Isle of Anglesey, Gwynedd
OS Map 114: NGR SH 395724

DINEFWR CASTLE
1m W of Llandeilo, off A40, Dyfed
Limited access during conservation works
OS Map 159: NGR SN 612217

DIN LLIGWY HUT GROUP
¾m N of Llanallgo, off A5025, Isle of
Anglesey, Gwynedd
OS Map 114: NGR SH 497861

DOLBADARN CASTLE
½m SE of Llanberis, on A4086, Gwynedd
OS Map 115: NGR SH 586598

DOLFORWYN CASTLE
1m W of Abermule, 3¼m NE of Newtown, off A483, Powys
Limited access during excavation and conservation works
OS Map 136: NGR SO 152950

DOLWYDDELAN CASTLE*
1m W of Dolwyddelan, on A470, Gwynedd
OS Map 115: NGR SH 721523

DRYSLWYN CASTLE
5m W of Llandeilo, on B4297, Dyfed
Limited access during excavation and conservation works
OS Map 159: NGR SN 555204

DYFFRYN ARDUDWY BURIAL CHAMBER
Dyffryn Ardudwy, 5m S of Harlech, on A496, Gwynedd
OS Map 124: NGR SH 588228

DYFI FURNACE*
6m SW of Machynlleth, on A487, Dyfed
OS Map 135: NGR SN 685951

ELISEG'S PILLAR
2m N of Llangollen, on A542, near Valle Crucis Abbey, Clwyd
OS Map 117: NGR SJ 203445

EWENNY PRIORY
Ewenny, 1½m S of Bridgend, off A48, Mid Glamorgan
OS Map 170: NGR SS 912778

EWLOE CASTLE
1m NW of Ewloe, 2m NW of Hawarden, off A55, Clwyd
OS Map 117: NGR SJ 288675

FLINT CASTLE*
NE side of Flint, Clwyd
OS Map 117: NGR SJ 247733

GROSMONT CASTLE
Grosmont, on B4347, 10m NW of Monmouth, 9m NE of Abergavenny, Gwent
Tel: (0981) 240301 – Key keeper
OS Map 161: NGR SO 405244

GWYDIR UCHAF CHAPEL
½m SW of Llanrwst, off B5106, Gwynedd
OS Map 115: NGR SH 794609

HARLECH CASTLE*
Harlech, Gwynedd
Tel: (0766) 780552
OS Map 124: NGR SH 581312

HAVERFORDWEST PRIORY
S outskirts of town, Haverfordwest, Dyfed
Limited access during excavation and conservation works
OS Map 158: NGR SM 957152

HEN GWRT MOATED SITE
¼m ENE of Llantilio Crossenny, off B4233, 7m E of Abergavenny, Gwent
OS Map 161: NGR SO 396151

HOLYHEAD MOUNTAIN HUT GROUP
2¼m W of Holyhead, Isle of Anglesey, Gwynedd
OS Map 114: NGR SH 212820

KIDWELLY CASTLE*
Kidwelly, Dyfed
Tel: (0554) 890104
OS Map 159: NGR 409071

LAMPHEY BISHOP'S PALACE*
Lamphey, 2½m E of Pembroke, off A4139, Dyfed
Tel: (0646) 672224
OS Map 158: NGR SN 018009

LAUGHARNE CASTLE
Laugharne, on A4066, 14m SW of Carmarthen, Dyfed
Limited access during excavation and conservation works
OS Map 159: NGR SN 302107

LLANGAR OLD PARISH CHURCH
1m SW of Corwen, off B4401, Clwyd
Limited access during conservation works
OS Map 125: NGR 063424

LLANMELIN WOOD HILLFORT
1¼m NW of Caerwent, off A48, 6m W of Chepstow, Gwent
OS Map 171: NGR ST 461925

LLANSTEFFAN CASTLE
Llansteffan, on B4312, 8m SW of Carmarthen, Dyfed
OS Map 159: NGR SN 352102

LLANTHONY PRIORY
9m N of Abergavenny, off A465, Gwent
Tel: (0873) 890311 – Key keeper
OS Map 171: NGR SO 289278

LLAWHADEN CASTLE*
Llawhaden, off A40, 3m NW of Narberth, 10m
E of Haverfordwest, Dyfed
A key can be collected at the 'Post Office',
Llawhaden
Tel: (099 14) 201 – Key keeper
OS Map 158: NGR SN 073175

LLIGWY BURIAL CHAMBER
¾m N of Llanallgo, off A5025, Isle of
Anglesey, Gwynedd
OS Map 114: NGR SH 501860

LOUGHOR CASTLE
Loughor, on A4070, 7m NW of Swansea, West
Glamorgan
OS Map 159: NGR SS 564980

MAEN ACHWYFAN CROSS
1m WNW of Whitford, off A5151, 5m NW of
Holywell, Clwyd
OS Map 116: NGR SJ 129788

MARGAM STONES MUSEUM
Margam, 4m SE of Port Talbot, off A48,
adjacent to Margam Country Park, West
Glamorgan
Tel: (0656) 742678 – Key keeper
OS Map 170: NGR SS 801864

MONMOUTH CASTLE
Monmouth, Gwent
OS Map 162: NGR SO 507129

MONMOUTH, GREAT CASTLE HOUSE
Monmouth, Gwent
Viewing from exterior only
OS Map 162: NGR SO 507129

MONTGOMERY CASTLE
Montgomery, Powys
Tel: (068 681) 370 – Key keeper
OS Map 137: NGR SO 221967

NEATH ABBEY*
1m W of Neath, off A465, West Glamorgan
Tel: (0792) 812387 – Key keeper
OS Map 170: NGR SS 737974

NEWCASTLE CASTLE
Bridgend, Mid Glamorgan
A key can be collected at 'The Shop', 62
Newcastle Hill, Bridgend
Tel: (0656) 652964 – Key keeper
OS Map 170: NGR SS 902801

NEWPORT CASTLE
Newport, Gwent
OS Map 171: NGR ST 312884

OGMORE CASTLE
2½m SW of Bridgend, on B4524, Mid
Glamorgan
Tel: (0656) 653435 – Key keeper
OS Map 170: NGR SS 882769

OXWICH CASTLE
Oxwich, off A4118, Gower peninsula 11m SW
of Swansea, West Glamorgan
Limited access during conservation works
OS Map 159: NGR SS 497862

PARC LE BREOS BURIAL CHAMBER
½m NW of Parkmill, off A4118, Gower
peninsula, 8m SW of Swansea, West Glamorgan
OS Map 159: NGR SS 537898

PENMON CROSS
3½m NE of Beaumaris, off B5109, in St
Seiriol's Church, Penmon, Isle of Anglesey,
Gwynedd
OS Map 114: NGR SH 630808

PENMON DOVECOT
3½m NE of Beaumaris, Isle of Anglesey,
Gwynedd
OS Map 114: NGR SH 632807

PENMON PRIORY
3½m NE of Beaumaris, Isle of Anglesey,
Gwynedd
OS Map 114: NGR SH 630807

PENMON, ST SEIRIOL'S WELL
3½m NE of Beaumaris, Isle of Anglesey,
Gwynedd
OS Map 114: NGR SH 631808

PENNARTH FAWR MEDIEVAL HOUSE
5m W of Criccieth, off A497, Gwynedd
OS Map 123: NGR SH 419376

PENRHOS FEILW STANDING STONES
1¾m SW of Holyhead, Isle of Anglesey,
Gwynedd
OS Map 114: NGR SH 227809

PENTRE IFAN BURIAL CHAMBER
2m SE of Nevern, 3½m SE of Newport, off
A487, Dyfed
OS Map 145: NGR SN 099370

PONT MINLLYN
Near Dinas Mawddwy, on A470, Gwynedd
OS Map 124: NGR SH 859138

PRESADDFED BURIAL CHAMBER
1m NE of Bodedern, off B5109, Isle of
Anglesey, Gwynedd
OS Map 114: NGR SH 347809

RAGLAN CASTLE*
½m N of Raglan, 7m SW of Monmouth, off
A40, Gwent
Tel: (0291) 690228
OS Map 161: NGR SO 414083

RHUDDLAN CASTLE*
Rhuddlan, 3m S of Rhyl, Clwyd
Tel: (0745) 590777
OS Map 116: NGR SJ 024779

RHUDDLAN, TWTHILL
Near Rhuddlan Castle, 3m S of Rhyl, Clwyd
OS Map 116: NGR SJ 026777

RÛG CHAPEL
1m WNW of Corwen, off A494, Clwyd
Limited access during conservation works
OS Map 125: NGR SJ 064438

RUNSTON CHAPEL
1m NE of Crick, 3m SW of Chepstow, off A48,
Gwent
OS Map 162: NGR ST 495916

ST CYBI'S WELL
Llangybi, 6m NW of Criccieth, off B4354,
Gwynedd
OS Map 123: NGR SH 427413

ST DAVIDS BISHOP'S PALACE*
St Davids, Dyfed
Tel: (0437) 720517
OS Map 157: NGR SM 750254

ST DOGMAELS ABBEY
St Dogmaels, 1m W of Cardigan, on B4546,
Dyfed
Tel: (0239) 612563 – Key keeper
OS Map 145: NGR SN 163458

ST LYTHANS BURIAL CHAMBER
1½m S of St Nicholas, off A48, 6m SW of
Cardiff, South Glamorgan
OS Map 171: NGR ST 100722

ST NON'S CHAPEL
½m S of St Davids, Dyfed
OS Map 157: NGR SM 752243

**ST WINIFRED'S CHAPEL AND HOLY
WELL**
Holywell, Clwyd
Tel: (0352) 713054 – Key keeper
OS Map 116: NGR SJ 185763

SEGONTIUM ROMAN FORT
On outskirts of Caernarfon, off A4085,
Gwynedd
OS Map 115: NGR SH 485624

SKENFRITH CASTLE
Skenfrith, 6m NNW of Monmouth, on B4521,
Gwent
OS Map 161: NGR SO 457202

STRATA FLORIDA ABBEY*
1¼m SE of Pontrhydfendigaid, off B4343, 14m
SE of Aberystwyth, Dyfed
Tel: (097 45) 261
OS Map 135: NGR SN 746657

SWANSEA CASTLE
Swansea, West Glamorgan
OS Map 159: NGR SS 657931

TALLEY ABBEY*
Talley, on B4302, 6m N of Llandeilo, Dyfed
Tel: (055 83) 444 – Key keeper
OS Map 146: NGR SN 632327

TINKINSWOOD BURIAL CHAMBER
¾m S of St Nicholas, off A48, 6m WSW of
Cardiff, South Glamorgan
OS Map 171: NGR ST 092773

TINTERN ABBEY*
Tintern, on A466, 5m N of Chepstow, Gwent
Tel: (029 18) 251
OS Map 162: NGR SO 533000

TREFIGNATH BURIAL CHAMBER
1½m SSE of Holyhead, off B4545, Isle of
Anglesey, Gwynedd
OS Map 114: NGR SH 258805

TREGWEHELYDD STANDING STONE
1¾m NE of Bodedern, off B5109, Isle of
Anglesey, Gwynedd
OS Map 114: NGR SH 340831

TRETOWER CASTLE*
Tretower, off A40, 3m NW of Crickhowell,
Powys
OS Map 161: NGR SO 185212

TRETOWER COURT*
Tretower, off A40, 3m NW of Crickhowell,
Powys
Tel: (0874) 730279
OS Map 161: NGR SO 186211

TŶ MAWR STANDING STONE
1m SE of Holyhead, off B4545, Isle of
Anglesey, Gwynedd
OS Map 114: NGR SH 253809

TŶ NEWYDD BURIAL CHAMBER
¾m NE of Llanfaelog, off A4080, Isle of
Anglesey, Gwynedd
OS Map 114: NGR SH 344738

VALLE CRUCIS ABBEY*
1½m NW of Llangollen, on A542, Clwyd
Tel: (0978) 860326
OS Map 117: NGR SJ 205442

WEOBLEY CASTLE*
2m W of Llanrhidian, off B4271, 11m W of
Swansea, Gower peninsula, West Glamorgan
Tel: (0792) 390012
OS Map 159: NGR SS 478927

WHITE CASTLE*
6m SSE of Abergavenny, off B4233, Gwent
Tel: (060 085) 380
OS Map 161: NGR SO 379167

Further Reading

The list of books, articles and specialist papers consulted during the preparation of this text is very large. Once again, I must apologise to all those scholars who have studied the archaeology and history of these monuments over many years, and whose work I have of necessity drawn upon anonymously. Alas, however much it goes against scholarly principle, it is not in the nature of such volumes to include an extensive list of references. The following is merely intended as a guide to the more important general sources. The reader particularly interested in following up more of the source material will find much fuller bibliographies in many of the volumes listed here.

PREHISTORY
R. Bradley, *The Social Foundations of Prehistoric Britain* (London 1984).
D.V. Clarke, T.G. Cowie and A. Foxon, *Symbols of Power at the Time of Stonehenge* (Edinburgh 1985).
T. Darvill, *Prehistoric Britain* (London 1987).
F.M. Lynch, *Prehistoric Anglesey* (Langefni 1970).

J.V.S. Megaw and D.D.A. Simpson, editors, *Introduction to British Prehistory* (Leicester 1979).
J.A. Taylor, editor, *Culture and Environment in Prehistoric Wales* (Oxford 1980).

ROMAN
G.C. Boon, *The Legionary Fortress of Caerleon-Isca: A Brief Account* (Caerleon 1987).
P. Clayton, editor, *A Companion to Roman Britain* (Oxford 1980).
S.S. Frere, *Britannia: A History of Roman Britain*, third edition (London 1987).
V.E. Nash-Williams, *The Roman Frontier in Wales*, second edition, revised by M.G. Jarrett (Cardiff 1969).
P. Salway, *Roman Britain* (Oxford 1981).
M. Todd, *Roman Britain 55 B.C.–A.D. 400* (London 1981).
G. Webster, *The Roman Imperial Army*, third edition (London 1985).

EARLY MEDIEVAL
L. Alcock, *Economy, Society and Warfare Among the Britons and Saxons* (Cardiff 1987).

W. Davies, *Wales in the Early Middle Ages* (Leicester 1982).

N. Edwards and A. Lane, editors, *Early Medieval Settlements in Wales AD 400–1100* (Bangor and Cardiff 1988).

V.E. Nash-Williams, *Early Christian Monuments of Wales* (Cardiff 1950).

C. Thomas, *Celtic Britain* (London 1986).

MEDIEVAL AND LATER

R. Avent, *Castles of the Princes of Gwynedd* (Cardiff 1983).

R.A. Brown, *English Castles*, third edition (London 1976).

R.R. Davies, *Conquest, Coexistence and Change: Wales 1063–1415* (Oxford 1987).

D.M. Rees, *The Industrial Archaeology of Wales* (Newton Abbot 1975).

R. Gilyard-Beer, *Abbeys: An Illustrative Guide to the Abbeys of England and Wales*, second edition (London 1976).

R. Haslam, *The Buildings of Wales: Powys* (Harmondsworth and Cardiff 1979).

E. Hubbard, *The Buildings of Wales: Clwyd* (Harmondsworth 1986).

D.J.C. King, *The Castle in England and Wales* (London 1988).

C. Platt, *The Castle in Medieval England and Wales* (London 1982).

C. Platt, *The Abbeys and Priories of Medieval England* (London 1984).

M. Prestwich, *Edward I* (London 1988).

A. Taylor, *The Welsh Castles of Edward I* (London 1986).

D. Stephenson, *The Governance of Gwynedd* (Cardiff 1984).

P. Smith, *Houses of the Welsh Countryside: A Study in Historical Geography*, second edition (London 1988).

D.H. Williams, *The Welsh Cistercians*, second edition, 2 volumes (Caldey Island 1984).

G. Williams, *The Welsh Church from Conquest to Reformation*, second edition (Cardiff 1976).

G. Williams, *Recovery, Reorientation and Reformation: Wales c. 1415–1642* (Oxford 1987).

THE ROYAL COMMISSION ON ANCIENT AND HISTORICAL MONUMENTS IN WALES

The inventories of the Royal Commission include detailed information on many of the sites in State care. Particular attention is drawn to the following volumes:

An Inventory of the Ancient Monuments in Anglesey (London 1937).

An Inventory of the Ancient Monuments in Caernarvonshire, I: *East* (London 1956).

An Inventory of the Ancient Monuments in Caernarvonshire, II: *Central* (London 1960).

An Inventory of the Ancient Monuments in Caernarvonshire, III: *West* (London 1964).

An Inventory of the Ancient Monuments in Glamorgan, I, iii: *The Early Christian Period* (Cardiff 1976).

An Inventory of the Ancient Monuments in Glamorgan, IV, i: *The Greater Houses* (Cardiff 1981).

An Inventory of the Ancient Monuments in Brecknock (Brycheiniog) – The Prehistoric and Roman Monuments, ii: *Hill-forts and Roman Remains* (London 1986).

CADW OFFICIAL GUIDEBOOKS

Cadw: Welsh Historic Monuments is currently engaged in the production of a new series of guidebooks to all those monuments in State care. The titles published to date are:

R. Avent, *Criccieth Castle – Pennarth Fawr Medieval Hall-House – St Cybi's Well* (Cardiff 1989).

D.H. Evans and J.K. Knight, *Valle Crucis Abbey – The Pillar of Eliseg* (Cardiff 1987).

J.R. Kenyon, *Kidwelly Castle* (Cardiff 1986).

J.R. Kenyon, *Raglan Castle* (Cardiff 1988).

J.K. Knight, *Blaenavon Ironworks* (Cardiff 1989).

J.K. Knight, *Caerleon Roman Fortress* (Cardiff 1988).

J.K. Knight, *Chepstow Castle* (Cardiff 1986).

D.F. Renn, *Caerphilly Castle* (Cardiff 1989).

D.M. Robinson, *Tintern Abbey* (Cardiff 1986).

S. Rousham, *Castell Coch*, revised edition (Cardiff 1987).

A. Taylor, *Beaumaris Castle*, revised edition (Cardiff 1988).

A. Taylor, *Caernarfon Castle and Town Walls*, revised edition (Cardiff 1989).

A.J. Taylor, *Conwy Castle and Town Walls* (Cardiff 1986).

A. Taylor, *Harlech Castle*, revised edition (Cardiff 1988).

A. Taylor, *Rhuddlan Castle* (Cardiff 1987).

INDEX

Reference to photographs and illustrations appears in *italic* script.